Chartered Institut
Management Account

This book comes with free EN-gage online resources so that you can study anytime, anywhere. This free online resource is not sold separately and is included in the price of the book.

## How to access your on-line resources

You can access additional online resources associated with this CIMA Official book via the EN-gage website at: **www.EN-gage.co.uk**.

## Existing users

If you are an **existing EN-gage user**, simply log-in to your account, click on the 'add a book' link at the top of your homepage and enter the ISBN of this book and the unique pass key number contained above.

## New users

If you are a new EN-gage user then you first need to register at: **www.EN-gage.co.uk**. Once registered, Kaplan Publishing will send you an email containing a link to activate your account - please check your junk mail if you do not receive this or contact us using the phone number or email address printed on the back cover of this book. Click on the link to activate your account. To unlock your additional resources, click on the 'add a book' link at the top of your home page. You will then need to enter the ISBN of this book (found on page ii) and the unique pass key number contained in the scratch panel below:

Then click 'finished' or 'add another book'.
Please allow 24 hours from the time you submit your book details for the content to appear in the My Learning and Testing area of your account.

## Your code and information

This code can only be used once for the registration of one book online. This registration will expire when this edition of the book is no longer current - please see the back cover of this book for the expiry date.

## Existing users

If you are an **existing EN-gage user**, simply log-in to your account, click on the 'add a book' link at the top of your homepage and enter the ISBN of this book and the unique pass key number contained above.

# CIMA

Case Study

Strategic Level

Study Text

Published by: Kaplan Publishing UK

Unit 2 The Business Centre, Molly Millars Lane, Wokingham, Berkshire RG41 2QZ

Copyright © 2015 Kaplan Financial Limited. All rights reserved.

No part of this publication may be reproduced, stored in a retrieval system or transmitted in any form or by any means electronic, mechanical, photocopying, recording or otherwise without the prior written permission of the publisher.

**Acknowledgements**

We are grateful to the CIMA for permission to reproduce pilot papers and their answers.

**Notice**

The text in this material and any others made available by any Kaplan Group company does not amount to advice on a particular matter and should not be taken as such. No reliance should be placed on the content as the basis for any investment or other decision or in connection with any advice given to third parties. Please consult your appropriate professional adviser as necessary. Kaplan Publishing Limited and all other Kaplan group companies expressly disclaim all liability to any person in respect of any losses or other claims, whether direct, indirect, incidental, consequential or otherwise arising in relation to the use of such materials.

**British Library Cataloguing in Publication Data**

A catalogue record for this book is available from the British Library

ISBN: 978-1-78415-409-7

Printed and bound in Great Britain.

# Contents

| | | Page |
|---|---|---|
| **Chapter 1** | Introduction to case study exams | 1 |
| **Chapter 2** | Understanding competencies | 13 |
| **Chapter 3** | Integrating skills and knowledge | 41 |
| **Chapter 4** | Preseen information for the pilot case | 51 |
| **Chapter 5** | Analysing the pre-seen | 99 |
| **Chapter 6** | Summary of the pre-seen | 119 |
| **Chapter 7** | Practice triggers and tasks | 135 |
| **Chapter 8** | Exam day techniques | 193 |
| **Chapter 9** | Unseen information for the pilot case | 211 |
| **Chapter 10** | Walkthrough of the pilot exam | 221 |
| **Chapter 11** | Review of solution to pilot case and marking guide | 241 |
| **Chapter 12** | Pre-seen Material – Look | 261 |
| **Chapter 13** | Summary of the Pre-seen – Look | 287 |
| **Chapter 14** | Unseen Material – Look | 299 |
| **Chapter 15** | Walk through of the unseen – Look | 307 |
| **Chapter 16** | Analysis of marking key – Look | 325 |

# Paper Introduction

**Acknowledgements**

Every effort has been made to contact the holders of copyright material, but if any here have been inadvertently overlooked the publishers will be pleased to make the necessary arrangements at the first opportunity.

# How to Use the Materials

**Icon Explanations**

**Supplementary reading** – These sections will help to provide a deeper understanding of core areas. The supplementary reading is **NOT** optional reading. It is vital to provide you with the breadth of knowledge you will need to address the wide range of topics within your syllabus that could feature in an assessment question. **Reference to this text is vital when self studying.**

**Test Your Understanding** – Following key points and definitions are exercises which give the opportunity to assess the understanding of these core areas

**Illustration** – To help develop an understanding of particular topics. The illustrative examples are useful in preparing for the Test your understanding exercises.

**Exclamation mark** – This symbol signifies a topic which can be more difficult to understand. When reviewing these areas, care should be taken.

Quality and accuracy are of the utmost importance to us so if you spot an error in any of our products, please send an email to mykaplanreporting@kaplan.com with full details, or follow the link to the feedback form in MyKaplan.

Our Quality Co-ordinator will work with our technical team to verify the error and take action to ensure it is corrected in future editions.

## Exam Introduction

To complete the CIMA qualification and be able to use the designatory letters of ACMA and CGMA, candidates for this prestigious award need to achieve three things:

- attain the entry requirements for the professional level qualification
- study for and complete the relevant professional level assessments and examinations
- complete three years of relevant practical experience

This text concentrates on the second of these requirements, and in particular to study for and complete the management case study exam.

## Overview of exam

The integrated case study exam will be available four times a year. The purpose of this exam is to consolidate learning at each level by reflecting real-life work situations. The exam is human marked.

This approach allows a wide range of knowledge and skills to be tested including research and analysis, presentation of information and communication skills whilst still ensuring competence in key skills.

CIMA believe that this new format will provide the commitment to delivering the competencies which employers desire thereby improving 'employability'.

For example, the strategic level case study exam will be set within a simulated business context, placing the candidate in the job role matched to the competency level. In the case of the strategic level, your job role is that of a senior manager communicating to the CFO and the rest of the senior management team with an emphasis on the following:

- Advising top level management, as they set the strategy for the business.
- Analysing strategic options – the various courses of action the business can take – based on the organisation's environment and its current strategic position.
- Considering risks – they need to be identified, classified, evaluated and then managed/reported.
- Advising on where to source finance for the strategies.

The exam is intended to replicate "a day in the life" of a finance professional operating at the strategic level and provide a simulated environment for candidates to demonstrate the required level of proficiency in each of the competency areas. Consequently, the exam will be set and marked according to the competency weightings at the level.

The integrated case study exam is 3 hours in duration and is made up of a series of timed tests. Candidates will be provided with access to pre-seen information approximately seven weeks before the real exam.

**Assessment aims and strategy**

The integrated Case Study examinations combine the knowledge and learning from across the three pillars of the syllabus set in a simulated business context relating to one or more fictional business organisations which are in turn based on a real business or industry.

The integrated case study is three hours long. The case study will include both pre-seen and un-seen material, the latter being made available during the examination. They will incorporate short written answers, emails, letters and any form of appropriate communication required within the tasks set.

The focus is on application, analysis and evaluation which are levels 3, 4 and 5 of the CIMA hierarchy of verbs (see below).

Simulated business issues in the integrated case studies provide candidates with the opportunity to demonstrate their familiarity with the context and interrelationships of the level's technical content. This reflects the cross functional abilities required in the workplace. Skills will include research, analysis, presentation of both financial and non-financial information and communication skills.

Feedback will be provided to candidates with their results. Exam sittings for the case studies will occur every three months. Candidates must have completed or be exempt from the three objective tests at a particular level before attempting the relevant integrated case study.

## Learning outcomes

Each syllabus topic from the objective test subjects contains one or more lead learning outcomes, related component learning outcomes and indicative syllabus content. This provides a guide for the likely content of the case study exam.

Each lead learning outcome:

- defines the skill or ability that a well-prepared candidate should be able to exhibit in an examination
- is examinable and demonstrates the approach likely to be taken in examination questions

The lead learning outcomes are part of a hierarchy of learning objectives. The verbs used at the beginning of each learning outcome relate to a specific learning objective as illustrated in the detail below. You will not necessarily see these verbs reflected in the case study requirements but they indicate the depth of knowledge required for particular topics. Requirements in the case study may be presented as requests for reports, presentations, etc, as well as simple tasks. The case study exam will focus on Levels 3, 4 and 5.

### Level 1

Learning objective – Knowledge (What you are expected to know)

- List – Make a list of
- State – Express, fully or clearly, the details/facts of
- Define – Give the exact meaning of

### Level 2

Learning objective – Comprehension (What you are expected to understand)

- Describe – Communicate the key features of
- Distinguish – Highlight the differences between
- Explain – Make clear or intelligible/State the meaning or purpose of
- Identify – Recognise, establish or select after consideration
- Illustrate – Use an example to describe or explain something

### Level 3

Learning objective - Application (How you are expected to apply your knowledge)

- Apply – Put to practical use
- Calculate – Ascertain or reckon mathematically
- Demonstrate – Prove with certainty or exhibit by practical means
- Prepare – Make or get ready for use
- Reconcile – Make or prove consistent/compatible
- Solve – Find an answer to
- Tabulate – Arrange in a table

### Level 4

Learning objective – Analysis (How you are expected to analyse the detail of what you have learned)

- Analyse – Examine in detail the structure of
- Categorise – Place into a defined class or division
- Compare and contrast - Show the similarities and/or differences between
- Construct – Build up or compile
- Discuss – Examine in detail by argument
- Interpret – Translate into intelligible or familiar terms
- Prioritise – Place in order of priority or sequence for action

- Produce – Create or bring into existence

## Level 5

Learning objective – Evaluation (How you are expected to use your learning to evaluate, make decisions or recommendations)

- Advise – Counsel, inform or notify
- Evaluate – Appraise or assess the value of
- Recommend – Propose a course of action

## How to use the material

These Official CIMA learning materials brought to you by CIMA and Kaplan Publishing have been carefully designed to make your learning experience as easy as possible and give you the best chances of success in your Integrated Case Study Examinations.

This Study Text has been designed with the needs of home study and distance learning candidates in mind. However, the Study Text is also ideal for fully taught courses.

The aim of this textbook is to walk you through the stages to prepare for, and to answer, the requirements of the Case Study Examination.

Practical hints and realistic tips are given throughout the book making it easy for you to apply what you've learned in this text to your actual Case Study Exam.

Where sample solutions are provided, they must be viewed as just one interpretation of the case. One key aspect, which you must appreciate early in your studies, is that there is no single 'correct' solution.

Your own answer might reach different conclusions, and give greater emphasis to some issues and less emphasis to others, but score equally as well if it demonstrates the required skills.

If you work conscientiously through the official CIMA Study Text according to the guidelines above, as well as analysing the pre-seen information in full, you will be giving yourself an excellent chance of success in your examination. Good luck with your studies!

## Planning

To begin with, formal planning is essential to get the best return from the time you spend studying. Estimate how much time in total you are going to need for each subject you are studying for the Case Study Examination. You may find it helpful to read "Pass First Time!" second edition by David R. Harris ISBN 978-1-85617-798-6.

This book will provide you with proven study techniques. Chapter by chapter it covers the building blocks of successful learning and examination techniques and shows you how to earn all the marks you deserve, and explains how to avoid the most common pitfalls.

With your study material before you, decide which chapters you are going to study in each week, which weeks you will devote to practising past exams, and which weeks you will spend becoming familiar with your case study pre-seen material.

Prepare a written schedule summarising the above and stick to it! Students are advised to refer to articles published regularly in CIMA's magazine (Financial Management), the student e-newsletter (Velocity) and on the CIMA website, to ensure they are up to date with relevant issues and topics.

## Tips for effective studying

(1) Aim to find a quiet and undisturbed location for your study, and plan as far as possible to use the same period of time each day. Getting into a routine helps to avoid wasting time. Make sure that you have all the materials you need before you begin so as to minimise interruptions.

(2) Store all your materials in one place, so that you do not waste time searching for items around your accommodation. If you have to pack everything away after each study period, keep them in a box, or even a suitcase, which will not be disturbed until the next time.

(3) Limit distractions. To make the most effective use of your study periods you should be able to apply total concentration, so turn off all entertainment equipment, set your phones to message mode, and put up your 'do not disturb' sign.

(4) Your timetable will tell you which area to study. However, before diving in and becoming engrossed in the finer points, make sure you have an overall picture of all the areas that need to be covered by the end of that session. After an hour, allow yourself a short break and move away from your Study Text. With experience, you will learn to assess the pace you need to work at.

(5) Work carefully through each chapter, making notes as you go. When you have covered a suitable amount of material, vary the pattern by attempting a practice exercise. When you have finished your attempt, make notes of any mistakes you made, or any areas that you failed to cover or covered more briefly.

(6) Make notes as you study, and discover the techniques that work best for you. Your notes may be in the form of lists, bullet points, diagrams, summaries, 'mind maps', or the written word, but remember that you will need to refer back to them at a later date, so they must be intelligible. If you are on a taught course, make sure you highlight any issues you would like to follow up with your lecturer.

(7) Organise your notes. Make sure that all your notes, calculations etc can be effectively filed and easily retrieved later.

(8) Attempt practice exercises and write out full answers. Reviewing these and reflecting on suggested solutions is a crucial part of your studies.

**Relevant practical experience**

In order to become a Chartered Global Management Accountant (ACMA, CGMA), you need a minimum of three years' verified relevant work-based practical experience.

Read the 'Applying for Membership' brochure for full details of the practical experience requirements (PER). At the time of print CIMA were in the process of updating these requirements for 2015.

# chapter 1

# Introduction to case study exams

## Chapter learning objectives

- To gain an overview of the case study exam, its purpose, structure, marking and process involved.

# Introduction to case study exams

## 1 Why a Case Study Examination?

The Case Study Examination is an attempt to simulate workplace problem solving, and allows examiners to move one step closer to the assessment of competence than is possible with objective test questions. It is a test of your professional competence.

CIMA wishes to assess:

- your possession of skills such as research, synthesis, analysis and evaluation, in addition to;
- your technical knowledge, and
- your skill in presenting and communicating information to users.

Since the examination tests a range of different skills, preparing for this examination needs to be different from studying for a 'traditional' examination. The purpose of this text is to suggest how you might prepare for the examination by developing and practising your skills.

## 2 Your role

Each case study exam will be set within a simulated business context, placing the candidate in the job role matched to the competency level.

In the case of the strategic level the job role is that of a senior manager reporting to the CFO and other members of the senior management team within the organisation. Key elements of the case are likely to focus on the following:

- Advising top level management, as they set the strategy for the business.
- Analysing strategic options – the various courses of action the business can take – based on the organisation's environment and its current strategic position.
- Considering risks – they need to be identified, classified, evaluated and then managed/reported.
- Advising on where to source finance for the strategies.

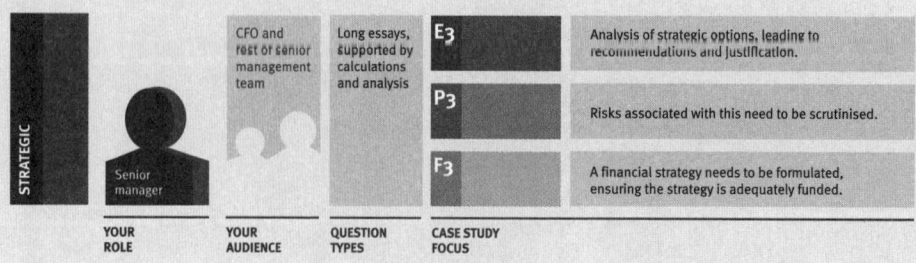

## 3 CIMA's Competency Framework

CIMA has developed a competency framework which explains the skills which a finance professional needs to possess in order to drive their organisation forward. This framework highlights the importance of not just accounting techniques but also wider business management skills. It also emphasises the need for complete integration of these many and varied skills. It is no longer sufficient for a finance professional to only display relevant technical ability.

The technical competencies are still important but in addition the accountant must have a good understanding of the organisation, it's environment and other relevant commercial knowledge. It is also important to possess the relevant people and leadership skills to ensure that technical and business knowledge is applied appropriately and effectively throughout the organisation.

The four generic competencies can be summarised as:

(1) Technical skills ('Do accounting and finance work')
(2) Business skills ('in the context of the business')
(3) People skills ('to influence people')
(4) Leadership skills ('and lead within the organisation')

# Introduction to case study exams

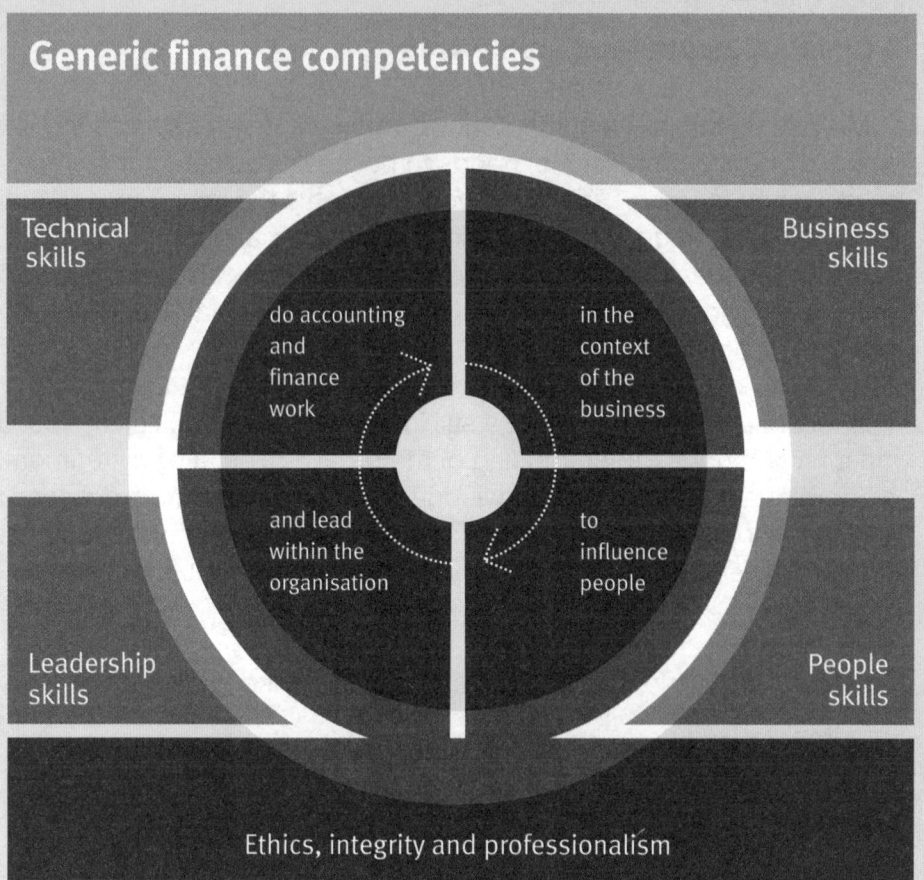

CIMA recognise that the relevance of each of these competence areas will depend on the level a professional has progressed to within the organisation.

So for an entry level role (broadly equivalent to operational level), the core accounting and finance skills will form a large part of the role and only a small amount of leadership skill will be expected. This is reflected in the syllabus weightings. As you progress to management level it is anticipated that your role is more in line with a manager and therefore you will be expected to display a greater understanding of the business context and have developed more people and leadership skills.

At the strategic level the weightings for each of the four areas of competency are equal, reflecting the fact that as a senior manager you need to balance a broad range of skills.

Whilst the objective tests will examine your knowledge and ability to apply the underlying technical, business, people and leadership skills, the case study exam aims to test your ability to demonstrate and integrate these skills as a rounded finance professional.

# chapter 1

## 4 How the Case Study Examination works

The Case Study Examination is a computer based examination of three hours.

Candidates cannot take the examination until they have successfully completed all the Objective Test Examinations for the relevant level. The Case Study Examination is made up of a series of requirements which aim to integrate and apply the technical knowledge tested in the Objective Test Examinations.

The exam is based on:

- pre-seen material issued in advance of the exam day, supplemented by
- additional, previously unseen material given to you in the exam room.

There will be several sections, comprising:

(a) Triggers – information and updates regarding situations in which the company finds itself
(b) Tasks – work you will need to carry out based on the trigger

## 5 The pre-seen

CIMA releases the pre-seen material approximately seven weeks before the examination. This is posted on the student area of the CIMA website (www.cimaglobal.com) and it is your responsibility to download it.

The pre-seen material is an extended scenario consisting of approximately 15 exhibits giving information about a business organisation. You will be taking on the role of a senior manager who works for the organisation, and your responses to the tasks will usually be addressed to your superior.

The pre-seen information for the Strategic level pilot exam (which concerns a retailer with a long history who has recently moved into on line retailing) comprises:

- An introduction to the company, its history, strategy, products, market, structure and processes
- Industry analysis
- Risk factors
- Mission statement and strategy
- Directors biographies
- Financial statements for current and previous years – including notes to the accounts

# Introduction to case study exams

- Corporate Social Responsibility Report
- Company press release
- Business news extract
- Competitor analysis
- Share price of two competitor companies
- Extracts of financial statements for two competitor companies

As you can see there is information relevant to all three strategic level technical subjects as well as information relevant to earlier papers.

The purpose of giving you access to this information in advance of the exam is to enable you to prepare notes, analyse and become very familiar with the organisation(s) and industry described. Remember, you have the role of a senior manager within this organisation and so you should use the pre-seen material to get a similar background knowledge as would be expected from someone in this situation.

## Suggested approach to analysing the pre-seen information

(1) Detailed exhibit by exhibit analysis

As you review each exhibit ask yourself questions about what each piece of information means and what the implications of it might be for the organisation. Try to consider why the examiner might have provided this information.

(2) Technical analysis

Now it's time to apply many of the techniques you studied for the Objective Test Examinations to help you understand the organisation and the industry in which it operates in more depth. Some suggestions of what you could perform:

- Ratio analysis of financial statements and financial plans.
- Business strategy analysis, including generation of strategic options.
- Management accounting analysis, including costing, pricing and performance measurement.

It is important to bear in mind that this analysis will aid your understanding of the case study but you should not be determined to include the analysis in your responses unless clearly relevant to the requirement.

(3) Researching the industry involved

To ensure you have a good understanding of the context of the case, you could carry out some wider reading including researching the industry in which the organisation operates. For example, you could look at some of the real life key players and see what strategies they are adopting. Also consider key trends within the industry and the risks that have to be addressed. Finally you could consider what impact the economic climate or broader business influences (such as the political or regulatory environments) may be having on the industry.

You should not aim to spend too much time on this research as the pre-seen should be sufficient for your understanding of the industry. However a general appreciation of the 'real-world' should help to ensure you give sensible, commercial responses.

(4) Overall position analysis

Once you have completed all of the above, you should be able to stand back and see the bigger picture of the organisation within the case material. You should complete a position audit, including a SWOT analysis so you have a clear understanding of where the organisation is and where it might want to go.

(5) Identification of key issues

Using your SWOT analysis, you should now be able to identify a short list of key issues facing the organisation. An appreciation of these will assist you when understanding the issues introduced in the unseen material in the exam.

## 6 The unseen

In the examination you will be provided with:

- an on-screen version of the pre-seen material
- additional unseen material, which contains both triggers (new information) and tasks (what you need to do).
- an on-screen calculator
- space to complete your answers

The unseen material will be a continuation of the pre-seen and will usually bring the scenario up to date. The unseen may focus on a number of issues that appeared in the pre-seen or it may just focus on one or two; either way it will provide the basis for the content of your answers.

# Introduction to case study exams

A common mistake made by weaker students is that they place too much emphasis on their analysis of the pre-seen material and do not develop the information in the unseen material adequately. The key points to be referred to in your answer should be driven by the new information and specific tasks in the unseen material.

## 7 Triggers

Each section in the unseen material will begin with a **trigger**.

This will be information provided as an introduction to the work that you are required to complete.

The information may be in the form of a briefing by your superior, a newspaper article, some financial information or extracts from internal reports. You will be expected to integrate this new information with the analysis you have performed on the pre-seen material to produce a coherent and well informed response.

Here is an example of a trigger from the pilot exam:

### Example trigger from pilot exam

**Trigger 1**

**Today is 16th May 2015. You are a senior manager advising Judith, the new Group CEO, on issues relating to shareholders. The current position is as follows:**

Cast is a private company and so its shares are not freely traded. The company was established as a family business, but there are now 40 shareholders. There are no close family ties holding the shareholders together. Over the years the shares have changed hands because of inheritance. The present shareholders are not closely related.

The only significant shareholder is Arnold, who is the great grandson of the shopkeeper who founded the business. Arnold owns 30% of Cast's shares.

Cast's constitution forbids the sale of shares to anyone other than an existing shareholder. That creates two problems. First of all, shareholders cannot liquidate any of their shareholding unless they can find a willing buyer amongst the other shareholders. There is a feeling that the few sales that have occurred have tended to be for less than the real value of the company's shares. Secondly, there is a tax charge when shares change hands because of inheritance. This requires a fair value to be negotiated with the tax authorities and that has created significant problems over the past few years.

> Several shareholders believe that Judith's appointment is an ideal time for Cast to seek a stock market quotation. The company is large enough to be in the top 250 companies in its national stock exchange in the event that it is quoted. These shareholders have written to the company with a formal request that the directors begin the process of seeking a quotation. Arnold is aware of this request and has spoken to Judith to express his reluctance to see the company seek a quotation.
>
> **Judith has asked you to step into her office to discuss something important.**

## 8 Tasks

Within each section of the examination, there will be a task or tasks that you will be asked to perform, usually by your superior. These tasks can take various different forms, the most common are likely to be reports and email responses.

There is a time limit attached to each task and an onscreen timer will show you the time remaining for the task you are working on. Once you have submitted a task (or the time limit is reached, whichever is sooner) **you will not be able to return to that task**. If you still have time remaining you will be prompted to confirm you wish to move on to the next task before the previous task is completed and locked. This should reduce the problem of not completing the paper but does mean you will need to be very disciplined when attempting each task.

The Strategic level pilot exam comprises the following requirements:

- A briefing note covering the analysis of stakeholders affected by a business decision
- A briefing note suggesting a strategy for dealing with major shareholder
- A paper discussing the suitability of a range of company valuation models
- A paper covering the governance issues associated with company floatation
- A paper covering the ethical implications for the company in relation to its employment practices
- A paper covering the implications of the resistance of a major shareholder and the employment practices for a share issue price

## Introduction to case study exams

Here is an example of a task from the pilot exam:

**Example task from pilot exam**

**Task 1a**

**Judith hands you a copy of a letter which can be accessed in the reference material above.**

**Reference material – letter**

> To the board of Cast,
>
> We write as the owners of more than 40% of Cast's equity.
>
> Our company has had a long and distinguished history. It had humble beginnings, but through hard work and imaginative management it has grown from a single shop to one of the country's leading retailers.
>
> In the past, we have prided ourselves on being one of the country's largest unquoted companies. We have valued our independence and the freedom to take decisions without being held accountable to a widespread and transient body of market participants. Unfortunately, we no longer feel that the advantages of our unquoted status outweigh the disadvantages. We believe that Cast cannot expand unless we seek a stock market quotation.
>
> We urge the board to commence the process of registering the company with the stock exchange. Clearly, this will be a challenging and expensive process. We believe that the costs will be more than compensated by the benefits.
>
> Yours sincerely,
>
> Simon and eight other shareholders.

## 9 Marking the Case Study

The Case Study Exams will be marked against the competencies summarised in section 2 of this chapter.

For the strategic level the weightings applied to these competencies are shown in the following diagram:

STRATEGIC LEVEL

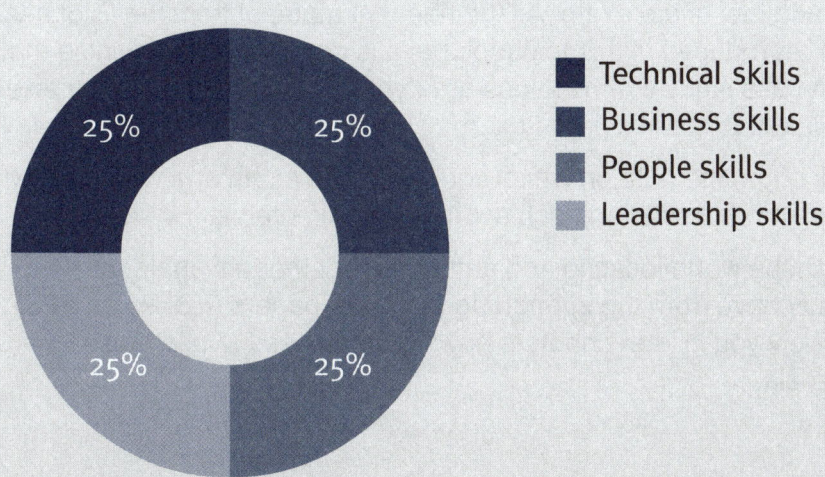

- Technical skills 25%
- Business skills 25%
- People skills 25%
- Leadership skills 25%

As you can see there is significantly less focus on your technical skills as compared to the Operational and Management Case Study and a greater focus on developing your people and leadership skills.

This reflects the syllabus content for the exams within the Strategic level.

The following two chapters will explain further how these competencies relate to each syllabus and will also show the importance of integrating your knowledge of the three technical papers where possible and appropriate. You can also see in Chapter 11 how the competencies are applied in the marking of the pilot paper.

## 10 Summary

You should now have a basic understanding of how the case study works. All of the ideas presented in this chapter will be explored further in the remainder of this textbook.

**Next steps:**

(1) It is a good idea to register with Pearson Vue to see the online version of the Pilot exam as this will allow you to become more familiar with the look and feel of the exam. All the relevant material from the Pilot has been reproduced in this textbook but it is important to recognise that the CIMA case study examinations are dynamic and shouldn't be viewed as equivalent to a static paper exam.

(2) Think about the date on which you will sit the exam and work backwards to create a sensible and achievable study timetable.

(3) It might be worth locating and gathering together any materials you already have from the supporting technical papers (E3, P3 and F3). We will show you in later chapters how you may need to use these materials.

chapter 2

# Understanding competencies

## Chapter learning objectives

- To understand how the learning outcomes from individual papers can be interpreted in terms of the competencies required for the case study exam.

## 1 Relevance of the Strategic level syllabus

Let us start by recapping the learning outcomes covered in the three individual strategic level papers.

### E3 – Strategic Management

**Syllabus area A: Interacting with the organisation's environment (20%)**

| You must understand and be able to apply the following: | CIMA Official Study Text Chapter |
|---|---|
| • Non-market strategy and forms of corporate political activity<br>• Stakeholder management<br>• Building stakeholder alliances<br>• Vision and mission statements | Chapter 2 – Strategic analysis: Mission, vision and stakeholders |
| • External demands for sustainability and responsible business practices and ways to respond to these<br>• Business ethics and the CIMA Code of Ethics | Chapter 3 – Strategic analysis: Ethics and corporate social responsibility |
| • Different organisation environments<br>• The key environmental drivers of organisational change<br>• Explain and apply e.g. PEST, Five Forces, Product Lifecycle, Porter's National Diamond | Chapter 4 – Strategic analysis: External environment |
| • Supply chains<br>• Customer analysis and behaviour<br>• Building strategic alliances | Chapter 11 – Customers, suppliers and supply chain management |

## Syllabus area B: Evaluating strategic position and strategic options (30%)

| You must understand and be able to apply the following: | CIMA Official Study Text Chapter |
|---|---|
| • The process of strategy formulation (the approaches/types of strategy within an organisation)<br>• The roles and responsibilities of directors and senior managers in making strategic decisions<br>• The role of Chartered Management Accountants in strategy formulation | Chapter 1 – The process of strategy formulation |
| • Vision and mission statements and how they orient the organisation's strategy | Chapter 2 – Strategic analysis: Mission, vision and stakeholders |
| • Audit of resources, competences and capabilities<br>• Critical success factors (CSFs) and objectives<br>• Value drivers and value chain analysis | Chapter 5 – Strategic analysis: internal environmental analysis |
| • Game theory<br>• Real options<br>• Scenario planning<br>• Forecasting | Chapter 6 – Position and gap analysis |
| • The identification and evaluation of strategic options, including the use of: Ansoff, Porter's generic strategies and the BCG matrix<br>• Diversification and joint methods of expansion<br>• Evaluation of strategies using the suitability, acceptability, feasibility (SAF) framework | Chapter 7 – Strategic options and choice |

# Understanding competencies

## Syllabus area C: Leading Change (20%)

| You must understand and be able to apply the following: | CIMA Official Study Text Chapter |
|---|---|
| • Internal and external triggers for change<br>• Classifications (types) of change<br>• Culture – especially the McKinsey 7S model and the cultural web<br>• Resistance to change | Chapter 12 – Change management – understanding the context of change |
| • Models of change management – Lewin's three step model and Force Field analysis<br>• Beer and Nohria – Theory E and O<br>• Change leadership – Kotter's 8 steps, group and team formation, executive mentoring and coaching, Kotter and Schlesinger's leadership styles<br>• Change agents<br>• Decline<br>• Change-adept organisations | Chapter 13 – Change management – managing the change process |

## Syllabus area D: Implementing strategy (15%)

| You must understand and be able to apply the following: | CIMA Official Study Text Chapter |
|---|---|
| • Financial and non-financial performance measures<br>• The balanced scorecard<br>• The performance pyramid<br>• Fitzgerald and Moon<br>• Benchmarking<br>• Divisional performance – EVA/SVA/Triple bottom line<br>• Communication and stretch targets | Chapter 8 – The performance measurement mix |

## Syllabus area E: The role of information systems in organisational strategy (15%)

| You must understand and be able to apply the following: | CIMA Official Study Text Chapter |
|---|---|
| • Earl's three levels of information strategy<br>• IT's strategic context (i.e. link to SWOT/Five Forces/Value chain)<br>• McFarlan's grid<br>• Benefits and drawbacks of e-business<br>• Web 2.0 and other modern developments in the commercial use of the internet | Chapter 9 – Information technology and e-business |
| • Classifications of knowledge and knowledge management<br>• Data warehousing and mining<br>• Big Data | Chapter 10 – Information for advantage and knowledge management |

## P3 – Risk Management

### Syllabus area A: Identification, classification and evaluation of risk (20%)

| You must understand and be able to apply the following: | CIMA Official Study Text Chapter |
|---|---|
| • Risk identification and classification | Chapter 1 – Risk |
| • Frameworks for risk management – ERM, risk management cycle<br>• Risk strategies – e.g. considering risk appetite<br>• Risk evaluation, for example, using risk maps<br>• Recommending responses, say, using TARA<br>• Roles of risk managers, risk committees and risk registers | Chapter 2 - Risk Management |
| • Board responsibility for risk management – especially in setting up a system of controls and the control environment<br>• Turnbull Report<br>• Risk reporting | Chapter 3 – Internal Control |

# Understanding competencies

## Syllabus area B: Responses to Strategic Risk (20%)

| You must understand and be able to apply the following: | CIMA Official Study Text Chapter |
|---|---|
| • The key risks associated with computer/information systems<br>• The controls that can be put in place to mitigate those risks<br>• Systems development risks and their management | Chapter 4 – Risk and control of information systems |
| • Identifying CSFs and their associated KPIs as a basis for control systems to ensure the firm achieves its strategic targets<br>• Information systems (e.g. EIS)<br>• Information strategies (e.g. use of big data) | Chapter 5 – Information Strategy |
| • Systems theory<br>• Behavioural implications of control systems<br>• Responsibility accounting<br>• Problems with typical measures, such as ROI or RI<br>• Use of NFPIs v FPIs<br>• Problems associated with transfer pricing<br>• Problems with traditional management accounting techniques and "Beyond budgeting" as a response to these<br>• Modern manufacturing techniques<br>• Strategic Management Accounting | Chapter 6 – Management Control Systems |
| • History and definition of corporate governance<br>• Principles of good governance – e.g. board composition, directors' powers, NEDs, roles of committees, remuneration, etc<br>• UK Corporate Governance Code<br>• SOX<br>• Corporate governance and internal controls – Turnbull<br>• CSR | Chapter 9 – Corporate Governance |

## Syllabus area C: Internal Controls to Manage Risk (20%)

| You must understand and be able to apply the following: | CIMA Official Study Text Chapter |
|---|---|
| - Control systems and their design<br>- Turnbull Report<br>- COSO model of internal control<br>- Details of control activities for specific business areas | Chapter 3 – Internal Control |
| - The nature of, and prerequisites for, fraud<br>- Fraud risk management – especially what controls can reduce the risk of fraud occurring<br>- Fraud policy statements<br>- Whistleblowing | Chapter 7 – Fraud |
| - CIMA code of ethics – fundamental principles, threats and safeguards<br>- Ethical dilemmas and resolution<br>- Ethical issues as a source of risk | Chapter 8 – Ethics |
| - The role(s) of internal audit<br>- Forms of internal audit – e.g. VFM audit<br>- Operation of internal audit – e.g. risk assessment, analytical review, the use of CAATs<br>- Effective management of internal audit<br>- Reports | Chapter 10 – Audit |

# Understanding competencies

**Syllabus area D: Managing risks associated with cash flows (20%)**

| You must understand and be able to apply the following: | CIMA Official Study Text Chapter |
|---|---|
| • Political risk and its sources<br>• Credit risk and its sources<br>• Foreign currency risk and its sources<br>• Interest rate risk and its sources<br>• Use of financing packages to split risk | Chapter 11 – Financial Risk |
| • Determinants of exchange rates – parity theories<br>• Evaluation of currency risk exposure<br>• The use, advantages and disadvantages of<br>  – Internal techniques<br>  – Forwards<br>  – Money Market Hedges<br>  – Futures<br>  – Options<br>  – Swaps<br>  – Netting centres<br>• Arbitrage | Chapter 12 – Currency Risk Management |
| • Evaluation of interest rate risk exposure<br>• The use, advantages and disadvantages of<br>  – Internal techniques<br>  – FRAs<br>  – IRGs<br>  – Futures<br>  – Options<br>  – Swaps<br>• Arbitrage | Chapter 13 – Interest rate risk management |

# chapter 2

**Syllabus area E: Managing risks associated with capital investment decisions (20%)**

| You must understand and be able to apply the following: | CIMA Official Study Text Chapter |
|---|---|
| - Choice of which investment appraisal method to use<br>- WACC<br>- CAPM<br>- Risk-adjusted WACC<br>- APV<br>- Certainty equivalents<br>- Sensitivity analysis<br>- Use of expected values<br>- Real options | Chapter 14 – Cost of Capital and Capital Investment Decisions |
| - Stakeholder conflicts and their resolution<br>- Conflicts due to choice of KPIs<br>- How to monitor projects<br>- Post completion audits | Chapter 15 – Managing conflict, implementation and post completion |

# Understanding competencies

## F3 – Financial Strategy

### Syllabus area A: FORMULATION OF FINANCIAL STRATEGY (25%)

| You must understand and be able to apply the following: | CIMA Official Study Text Chapter |
|---|---|
| • Explain the characteristics of different types of entity (e.g. incorporated, unincorporated, quoted, unquoted, private sector, public sector, for-profit and not-for-profit)<br>• Discuss what types of financial and non-financial objectives these different entities might have<br>• Comment on calculations and interpret financial ratios, in order to assess whether financial objectives have been achieved. | Chapter 1 – Objectives |
| • Discuss the limitations of using just financial statements to appraise the performance of an entity<br>• Understand and explain the concept of Integrated Reporting (<IR>)<br>• Discuss the need to present additional information in line with the <IR> Framework and/or the Global Reporting Initiative's (GRI's) G4 Guidelines | Chapter 2 – Integrated Reporting |
| • Explain the links between investment decisions, financing decisions and dividend decisions<br>• Explain how lenders assess creditworthiness | Chapter 3 – Development of Financial Strategy |
| • Explain the hedge accounting rules as per IAS 39<br>• Prepare journal entries to show the effect on the financial statements of a fair value hedge, cash flow hedge of net investment hedge<br>• Explain the key disclosures required as per IFRS 7 | Chapter 4 – Hedge Accounting |

chapter 2

| | |
|---|---|
| • Comment on and interpret financial ratios before and after investment decisions, financing decisions and/or dividend decisions in order to assess the impact on things such as debt covenants and attainment of financial objectives | Chapter 9 – Financial Performance Measurement |

**Syllabus area B: FINANCING AND DIVIDEND DECISIONS (35%)**

| You must understand and be able to apply the following: | CIMA Official Study Text Chapter |
|---|---|
| • Explain the various methods of flotation (Initial Public Offering (IPO), introduction) and implications for the management of the entity and for its stakeholders<br>• Discuss the use of rights issues, including choice of discount rate and impact on shareholder wealth<br>• Comment on and interpret TERP (the theoretical ex rights price) and yield-adjusted TERP | Chapter 5 – Financing – Equity Finance |
| • Explain the features of different types of debt finance (e.g. bank borrowings, bonds, convertible bonds, commercial paper)<br>• Explain the procedures for issuing debt securities<br>• Discuss debt covenants<br>• Evaluate a lease or buy decision | Chapter 6 – Financing – Debt Finance |
| • Discuss the likely impact on weighted average cost of capital (WACC) of a change in capital structure, according to the theories of Modigliani and Miller (both with and without tax) and the traditional view of gearing<br>• Comment on and interpret cost of equity or WACC to reflect a change in capital structure | Chapter 7 – Financing – Capital Structure |

# Understanding competencies

| | |
|---|---|
| • Comment on and interpret financial ratios to assess the impact of a change in capital structure on financial statements and key performance measures<br><br>• Comment on and interpret the impact of scrip dividends and share repurchases on shareholder value and entity value/financial statements/performance measures | Chapter 9 – Financial Performance Measurement |
| • Discuss the implications for shareholder value of alternative dividend policies including Modigliani and Miller's theory of dividend irrelevancy | Chapter 8 – Dividend Policy |

## Syllabus area C: CORPORATE FINANCE (40%)

| You must understand and be able to apply the following: | CIMA Official Study Text Chapter |
|---|---|
| • Discuss the main reasons for and against acquisitions, mergers and divestments (e.g. strategic issues, synergy, big data, risks and tax implications)<br><br>• Explain the process and implications of a management buy-out, including potential conflicts of interest<br><br>• Describe the role of competition authorities in relation to mergers and acquisitions | Chapter 10 – Financial and Strategic Implications of Mergers and Acquisitions |
| • Comment on and interpret the value of an entity using various valuation methods (asset valuation, earnings valuation, dividend valuation, discounted free cash flow valuation)<br><br>• Comment on and interpret an appropriate cost of capital for use in discounted cash flow analysis (e.g. cost of equity or WACC) by reference to the nature of the transaction (e.g. division or an entire entity), including use of CAPM, dividend valuation model and Modigliani and Miller's WACC formula<br><br>• Explain the strengths and weaknesses of each valuation method | Chapter 11 – Business Valuation |

| | |
|---|---|
| • Evaluate forms of consideration and terms for acquisitions (e.g. cash, shares, convertibles and earn-out arrangements), and their impact on shareholders<br>• Comment on and interpret potential post-transaction value for both acquirer and seller (e.g. taking into account synergistic benefits, forecast performance and market response) | Chapter 12 – Pricing Issues and Post-transaction Issues |

## 2 Introduction to strategic level case study competencies

For the case study exam, the individual paper learning outcomes are augmented/supplemented by four generic competencies to aid focus.

As we explained in Chapter 1, at this level you will be tested on those competencies expected of a senior manager.

The weightings for the generic competencies are:

- Technical skills – 25%
- Business skills – 25%
- People skills – 25%
- Leadership skills – 25%

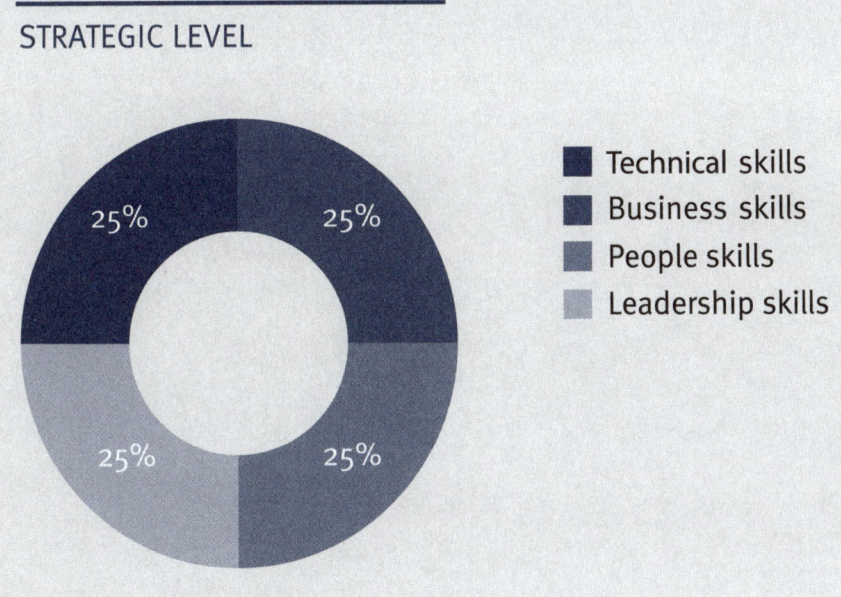

# Understanding competencies

You will be expected to show core accounting and finance skills such as evaluating finance requirements from your F3 paper ('doing accounting and finance work') whilst taking into account the business context such as your understanding of the market environment from E3 ('in the context of the business'). You may then need to make decisions and communicate them such as a decision to undertake a joint venture using techniques learnt in P3, F3 and E3 ('to influence people') and potentially advise on managing the resulting change process using skills learnt in E3 ('whilst leading within the organisation').

You should aim to be comfortable with the whole syllabus for all three subjects and should be ready to attempt the whole paper as there is a limit to the extent to which strength in one topic can compensate for weakness in another.

Let's examine each generic competency in more detail before thinking about integrating these skills. Remember a competency focuses on what you can DO rather than what you KNOW and so you need to think about this in terms of ability rather than simply knowledge.

## 3 The competencies in more detail

The generic competencies and individual paper learning outcomes can be correlated as follows:

| CIMA COMPETENCY FRAMEWORK | | | |
|---|---|---|---|
| Competencies | Syllabus area | | |
| **Technical skills** | E3 | P3 | F3 |
| Financial accounting and reporting | | | |
| Cost accounting and management | | | |
| Planning and control | | | |
| Management reporting and analysis | E3 | | |
| Corporate finance and treasury management | | | F3 |
| Risk management and internal control | | P3 | |
| Taxation | | P3 | F3 |
| Accounting information systems | | P3 | |
| **Business skills** | | | |
| Strategy | E3 | | |
| Market environment | E3 | | |
| Process management | E3 | | |
| Business relations | E3 | | |
| Project management | | | |
| Regulatory environment | | | |
| Macro-economic anlaysis | E3 | | F3 |
| **People skills** | | | |
| Influence | | | |
| Negotiation | | | |
| Decision making | E3 | P3 | F3 |
| Communication | E3 | | |
| Collaboration and partnering | | | |
| **Leadership skills** | | | |
| Team building | E3 | | |
| Coaching and mentoring | E3 | | |
| Driving performance | E3 | | |
| Motivating and inspiring | E3 | | |
| Change management | E3 | | |
| Underpinned by ethics, integrity and professionalism | | | |

It is important to recognise a significant change at the strategic level from the operational and management levels which is reflected by a greater focus on the use of higher level verbs.

# Understanding competencies

There is more emphasis on appraising or assessing the value of a course of action, informing the board of directors of the decision and making fully justifiable recommendations on the options chosen as appropriate. The verbs used in this context are evaluate, advise and recommend.

## Technical skills

At the strategic level these skills will be drawn from the syllabus for papers E3, F3 and P3. Here is a sample of some of the competencies which you may be expected to demonstrate:

- I can evaluate the limitations of current financial statements in reflecting business value
- I can advise on new developments in reporting to inform stakeholders of relevant information to reflect real business value

### Illustration 1

*Trigger*

At a recent AGM the board of X company has received criticism over the quality of the annual report. They are considering revising their current system and have asked you to provide advice as to the suitability of a new approach called integrated reporting.

*Task*

Evaluate the use of integrated reporting for the board of X.

*Suggested Approach*

- Make a note of as many advantages and disadvantages as you can of integrated reporting
- Look for clues in the pre seen and unseen such as availability of information which will be used to generate the necessary reports
- Discuss the pros and cons MOST RELEVANT to the company situation bringing in information from the pre-seen and unseen where possible.

- I can evaluate the impact of changes to financing requirements
- I can advise on financial strategy

### Illustration 2

*Scenario/Trigger*

J company is considering investing in new technology for its production facility in Country X. It is expected that the investment will require significant finance but the FD is unsure about the options available.

*Task*

Evaluate the current financial structure of the business and advise on the most efficient combination and source of finance to ensure that sufficient funds are available for the duration of the new project.

*Suggested Approach*

- Review and evaluate the current debt to equity structure
- Determine financing requirements for the new technology project
- Advise on the interests of relevant stakeholders in the financing decision
- Advise on the availability of finance given current external influence
- Recommend the most appropriate method of raising finance and justify your selection

- I can advise on the value of a business entity
- I can evaluate the appropriateness of a range of different valuation methods

# Understanding competencies

### Illustration 3

*Scenario/Trigger*

C company, a growing retail business, wishes to acquire one of its main competitors. The FD is unsure as to which valuation method would provide the most acceptable price.

*Task*

Evaluate the suitability of the different valuation methods and recommend which would be most appropriate given the circumstances facing the business.

*Suggested Approach*

- Determine the most appropriate valuation methods given the circumstances depicted
- Evaluate and note down the strengths and weaknesses of each of the valuation methods
- Decide which are particularly relevant for the retailer
- Advise and recommend on the most appropriate method with full justification.

- I can evaluate an organisations exposure to risk from a financial and non-financial perspective
- I can advise and recommend on risk management responses
- I can advise on the influence of external factors on any revisions to an organisations risk profile

## Illustration 4

*Scenario/Trigger*

Y plc is involved in oil and gas exploration and wishes to take advantage of newly developed techniques to extract natural gas from recently discovered fields.

*Task*

Evaluate the risks for Y in the context of this new venture.

*Suggested Approach*

- Advise on the categories of risk which would need to be considered for the new venture
- Evaluate, financially and non-financially the effect on Y plc for each of these risks identified
- Advise on the likely stakeholder response should each risk materialise
- Advise on an appropriate strategies to manage the effects of the risks identified

---

- I can evaluate the ethical issue facing a business entity
- I can evaluate the risks associated with corporate governance
- I can advise senior managers of the solutions to risks identified

# Understanding competencies

### Illustration 5

*Scenario/Trigger*

X plc is involved in the production and supply of goods to companies in Europe. It is known to source raw materials from third world suppliers where working practices have recently been criticised via an independent television report for poor working conditions and treatment of staff. The CEO and Chairman Mr T has denied that these practises exist challenging anyone to question his judgement.

*Task*

Evaluate the risks facing X plc.

*Suggested Approach*

- Identify the stakeholders affected
- Evaluate the responsibilities of the board in the circumstances
- Advise the board as to the impact of not addressing the issues noted
- Recommend and fully justify appropriate and corrective course of action

## Business skills

At the strategic level the skills within this generic competence fall mainly within the E3 syllabus with a small amount also coming from F3.

Here is a sample of the competencies which you may be expected to demonstrate:

- I can evaluate developments in external factors influencing the organisations strategy
- I can evaluate the organisations interaction with its stakeholders
- I can advise on and recommend strategic options

# chapter 2

### Illustration 6

*Scenario Trigger*

Z company who compete in the computer games industry are concerned about the recent fall in sales and profitability. The board wishes to prepare a strategic response.

*Task*

Evaluate the circumstances facing Z company and the options available to correct the dip in sales and profits.

*Suggested Approach*

- Identify the factors affecting company Z from the information presented.
- Evaluate the factors identified and their effect on the success of Z
- Advise and evaluate the options available to Z to correct the downward trend in sales
- Recommend with full justification the most appropriate options given the facts as presented

- I can evaluate the process for strategic options generation
- I can evaluate strategic analysis tools in the process of strategy formulation

# Understanding competencies

### Illustration 7

*Scenario/Trigger*

The board of S company is considering holding an away day where a revision to the process by which strategy is developed within S will be discussed. The board are concerned as to their lack of understanding of the practical techniques available to use.

*Task*

Evaluate the current process and recommend alternative options as appropriate.

*Suggested Approach*

- Identify and note the current techniques and processes being used within S for strategy formulation
- Evaluate the alternatives available given information presented in the scenario
- Advise on the most appropriate techniques

- I can advise on the most relevant techniques for managing organisational change
- I can evaluate techniques for the management of change

# chapter 2

### Illustration 8

*Scenario/Trigger*

ABC company have set a key objective to improve production at one of their plants. This will involve the implementation of new processes and working practices resulting in significant change on behalf of the existing work force.

*Task*

Evaluate the options available to achieve this objective

*Suggested Approach*

- Note the most appropriate techniques to assess the impact of the change on the organisation
- Evaluate the use of each technique to achieve the required change
- Recommend on the most appropriate methodology given the facts presented company objectives.

---

- I can evaluate the strategic impact of information systems on an organisation
- I can evaluate the impact of information technology on strategy formulation
- I can advise on changes to the organisations value chain

# Understanding competencies

### Illustration 9

*Scenario/Trigger*

CCC, a major retailer has for some time been concerned as to the lack of sales and marketing information which it derives from its operational tilling system. Various solutions have been suggested to capture the information at source.

*Task*

Evaluate the options as presented and provide a justifiable recommendation based on the availability of resources.

*Suggested Approach*

- Determine the current operational systems strengths and weaknesses
- Identify available options based on information presented in the scenario
- Evaluate each option chosen in the context of adding value to CCC
- Advise and recommend on the chosen option and the management of the impact on current systems

## People Skills

At the strategic level the skills within this generic competence fall mainly within the E3 syllabus with a small amount also coming from F3 and P3. Here is a sample of the competencies which you may be expected to demonstrate:

- I can evaluate the significance of strategic relationships
- I can advise on how to manage and build alliance with key stakeholders

# chapter 2

> **Illustration 10**
>
> *Scenario Trigger*
>
> BL car company is planning to close operations in a European country and move its manufacturing base to Asia. The board are concerned that this move may alienate some stakeholder groups.
>
> *Task*
>
> Explain the techniques which can be used to influence these stakeholders and evaluate each alternative.
>
> *Suggested Approach*
>
> - List those stakeholder groups which may be affected by the proposed move
> - Determine the information needs of each stakeholder group affected and the impact on that group
> - Evaluate from the available information the influence each group may have over the decision
> - Advise on the most appropriate communication method for each stakeholder group identified

- I can collaborate with relevant stakeholders.

## Leadership Skills

At the management level the skills within this generic competency fall mainly within the E3 syllabus. Here is a sample of the competencies which you may be expected to demonstrate:

- I can evaluate the role of leadership
- I can evaluate strategies for managing the change process
- I can evaluate the role of the change leader to support strategy implementation

# Understanding competencies

**Illustration 11**

*Scenario/Trigger*

CL company trades as a retailer in several in town operations within a major European city. Recent changes in demographics have caused CL to develop some out of town stores with some members of staff being requested to travel to the new sites to deliver customer service support.

*Task*

The board have requested your opinion on the most appropriate leadership styles and an evaluation of the role of leadership to maintain and manage an effective team whilst implementing strategy.

*Suggested Approach*

- Identify from the information presented the type of change
- Determine those affected and how they are impacted
- Evaluate the most appropriate management style given the change required
- Recommend an appropriate leadership style within the organisational context

- I can coach and mentor staff
- I can participate in driving organisational performance
- I can motivate and inspire staff

# chapter 2

**Illustration 12**

*Scenario/Trigger*

X company is about to embark on a comprehensive programme of system upgrades within the finance department.

*Task*

Draft an email explaining these changes to the department..

*Suggested Approach*

- Think about how these changes will affect the department – what will their main concerns be?
- What will the benefits be to the department?
- Address the above two points in your email using a positive tone

---

- I can recommend techniques to manage resistance to change

## 4 Summary

You should now have a better understand of how the technical knowledge from previous studies may translate into what you need to be able to DO in the exam in the form of competencies. You should also now recognise if it is likely that you will have some gaps in your knowledge which you will need to revisit.

**Next steps:**

(1) You can begin to revisit and revise technical material from your previous studies according to the summaries given in this chapter. However we suggest you continue to do this alongside working through the rest of this book so you can also learn how you may need to apply the knowledge.

(2) Remember that you are unlikely to have to perform detailed calculations in the case study exam. However you may need to explain or interpret calculations and so an appreciation of how they are prepared is still relevant and useful.

# Understanding competencies

chapter 3

# Integrating skills and knowledge

**Chapter learning objectives**

- To understand how the learning outcomes and skills derived from the individual papers are integrated within the case study competencies and tasks.

# Integrating skills and knowledge

## 1 Triggers and tasks – integrating the skills

In the previous chapter we considered each competency in isolation. It is important that you understand how these competencies will be linked in the examination. We can now bring together these skills into a series of integrated tasks.

Consider the following short scenario:

### Scenario – Company XYZ

XYZ Ltd is a privately owned travel company operating out of ten travel shops based in major towns in the South East of the UK. For some time now the board have been concerned as to the downward trend in customers visiting their shops and were considering rationalising their high street presence and staffing numbers.

The company offers a range of holidays focussing on the mass and cheaper end of the market. Sales have grown for each of the last five years at 10% per annum but unfortunately profits have not risen at the same rate. The company has used price as the main source of competitive advantage being more concerned with financial results than customer service. Many of the processes associated with holiday bookings operated by XYZ are manual and there is still a significant amount of face to face customer contact, the details of which often go unrecorded.

Customer complaints are rising with some 15% of recent customers registering complaints which include poor customer service, alterations to travel schedules, poor accommodation and flight delays.

A fall in advance bookings of 30% forcing the board to consider the urgent corrective action. As the senior management accountant to investigate they have asked you to investigate.

This is an example of what CIMA refer to in the Case study exam as a **trigger**. This information and the events occurring will give rise to one or more tasks. These tasks are likely to come from a range of different generic competency areas.

# chapter 3

### Technical skills

So the first task you may be asked to complete could demonstrate your technical skills.

One of the skills here is to 'identify the types of risk facing an organisation '. So you may be asked to do the following:

**Task 1**

Prepare a briefing note for the Board explaining the risks involved with the current travel shop operations and advise on a suitable alternative.

Advise how the alternative would support or conflict with the overall financial objectives of XYZ.

Given the information in the trigger (and much more detailed company and environmental information provided in the pre-seen information) you are likely to conclude that a company such as XYZ should be using technology much more to provide a more effective and effective service. In addition it may be possible, depending on the information available, to calculate the cost of the manual operation and draw comparisons for future investment in the automation of some or all of the processes. This could have an impact on the charge for the service, future cost savings and hence profitability.

### Business Skills

As part of the Business skills competency you need to show that you can 'evaluate the influence and impact of the external environment'. This may include recognising that other external factors will affect the operation of XYZ.

The next task could thus be:

**Task 2**

Evaluate the external factors which XYZ needs to take into account when planning for changes to the business operations.

### People Skills

Another key generic competency that you will be required to demonstrate involves People Skills such as the ability to 'manage critical periods of adaptive, evolutionary, reconstructive and revolutionary change'. It is possible that you will be tested on your understanding of relevant theory and techniques explaining how to identify and manage such change.

# Integrating skills and knowledge

However it is also likely that you will show your ability through actually influencing relevant stakeholders through the task.

So the above task could be rewritten as:

### Task 2 – Version 2

Write a report to advise the Board on the alternatives available to revise the current business operations at XYZ.

Your report should include an evaluation of the external factors that Z needs to take into account when implementing suitable revisions to operations

## Leadership skills

The final generic competency is leadership.

As with people skills there is knowledge which you may have to show and apply in the case study, for example showing you can 'recommend appropriate leadership styles within organisational change context'.

The following task may be required:

### Task 3

Evaluate the impact on the XYZ organisation of moving towards the greater use of technology and advise how such a change may be managed.

This tests your knowledge and application of change management techniques. Leadership also includes skills such as an ability to 'motivate and inspire staff'.

With this in mind you may also have to demonstrate leadership through completion of a task such as :

### Task 4

Write a letter to the employees of XYZ explaining the move towards an new automated operating system, clearly showing the reasons for the move and the likely impact it will have on the staff and the organisation.

So to summarise the progression here:

> Prepare a briefing note for the Board explaining the risks involved with the current travel shop operations and advise on a suitable alternative. Advise how the alternative would support or conflict with the overall financial objectives of XYZ.

*Do accounting and finance work*

↓

> Evaluate the external factors which XYZ needs to take into account when planning for changes to the business operations.

*In the context of the business*

↓

> Write a letter to the employees of XYZ explaining the move towards a new automated operating system, clearly showing the reasons for the move and the likely impact it will have on the staff and the organisation. Evaluate the impact on the XYZ organisation of moving towards the greater use of technology and advise how such a change may be managed.

*To influence people*

↓

> Write a letter to the employees of XYZ explaining the move towards a new automated operating system, clearly showing the reasons for the move and the likely impact it will have on the staff and the organisation

*And lead within the organisation*

## 2 Triggers and tasks – integrating the technical syllabi

As well as integrating the competencies it is useful to understand how the different technical papers on which the case study builds (E3, P3 and F3) are integrated in the exam.

# Integrating skills and knowledge

The above series of tasks can be mapped out as follows:

|  | P3 | E3 | F3 |
|---|---|---|---|
| Technical skills | Explain the risks involved with the current travel shop operations and advise on a suitable alternative. |  | Advise how the alternative would support or conflict with the overall financial objectives of XYZ. |
| Business skills |  | Evaluate the external factors which XYZ needs to take into account when planning for changes to the business operations |  |
| People skills |  | Evaluate the impact on the XYZ organisation of moving towards the greater use of technology and advise how such a change may be managed |  |
| Leadership skills |  | Explain the move towards an new automated operating system, clearly showing the reasons for the move and the likely impact it will have on the staff and the organisation |  |

As you can see this series of tasks addresses each of the syllabi at the strategic level with more emphasis on E3. It is important to remember however that the exam weightings for the case study are based on the competencies rather than the syllabi.

Let's look at another scenario:

> Despite continual growth even through recent recessionary periods CCC, a large retailer renowned for its customer service and based in Country X, has experienced a decrease in overall customer numbers in the past year of 2%. An ambitious expansion plan, developed by the board over the previous decade and supported by the main investors in CCC finds them operating in most major towns and cities of its home country.
>
> The board of CCC are aware of the growth and increasing prosperity of some parts of Asia and are keen to take advantage of these growth patterns and expand in these countries. As part of a planned expansion plan, the board has identified a potential takeover target BBB. They are however acutely aware of their lack of expertise in international expansion and are being cautiously ambitious in their planning.
>
> Following a recent exploratory visit by the CEO of CCC as part of a trade mission with country Z, the largest and most successful of the countries in the far East, she has become aware of an excellent opportunity to develop a retail operation in the capital city of country Z via an alliance with a large existing retailer DDD. DDD offer a different product range to CCC and tend to cater for the lower price market.
>
> The government of CCC's home country is keen to develop trade links with country Z and has given CCC its blessing to explore the opportunity even suggesting that there may be some financial support forthcoming if the right development package is put together. Not all of the board are enthusiastic however and they are supported by some store managers who are aware of the development and are worried that expansion of this sort could result in catastrophic job losses in future years.
>
> CCC's most recent results are 5% down on forecast. A recent letter received at CCC from one of the major shareholders indicates that they are expecting to see a revision to the current strategy to support a turnaround in the recent numbers. In addition the CEO is aware that unpublished management information suggests that a "like for like" fall in customer numbers of 10% when compared to the previous year.
>
> As the senior management accountant in the Retail Analysis and Strategy department the board have asked you to evaluate the opportunity and advise on and recommend any viable alternatives.

# Integrating skills and knowledge

A similar series of tasks to the first example, incorporating a different range of technical content, could be mapped as follows:

|  | P3 | E3 | F3 |
|---|---|---|---|
| Technical skills | (2) Evaluate the extent to which these options will affect future cash flows. | | |
| Business skills | (1) Identify and explain the risks associated with this potential change in growth strategy options. | | |
| People skills | | (3) Identify and explain suitable techniques which can be used in persuading senior management of the need to accept such a change in strategy. | |

| Leadership skills | | (4) Explain the move towards an international expansion strategy and recommend how to build relationships with stakeholders affected | |

## 3 Summary

You should now appreciate how the different technical areas from previous studies may integrate and form more complex triggers and tasks. You should also understand how you may see progression through the four generic competency areas.

**Next steps:**

(1) Return to the previous chapter and consider the range of competency statements which we gave you. Can you create your own integrated tasks using skills from each of the technical syllabi?

(2) Think about your own role at work. Where do you use Technical skills? What about Business skills? Do you have much opportunity to use People skills or even Leadership? Thinking about your own experiences is very useful in generating ideas in the exam.

# Integrating skills and knowledge

chapter

# 4

# Preseen information for the pilot case

**Chapter learning objectives**

## Introduction

The Case Study Examinations are like no other CIMA exam; there is no new syllabus to study or formulae to learn. The best way to be successful at this level is to practise using past case study exams and mock exams based on your real live case study. By reviewing previous case studies alongside your current case you will improve your commercial thought processes and will be more aware of what the examiner expects. By sitting mock exams, under timed conditions you can hone your exam techniques and, in particular, your time management skills.

This textbook is therefore based on this principle. It presents the pilot case study and uses this to demonstrate the skills and techniques that you must master to be successful. The first pilot case, Cast, will be used to walkthrough the processes and approach. The remainder of this chapter contains the Cast pre-seen material.

We would advise that you skim read this now before moving on to Chapter 5 where you will be provided with more guidance on how to familiarise yourself with the pre-seen material.

## 1 Reference material 1 – Intro

### The Cast Group

You are a senior manager who works for the Cast Group ("Cast"). You report directly to the parent company's board and advise on special projects and strategic matters. You have compiled the following facts about the company.

### Company history

In 1920, Frank Smith opened a shop that sold men's clothing. The shop sold good quality clothing at a reasonable price and sales grew. In 1922 Mr Smith moved to a larger shop and started to sell women's clothes and by 1925 the business had occupied the largest shop in town and was selling household goods.

Over the next ten years the business grew as Mr Smith opened new stores in neighbouring towns. Growth slowed during the Second World War, but the company was able to continue to trade throughout the War years.

When Frank Smith retired as chief executive in 1952 the company owned eleven department stores in the Northern region of its home country. The stores traded as "Frank Smith and Sons". Frank Smith's four sons took over the running of the company and started an ambitious expansion plan. Firstly, they changed the trading name of the business to Woodvale. Secondly, they started an aggressive expansion which led to the opening of a total of 65 Woodvale stores, spread across their home country.

The expansion programme implemented by Frank Smith's sons was financed largely by the use of commercial mortgages that were used to purchase Woodvale's shops. As a major retailer, Woodvale generated significant cash inflows and the mortgages were serviced out of trading income. All of the mortgages were paid off by 1990.

Frank Smith had incorporated the business as a company in 1920. The company has never sought a stock market quotation. The shareholdings have become increasingly widespread because of inheritance. Succeeding generations of the founder's family have tended to leave the running of the company to professional managers. None of the present board members are members of Frank Smith's family.

During the 1990s, the Woodvale stores were a major presence in virtually every large town's shopping centre. The shops still sold ranges of clothing and household goods. They aimed for the mass market by selling goods that were towards the bottom end of the market in terms of pricing, but were still of reasonable quality. Sales started to decline, partly because consumer tastes were changing. Most of Woodvale's competitors moved upmarket and sold better quality items that were more fashionable. At the same time, some newcomers started to undercut Woodvale's prices at the bottom end of the market. Many supermarkets started to sell inexpensive clothes in their larger branches and some new retail chains started to offer admittedly low quality goods at very cheap prices.

Woodvale's initial response to these changes in the market was to aim to hold the middle ground and to aim to retain their existing customer base. That strategy failed because younger customers were attracted by the cheaper prices on offer from the low-cost entrants to the market while older customers moves slightly upmarket to buy from Woodvale's traditional rivals.

The retail market was also changing in another significant way. Retail parks were opening on the outskirts of town and city centres. These offered customers the convenience of easy parking and a wide range of shops. Woodvale would have found it difficult to move out to these retail parks because it owned large town centre stores. It would have been expensive to sell those and to relocate to the retail parks.

Woodvale attempted to stem the loss of business by rebranding its stores. The emphasis on clothing was reduced and new lines were added. The company started to sell computer games and music CDs, cosmetics and other books. One strategy that it adopted was the purchase of a number of smaller retailers who had already established themselves in those markets. For example, the Smile chain had a cosmetics shop in almost every town centre, but was struggling to compete with larger competitors. Woodvale purchased all of Smile's equity and created a Smile "shop within a shop" within existing Woodvale stores. This strategy was used to create synergies with several other declining city centre retailers.

**Preseen information for the pilot case**

By the year 2010, Woodvale's sales revenues were declining rapidly. The company was still committed to town centre shops, that now faced increasing pressure from internet retailing. The directors agreed that it was becoming increasingly difficult to maintain sales revenue. Profits had declined to the point where Woodvale was barely breaking even and was expected to slip into loss within a year.

The directors called an extraordinary meeting of the shareholders to present a proposal for a radical change of strategy, as outlined below. The shareholders agreed unanimously that the present business model had to change and that the directors should be given their permission to pursue a new online retailing strategy.

### The present strategy

By 2011, Woodvale had sold all of its traditional stores. The cash that was generated was used to establish an online retailer. The company changed its trading name to "Cast".

*Note: To avoid confusion, it should be noted that Cast and Woodvale are different trading names for the same company. Any subsequent references to Woodvale are to this company in the period before 2010, when the company operated as a traditional, town centre retailer. Any references to Cast are to the period after 2010, after the company was restructured as an online retailer.*

Despite the decline in business during the 1990s and into the 2000s, Cast remains a significant company. It is still unquoted and it is the largest unquoted business based in its home country.

Cast operates as a single entity, with a single corporate office and a single logistics centre. It trades through six main trading names, each of which has its own website. Each website sells a different product line. Having six separate sites makes it easier for customers to browse for the items that they wish to buy. It also means that Cast can manage the separate retail brands independently in the hope of maximising consumer awareness and brand identity. It is no secret that all six trading names belong to Cast.

Cast trades as follows

| | |
|---|---|
| Cast Disk | Cast Disk sells DVDs, Blu-ray disks and music downloads. Cast Disk used to trade through Woodvale shops as Happy Music. When the decision was made to move to online retailing, the directors rebranded these stores as Cast Disk.<br><br>Cast Disk sells a wide range of popular entertainment media, including computer games. |
| Papercut | Papercut sells books.<br><br>In principle, customers can purchase almost any book that is in print. The logistical arrangements that are in place to make this possible are described below.<br><br>Woodvale did not sell books, but it was a very natural product line for Cast to sell because consumers were already familiar with buying books online. |
| Childsplay | Childsplay sells toys.<br><br>Childsplay's core business is the sale of branded toys and games. For example, one of the site's most successful products is a range of construction toys that is sold globally.<br><br>Childsplay also carries unbranded, generic products such as balls and skipping ropes.<br><br>The Childsplay website also sells computer games, both hardware and software. |
| Smile | Smile sells cosmetics.<br><br>Prior to 2010, as part of Woodvale, Smile specialised in inexpensive brands of cosmetics. Smile has offered a wider range of products, including higher quality and more expensive brands, since the creation of Cast. |
| Warm | Warm sells fashion clothes.<br><br>Warm aims at the market for men and women in the age range 18-35. All of the clothes sold are branded products.<br><br>These are the only clothes sold by Cast. Cast places far less emphasis on clothing than it did when it traded as Woodvale and it aims for a far narrower niche within the clothing market. |

| Zap | Zap sells consumer electronics. These range from computers and tablets to music players and cameras.

Customers can buy games consoles through the Zap website and so there is further overlap between this site and the Cast Disk and Childsplay websites. |

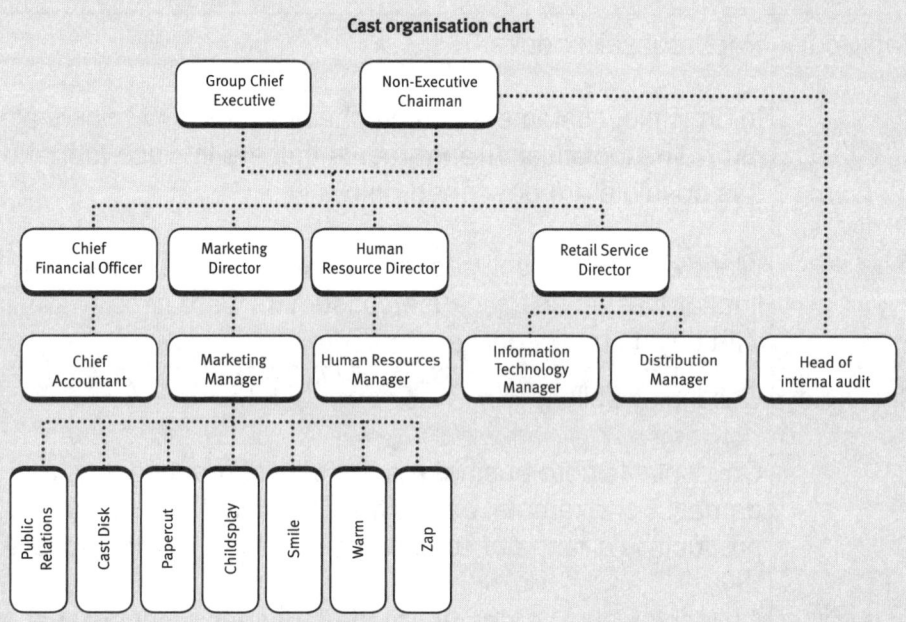

Cast organisation chart

## Organisation

Each of these trading names has its own website. Customers can select items for purchase by either making specific searches or by browsing online. The software uses cookies to track customers and both buying and browsing habits are recorded. If a customer places an order then the customer's email address is used to send personalised emails. For example, if a customer browses lipsticks on the Smile website but does not place an order then the system will send an email 48 hours later reminding the customer of the products that were viewed.

Customers are encouraged to leave feedback on their purchases. Thus, anybody who is unsure about a product's suitability can read reviews left by others who have already purchased that item. Each review starts with the customer's initial impression expressed as a mark out of five. The reviewer is then invited to expand on that score by leaving brief comments on their experiences.

Cast's retailing model is supported by a complex logistical operation. The group's head office is in the centre of the country and it hosts the servers from which the websites are run. There are three distribution centres, one beside the head office and one each in the North and in the South of the country. Cast holds inventories of many of its more popular lines. Orders for those goods are automatically forwarded to one of the distribution centres, provided it has the item or items in stock. Less popular items are supplied by manufacturers or by other online retailers. These companies pay Cast a commission for all orders received through Cast's website. They must also keep their inventory records up to date so that customers can check that an item is available before placing an order. Cast forwards the customer's payment, less commission, as soon as the supplier confirms the despatch of the goods.

Each of the websites has its own website management team. Each team is responsible for monitoring and managing sales from its site. The teams are also responsible for procurement and buying. The managers in charge of each team report directly to the marketing manager. The marketing manager also supervises Cast's public relations officer.

Cast's marketing director regards buying as an extension of the marketing function because sales depend on Cast buying products that will appeal to customers. Marketing managers within each website team spend a lot of their time reviewing potential new products to add to the products sold through their site.

Most of the sites sell branded products and the promotion of the products themselves is largely left to the manufacturers. Cast's marketing effort consists largely of designing web pages. Manufacturers often provide their own marketing materials, including product photographs and descriptive text, but Cast has to adapt that material in order to permit some consistency across the site,

Even though Cast does not advertise its products, marketing is a very important aspect of the business. It is possible to promote specific products or specific manufacturers by putting them on the opening page of a site. For example, a customer logging onto the Papercut site might be shown a recently-published book that is being sold at a discount. It is also possible to influence the order in which search results are displayed. For example, a customer entering the phrase "tablet computer" will be shown a wide range of computers, but the search algorithm will tend to place items that have a larger mark-up towards the top of the page so that the potential profit is maximised. Cast's research shows that careful management of the opening page and of the search algorithm can have a significant effect on profit. The website sales teams are evaluated on their sales revenues and contribution figures.

Each website management team includes a buying department. The buyers are responsible for maintaining good relations with suppliers and for placing orders. The buyers are also responsible for negotiating prices and terms of trade with new suppliers and for ensuring that these are kept under review. For example, if a product is selling well then the buyers may attempt to seek a larger discount from the supplier.

The Cast Disk team is responsible for computer games, both the hardware in the form of consoles and the software in the form of disks and cartridges. Most sales of these products originate from customers who started on the Cast Disk site. Having a single team for computer games ensures consistency in presentation and also ensures that manufacturers have a designated point of contact with Cast.

The website management teams have their own staff who are expert in web page design. They ensure that the web pages are up to date and then submit the new or revised pages to the information technology department for upload to the site itself.

The information technology (IT) department is responsible for the availability and security of the company websites. A single server supports the sites and provides all of the associated services, such as processing of customer credit and debit card payments.

The IT department also manages a recovery site that operates at a remote location. The recovery site maintains a full backup of all of the main site's files. It also has the hardware and software required to act as the primary site in the event that Cast's main server is forced to go offline for any reason.

The distribution department is responsible for the operation of the distribution centres.

The logistical arrangements are complicated.

Customer orders are analysed by a computer programme that determines the most efficient way of fulfilling the order. If Cast holds the goods in one or more of its distribution centres then it will forward the details to whichever centre can fulfil the order. It may choose between centres on the basis that orders for multiple items should be directed to the centre that has everything in stock so that only one package needs to be prepared and despatched. The software can also take account of the activity levels in different centres. If two or more centres could fulfil the order then the instructions will go to the centre that is least busy at the time.

If Cast does not have the goods in stock then it forwards the order to the third party who is responsible for that line.

The work undertaken within Cast's distribution centres combines both high technology with unskilled manual labour. Inventory is retrieved from storage areas using electrically-powered vehicles that are directed by messages transmitted by the inventory system. Screens on the vehicles instruct human operators to load specific items from each location and they scan barcodes on the packaging to confirm that the correct item that has been collected. Retrieved items are then delivered to the packing area where staff package goods in accordance with picking lists printed out by the inventory system and attach customer address labels, also printed automatically, to each package. Goods are packaged in cardboard boxes that have been designed to be sealed quickly once the goods have been placed inside. Staff are trained to select the most suitable box and to pack the goods securely.

Labelled packages are placed on a conveyor belt. Sensors read the barcodes on each package and direct it to the appropriate loading area. Customers can pay extra for an express courier delivery. Items that are not delivered by express courier are allocated either to a different courier if the package is bulky or to the postal service if it is small enough to be delivered by post. The distribution centres despatch so many packages that the courier companies and the postal service have their own loading bays that are staffed by their own employees.

**2 Reference material 2 – Industry analysis**

**Industry analysis**

Online retailing has grown rapidly over the past ten years, to the extent that it is the third most shopped channel in the US, after supermarkets and mass merchandisers, which are essentially discount retailers that aim to sell large quantities of goods quickly using techniques such as discounting, self-service and so on.

The rate of growth is slowing as the market reaches maturity, but it continues to grow. The following chart shows inflation adjusted sales in Cast's home market for the four years from 2010 to 2013:

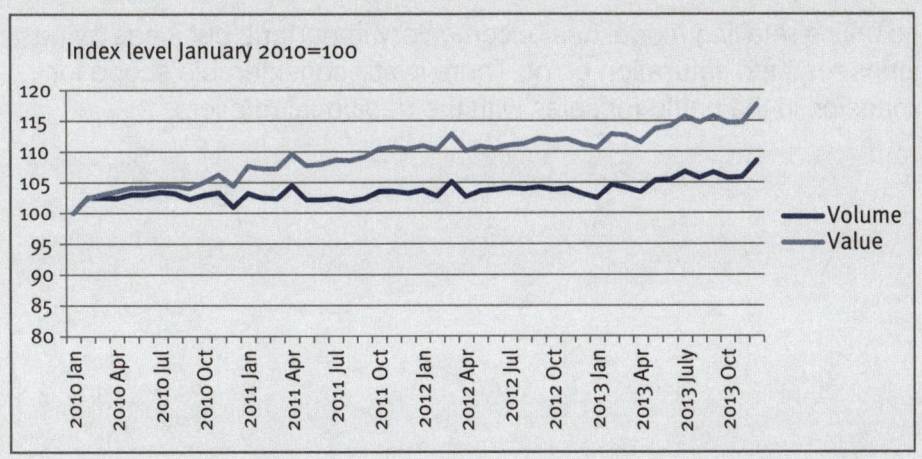

## Preseen information for the pilot case

Volume reflects the number of online sales while value expresses sales in monetary terms, index linked to exclude the effects of inflation. The average value of each sale made has increased because of growing consumer confidence in this medium, which has spurred retailers to offer "big ticket" items alongside traditional online goods such as books and music.

A much wider range of products is now sold online, with fashion, health, beauty and groceries all growing strongly. Once shoppers buy a product from a given category online they tend to become comfortable with such purchases and tend to buy further products.

Customers are attracted by the convenience of having bulky items delivered directly to their homes and, in many cases, lower prices than would be charged by traditional shops.

The move to online retail has had an impact on traditional retail models. Half of online shoppers purchase electronic goods online. Large electronics retailers are shedding capacity in their shops and moving towards their own internet stores in response to this shift.

Shoppers have adapted to internet-based shopping in other ways. Purchasing decisions are often informed by online research, with consumers reading reviews and comparing specifications in order to choose between competing products. Social media sites often influence buying decisions with opinions expressed by other shoppers being regarded as more reliable than advice offered by retail assistants.

The technology associated with online retailing has been developing too. There is a growing tendency towards the use of smartphones and tablets to make purchases. Many retailers have created apps that can be downloaded and used to place orders. The fact that these are portable can also mean that consumers will browse reviews and other information even while shopping in stores.

Smartphone apps open up the online market to consumers who were not previously regular internet users.

The online retailing model has become very important, but it has by no means reached saturation point. There is still considerable scope for expansion in the battle for sales with the traditional retailers.

## 3 Reference material 3 – Risk factors

Cast is not a quoted company and is not required to publish details concerning risk management. However, the following report has been obtained from the annual report of a quoted company in the same industry.

| Competition | Our businesses face a great deal of competition. Many of our competitors are large and powerful and are long-established. They may be able to use their buying power to secure better terms from suppliers and to undercut our selling prices. |
|---|---|
| Fluctuating operating results and growth rates | Many of the products that we sell are discretionary purchases for which demand declines in line with tightening of the economy. That can make it difficult to forecast sales because we are forced to predict both changes in the economy and also the elasticity of sales demand in response to such changes. It may prove impossible for us to sustain historical rates of growth. |
| Inefficiency in our distribution centres | Any failure to operate our distribution centres efficiently may impact our profitability:<br><br>• Any failure to meet customer expectations could lead to a loss of repeat sales.<br><br>• Mismanagement of inventory could lead to obsolescence and overstocking.<br><br>• Additional delivery costs could be incurred because we fail to combine part-orders. |
| Seasonal factors | Demand is always far higher in our fourth quarter. That forces us to hold larger quantities of inventory during the period leading up to our peak demand. That increases the risks associated with overstocking and obsolescence.<br><br>Failure to meet peak demand involve the opportunity costs associated with lost sales and also the reputational cost of failing to meet customer expectations. |

Preseen information for the pilot case

| | |
|---|---|
| Supplier relationships | We enjoy competitive advantage because we have good working relationships with key suppliers who are prepared to give us preferential terms on the sale of new products. We are often given the opportunity to comment upon new products under development and to order significant quantities during the period leading up to launch.

Maintaining these relationships can be complicated because we must invest a great deal of time and effort and must also be prepared to make significant purchases of unproven products. |
| IT security | Our sales are online and so our customers must be confident that we can maintain and protect their personal information.

We would also face significant losses in the event that failures in either hardware or software were to disrupt our ability to process sales.

Our IT systems are under constant threat from external threats such as hacking and denial of service and are also exposed to physical threats such as fire and flood. |
| Product liability | We sell a wide range of products, many of which could injure a customer, damage property or be implicated in an incident affecting a third party. |
| Payment-related risks | We accept payments made by debit cards, credit cards and bank transfers. New forms of payment terms are being developed and we must be willing and able to process those in order to remain competitive. This leaves us exposed to fraudulent abuse of cardholders' details by third parties. We could record sales and despatch products in good faith and then be required to reimburse the customer without being able to recover the goods.

We also face the risks of failure by card issuers and other financial institutions, who may be unable to settle the receivables due to us. |

# 4 Reference material 4 – Cast's Mission Statement and Strategy

## Cast mission statement

Our vision is to be the most customer-focussed company in our home market. We aim to offer a virtual location that offers consumers the products that they wish to buy at prices they are willing to pay.

## Cast strategy

Cast's most immediate strategic priority is to build sales volume. The company aims to dominate the markets that it serves. That is partly to make the best possible use on any economies of scale that it might exploit and also to deter competitors from entering the market segments that the company has chosen to serve.

Cast cannot afford to lose ground because switching costs for consumers are low. It is difficult to differentiate an online retailer on the basis of quality because most sales are of branded goods that are generally available from a range of competing outlets. It is equally difficult to differentiate on the basis of service because most online retailers aim to offer fast and reliable delivery.

Larger retailers can generally negotiate discounts from suppliers and can absorb the costs of the logistical infrastructure more easily. Smaller competitors will, therefore, struggle to gain market share in the face of lower selling prices.

Cast's directors have prepared the following outline SWOT analysis

| Strengths | Weaknesses |
|---|---|
| • Diversified product range<br>• Strong customer focus | • Dependence on suppliers<br>• Unquoted status limits undermines credibility when dealing with suppliers |
| **Opportunities** | **Threats** |
| • Growth prospects for e-commerce<br>• Potential to add further product lines | • Suppliers may develop their own online sales channels<br>• Foreign competitors may enter the home market |

## 5 Reference material 5 – Directors' biographies

**Cast Directors Biographies**

(1) Judith Anderson

**Group Chief executive**

Judith joined Cast on 1 December 2014. She started her career as a journalist with a national newspaper. She was promoted to deputy editor before leaving to take charge of the public relations department of a television production company. She had several roles with that company before joining its board as sales director.

(2) Arthur Brown

**Non-executive chairman**

Arthur joined the board of Cast on 4 August 2010 and was appointed chairman on 1 April 2011. He has held a variety of roles in the banking industry. He is also the trustee of a charity.

(**Note**: Cast is an unquoted company and, as such, is not required to have non-executive directors. The shareholders have agreed that Arthur should remain the only non-executive for the time being.)

(3) Brenda Carroll

**Retail Services**

Brenda was appointed to the board on 12 November 2009. Previously she had held a variety of senior management positions with several retailers, including a national retail chain.

Brenda is a non-executive director with Cablevision, a quoted internet service provider.

(4) Charles Denning

**Marketing**

Charles has worked for Cast since 1997. He was appointed to Cast's Board on 23 February 2006. Previously, he had worked for Cast as a senior sales manager.

Charles has also worked for the marketing departments of two other major retailers

(5) Dana Elliot

**Chief Financial Officer**

Dana started her career as a trainee accountant in a government department. She has since held a number of posts with organisations including a manufacturing company and a distributor. She was appointed to Cast's board on 1 January 2013. Dana is a non-executive director of an opera company.

(6) Earnest Fletcher

**Human Resources**

Earnest was appointed to Cast's board on 1 July 2009. He has held a number of management positions in human resources, working in three different countries in the course of his career.

## 6 Reference material 6 – Internal audit department

### Cast

### Internal audit department

> The internal audit department comprises eight members of professional staff and two administrators. Five of the professional staff are qualified accountants and the other three are training for professional exams. One of the five qualified accountants is an experienced IT auditor, although she is also available for non-IT related assignments.
>
> The head of internal audit reports to the non-executive chairman for administrative purposes.
>
> The internal audit department focuses on compliance matters, with particular emphasis on the application of control processes and procedures in the area of accounting and administration.
>
> The department prepares an annual work programme, which is reviewed by the non-executive chairman and the group chief executive. The work programme focuses on areas identified as either high-risk or of significant importance to the business operations.
>
> Audit investigations are conducted in accordance with relevant professional standards. The audit programmes and the results of all investigations are documented in sufficient detail for review by the head of internal audit. Copies of all internal audit reports are made available to the board and any major findings are discussed by the board.

## 7 Reference material 7 – Extracts of financial statements

### Cast

The following information has been extracted from Cast's financial statements for the year ended 31 March 2015

**Accounting policies (extract only)**

**Vendor Agreements**

Some of our vendors provide us with cash payments as rebates and reimbursements for cooperative marketing arrangements. We generally account for these as a reduction of the cost prices for our purchases and so we offset these receipts against the cost of purchased inventory.

Vendor rebates are typically awarded in response to us reaching minimum purchase thresholds. We evaluate the likelihood of reaching purchase thresholds using past experience and current year forecasts. When volume rebates can be reasonably estimated, we record a portion of the rebate as we make progress towards the purchase threshold. The amounts that we accrue in this way are shown under trade receivables until such time as the payment is received or the balance is written off.

When we receive direct reimbursements for costs incurred by us in advertising a vendor's products we offset the amounts received against "Distribution" in our consolidated statement of profit or loss.

**Segmental reporting**

The group's operating segmental format is by line of business, based on the company's management and internal reporting structure.

**Goodwill**

Goodwill arising from the acquisition of subsidiaries is shown under intangible non-current assets. We evaluate goodwill annually for impairment.

**Software**

Software costs that meet the recognition criteria set out in IAS 38 Intangible assets are capitalised as intangible non-current assets. These costs are amortised over the shorter of their estimated useful lives and the life of the licence agreement.

## Cast Group

**Consolidated Statement of Profit or Loss for the year ended 31 March 2015**

|  | Notes | 2015 $m | 2014 $m |
|---|---|---|---|
| Revenue | (1) | 2,985 | 2,687 |
| Cost of sales |  | (2,090) | (1,777) |
| Gross point |  | 895 | 910 |
| Distribution costs |  | (197) | (192) |
| Administration expenses |  | (174) | (171) |
| Operating profit | (1, 2) | 524 | 547 |
| Finance costs |  | (1) | (1) |
| Profit before taxation |  | 523 | 546 |
| Taxation | (4) | (128) | (126) |
| Profit for the year |  | 395 | 420 |

## Cast Group

**Consolidated Statement of Changes in Equity for the year ended 31 March 2015**

|  | Share capital $m | Share premium $m | Retained earnings $m | Total $m |
|---|---|---|---|---|
| Opening balance | 15 | 18 | 634 | 667 |
| Profit for year | – | – | 395 | 395 |
| Dividend | – | – | (350) | (350) |
| Closing balance | – | – | 679 | 712 |

**Cast Group**

**Consolidated Statement of Financial Position as at 31 March 2015**

|  | Notes | $m | 2014 $m |
|---|---|---|---|
| **ASSETS** |  | 18 |  |
| Non-current assets |  |  |  |
| Intangible | (5) | 90 | 86 |
| Property, plant and equipment | (6) | 387 | 349 |
|  |  |  |  |
| Current assets |  |  |  |
| Inventories |  | 297 | 256 |
| Trade receivables |  | 117 | 105 |
| Cash and short term deposits |  | 243 | 238 |
|  |  | 657 | 599 |
| **TOTAL ASSETS** |  | 1,134 | 1,034 |
|  |  |  |  |
| **EQUITY** |  |  |  |
| Share capital |  | 15 | 15 |
| Share premium |  | 18 | 18 |
| Retained earnings |  | 679 | 634 |
|  |  | 712 | 667 |
| **LIABILITIES** |  |  |  |
| Non-current liabilities |  |  |  |
| Deferred tax |  | 8 | 6 |
| Debenture loans |  | 100 | 100 |
|  |  | 108 | 106 |
| Current liabilities |  |  |  |
| Trade payables |  | 190 | 138 |
| Current tax |  | 124 | 123 |
|  |  | 314 | 261 |
| **TOTAL EQUITY + LIABILITIES** |  | 1,134 | 1,034 |

**Cast Group**

**Consolidated Statement of Cash flows for the year ended 31 March 2015**

|  | 2015 $m | 2014 $m |
|---|---|---|
| **Cash flows from operating activities** | | |
| Cash receipts from customers | 2,973 | 2,498 |
| Cash paid to suppliers and employees | (2,347) | (2,053) |
| Cash generated from operations | 626 | 445 |
| Income taxes paid | (125) | (123) |
| Net cash from operating activities | 501 | 322 |
| **Cash flows from investing activities** | | |
| Purchases of property, plant and equipment | (112) | (28) |
| Proceeds from disposal of property, plant and equipment | 2 | 12 |
| Purchases of non-current intangibles | (35) | – |
| Net cash used in investing activities | (145) | (16) |
| **Cash flows from financing activities** | | |
| Interest paid | (1) | (1) |
| Dividend paid | (350) | (325) |
| Net cash from financing activities | (351) | (326) |
| Net increase/(decrease) in cash and cash equivalents | 5 | (20) |
| **Cash and cash equivalents at beginning of period** | 238 | 258 |
| **Cash and cash equivalents at end of period** | 243 | 238 |

## Note 1 – Segmental analysis

The Cast Group is not subject to the requirements of IFRS 8 Operating Segments, but the directors have provided the following analyses to assist the shareholders.

*Revenue*

| Film and music $m | Toys $m | Cosmetics $m | Books $m | Clothing $m | Electronics $m | Total $m |
|---|---|---|---|---|---|---|
| 776 | 507 | 328 | 448 | 328 | 598 | 2,985 |

*Operating profit*

| Film and music $m | Toys $m | Cosmetics $m | Books $m | Clothing $m | Electronics $m | Total $m |
|---|---|---|---|---|---|---|
| 173 | 58 | 94 | 52 | 47 | 100 | 524 |

## Note 2 – Operating profit

|  | Year ended 31 March 2015 $m | Year ended 31 March 2014 $m |
|---|---|---|
| Operating profit is stated after charging: |  |  |
| • Depreciation of property, plant and equipment | 63 | 54 |
| • Loss on disposal of property, plant and equipment | 9 | 1 |
| • Amortisation of intangible non-current assets | 22 | 19 |
| • Impairment of intangible non-current assets | 9 | – |
| • Cost of inventory recognised as an expense | 1,489 | 1,248 |
| • Operating leases | 22 | 18 |
| • External auditor's remuneration | 1 | 1 |

# Preseen information for the pilot case

**Note 3 – Staff costs including directors' remuneration**

|  | Year ended 31 March 2015 Number of employees | Year ended 31 March 2014 Number of employees |
|---|---|---|
| By activity |  |  |
| • Distribution | 311 | 349 |
| • Information technology | 113 | 110 |
| • Administration | 82 | 86 |
|  | 506 | 545 |

Employee costs, including directors' remuneration:

|  | Year ended 31 March 2015 $m | Year ended 31 March 2014 $m |
|---|---|---|
| Tax on profit | 9 | 11 |
| • Wages and salaries | 4 | 3 |
| • Pension costs |  |  |
| • Total | 13 | 14 |

Aggregate compensation paid to board members, including pension costs:

|  | Year ended 31 March 2015 $m | Year ended 31 March 2015 $m |
|---|---|---|
| • Total | 2 | 2 |

**Note 4 – Tax expense**

|  | Year ended 31 March 2015 $m | Year ended 31 March 2014 $m |
|---|---|---|
| Tax on current year's profit | 124 | 123 |
| Adjustment in respect of prior year | 2 | 4 |
|  | 126 | 127 |
| Increase/(decrease) in deferred tax | 2 | (1) |
| Tax on profit | 128 | 126 |

**Note 5 – Intangible non-current assets**

|  | Goodwill $m | Software $m | Total $m |
|---|---|---|---|
| Cost at 1 April 2014 | 70 | 40 | 110 |
| Additions | – | 35 | 35 |
| Impairment |  | (10) | (10) |
| Cost at 31 March 2015 | 70 | 85 | 135 |
|  |  |  |  |
| Accumulated amortisation at 1 April 2014 | – | 24 | 24 |
| Charge for year | – | 22 | 22 |
| Impairment | – | (1) | (1) |
| Accumulated amortisation at 31 March 2015 | – | 45 | 45 |
|  |  |  |  |
| Net book value at 31 March 2015 | 70 | 20 | 90 |
|  |  |  |  |
| Net book value at 1 April 2014 | 70 | 16 | 86 |

## Note 6 – Property, plant and equipment

|  | Property $m | Plant and equipment $m | Total $m |
|---|---|---|---|
| Cost at 1 April 2014 | 120 | 271 | 391 |
| Additions | 11 | 101 | 112 |
| Disposals | – | (14) | (14) |
| Cost at 31 March 2015 | 131 | 358 | 489 |
| | | | |
| Accumulated depreciation at 1 April 2014 | 18 | 24 | 42 |
| Charge for year | 3 | 60 | 63 |
| Disposals | – | (3) | (3) |
| Accumulated depreciation at 31 March 2015 | 21 | 81 | 102 |
| | | | |
| Net book value at 31 March 2015 | 100 | 277 | 387 |
| | | | |
| Net book value at 1 April 2014 | 102 | 247 | 349 |

## 8 Reference material 8 – Cast corporate social responsibility

**Cast**
**Corporate Social Responsibility Report**
**(for year ended 31 March 2015)**

**Our values**

**Our approach to corporate social responsibility stems from two main values:**

- Our customers come first and we strive to delight them with our service
- We treat everyone in the same manner as we would wish to be treated ourselves – every stakeholder's interests matters to us.

Those values are amplified in the following commitments:

(1) We buy and sell our products responsibly
(2) We care for the environment
(3) We offer local communities our active support
(4) We offer our employees good jobs and genuine career prospects.

Cast sets specific targets for each of those commitments and measures performance. Managers at all levels are evaluated on their contribution to the achievement of those targets.

Corporate social responsibility is an important element of our overall strategic planning for Cast's development.

### Responsible buying and selling

We recognise that our customers want to buy products that have been sourced from suppliers who behave ethically and who respect the environment. Cast takes care to ensure that everybody in the supply chain is treated honestly and fairly and that care is taken to minimise the impact of manufacture and distribution on the environment.

Cast works in partnership with suppliers to ensure that every product sold is sourced responsibly. We have an ethical trade manager, who reports directly to the board of directors, whose responsibility is to ensure that Cast's standards are adhered to by each and every one of its suppliers.

Cast has had some success in persuading suppliers to modify their products or their packaging so that their environmental impact is reduced.

In 2012 Cast committed itself to reducing the carbon emissions of the products in its supply chain by 20% by 2020. The company is well on its way to achieving this target.

Cast actively avoids trading with companies that have exploitative employment practices. Every supplier must demonstrate its commitment to treating staff fairly and to ensure that all staff have a safe and pleasant working environment. Suppliers must document their acceptance of Cast's values and must provide verifiable evidence that they do not employ child labour and that health and safety practices are of a high standard.

Cast develops long-term relationships with key suppliers, which makes it easier to ensure that the supply chain operates in a clear and transparent manner with respect to these issues.

**Caring for the environment**

Our online retail model is inherently less harmful than traditional retail. Our distribution model avoids the transportation of bulk goods from a central warehouse to retail outlets. Customers place their orders from home instead of travelling to a store or a shopping centre. Goods are transported directly to customers using a mixture of courier and postal services.

Cast is constantly striving to minimise its impact on the environment. Our distribution centres are modern and efficient facilities that are designed to minimise energy use.

The buildings are heavily insulated and use solar panels to provide a large proportion of the energy used for heat and light. Two of our centres have wind turbines that make them totally self-sufficient with respect to electricity.

We have developed a range of packaging that minimises waste, while ensuring that customers receive a safe and reliable delivery. Our cardboard contains a high proportion of recycled wood pulp. Our packaging is designed to be opened easily and to be easily recycled by customers.

Customer orders are distributed using a combination of courier and postal services. These services are provides by companies who operate modern and fuel-efficient fleets of vehicles. We take care to ensure that collections are scheduled in the most efficient manner possible so that vehicle capacity is not wasted and so fuel is saved.

We have introduced a number of further initiatives to protect the environment. For example, we have a scheme whereby customers can use a free postage service to return used ink and toner cartridges for recycling.

Our staff are encouraged to assist in identifying ways to avoid waste. There is a "green champion" in every work team and we offer rewards and incentives to staff who make cost-effective suggestions for improved energy efficiency.

## Supporting local communities

Cast aims to be a good neighbour to local communities. Our distribution centres are major local employers in their locations and our behaviour has a significant impact on the lives of local residents. We actively encourage our staff to become involved in local charities through a variety of initiatives, such as matching donations, granting special leave and funding projects.

During the year ended 31 March 2015, these activities include:

- Staff at the Capital City distribution centre raised $10,000 for a local children's charity by completing a sponsored bicycle ride. Cast contributed an additional $2 for every $1 raised from sponsorship, so a total of $30,000 was raised.

- Members of staff from the North distribution centre operate a crèche at a local hospital, making it easier for patients who have small children to attend outpatients clinics. Cast grants each participating employee an additional day of annual leave for every two days spent working at the hospital.

- The South distribution centre has a large recreation centre, including playing fields.

This centre is made available to local schools for two days per week.

Cast has a number of further initiatives in place to assist the local community. There are regular meetings and focus groups for local residents. For example, residents living beside the North distribution centre were being disturbed by security lights along the centre's perimeter. Those lights were relocated so that residents were not being troubled.

Cast contributes to the wider community. For example, the company does not aggressively pursue tax avoidance schemes that would artificially reduce the effective tax rate being paid.

## Creating good jobs and careers

We make the following commitment to our employees:

- You will be treated with respect
- You will have an opportunity to develop
- Your manager will be supportive
- Your working environment will be safe and pleasant

To that end, we work closely with employees to ensure that there is a sense of mutual respect and understanding. We hold regular focus groups for staff to give employees the opportunity to give us feedback. We have an employee website to keep staff informed of all major developments. We send all staff a weekly newsletter by email.

We set wage rates in excess of the national minimum and we benchmark against the rates offered for comparable jobs. We aim to pay a realistic rate to each of our staff.

We are willing to consider requests for flexible working patterns to accommodate the needs of single parents and others whose personal responsibilities. We have more than 500 full-time equivalent staff, but a number of those posts are filled by two people who job share.

We provide our staff with other benefits, including a generous defined contribution pension scheme, a staff discount on all purchases.

Cast has a comprehensive training programme, including formal training for staff who are promoted to supervisory positions and into managerial roles. Staff are also free to undertake part-time study in their own time and the company will pay for their courses provided they are relevant to their roles.

Cast provides itself on being an equal employer. The workforce is racially diverse and there is a healthy gender balance at all levels within the company.

Health and safety is of paramount importance.

- Every new process is subject to a formal risk evaluation. All staff receive appropriate safety training on their induction and there is a compulsory training programme to ensure that knowledge remains up to date.
- Cast works closely with government agencies to ensure that our health and safety standards exceed all relevant requirements.
- All workplace accidents are investigated and the results of that investigation are documented and discussed by senior management.

Cast has a health and safety department which carries out regular inspections of every area of operations on a rotational basis.

### 9 Reference material 9 – Press release

**Cast Group**

*Press Release*

Cast Group appoints new chief executive

The Cast Group is pleased to announce that Ms Judith Anderson will join the company as its chief executive with immediate effect.

Ms Anderson joins the company at an interesting stage in its development. The move to online retailing has been completed successfully and the appointment of a new chief executive will assist the board in its deliberations concerning future strategies.

Ms Anderson has had a long and varied career. She has worked in a variety of industries, including newspapers and entertainment. She has previously served on the boards of two quoted companies. Firstly as the finance director of a footwear manufacturer and latterly as the chief executive of a telecommunications company.

The board believes that Ms Anderson's acceptance of this role indicates that the Cast Group has an exciting future.

Note to editors

This information is cleared for immediate publication.

Please address any queries to the Cast Group press office.

## 10 Reference material 10 – Article in Business Daily

# Business Daily

[25th May 2014]| No 7893                                  [Daily Business Paper]|[£2.50]

## New CEO at Cast

Yesterday's announcement that Cast Group has appointed Judith Anderson as its CEO comes at an interesting point in the company's development.

The Cast Group is, by far, the country's largest unquoted company. It has been sitting on a large and, so far, unproductive cash mountain since it sold its massive property portfolio and embraced the altogether more profitable online retailing model.

The company has made no attempt to signal its intentions for the future. The only thing that we can be sure of is that major change is inevitable. It is highly unlikely that Judith Anderson would have stood down from the board of one of the country's leading telecoms providers to take charge of a sleeping giant such as Cast unless the directors had promised her some fresh challenges.

Unconfirmed rumours suggest that one of the new CEO's first challenges will be to heal internal disagreements within Cast's board. There have been suggestions that a fresh appointment from outside was considered necessary because the existing board could not reach a consensus on the direction that Cast should take.

## 11 Reference material 11 – Competitor analysis

### Competitor analysis

It is difficult to identify Cast's competitors because no other company sells exactly the same range of products in Cast's home market. Furthermore, Cast competes with many different types of retailer in virtually all of its markets. For example, DVDs are sold by other online retailers, by specialist video shops and by supermarkets. Each of those channels presents a slightly different threat to Cast's revenues. For example, other online retailers can compete in a visible and transparent manner on price and may also attempt to compete in terms of the quality of service. Shops can offer personal service and advice from shop staff. Supermarkets often aim to offer a very narrow range of titles but to discount them heavily, so that they can match or even undercut Cast's prices on popular items.

Cast's board tend to benchmark themselves against Greatline and Fashionstore.

Greatline is an online retailer that offers a wide range of products, including books, DVDs and electronic goods, through a single website. Greatline operates in a number of different countries, including Cast's home country.

# Preseen information for the pilot case

Greatline's website handles literally millions of different products. It can be searched and browsed and it also gathers data on individual consumers' searches and their purchase history.

Fashionstore also operates internationally, but focuses on the sale of fashionable clothes. Fashionstore sells more than 70,000 products through its sites. Some carry the Fashionstore brand, but most are from established clothing labels.

Fashionstore attracts younger and more fashion-conscious customers by refreshing its product ranges frequently. Roughly 2,000 new styles are added to the site every week, with a similar number being withdrawn as sales decline or products are sold out.

Both Greatline and Fashionstore are quoted on the stock exchange in Cast's home country. Their share prices are followed closely, if only because they reflect consumer confidence in the wider economy.

## 12 Reference material 12 – Shareprice graph

The following statistics have been obtained:

|  | Greatline | Fashionstore |
| --- | --- | --- |
| Current share price ($) | 3.12 | 15.07 |
| Market capitalisation ($) | 142,870m | 3,876m |
| Price/earnings ratio | 4.9 | 1.1 |
| Beta | 0.9 | 1.2 |
| Number of employees | 14,000 | 1,462 |

## 13 Reference material 13 – Greatline financial statements

**Greatline**
**Extracts from financial statements**

**Greatline Group**
**Consolidated Statement of Profit or Loss for the year ended 31 March 2015**

|  | Notes | $m | 2014 $m |
|---|---|---|---|
| Revenue | (1) | 61,200 | 55,080 |
| Cost of sales |  | (46,400) | (41,720) |
| Gross point |  | 14,800 | 13,360 |
| Distribution costs |  | (2,600) | (2,430) |
| Administration expenses |  | (920) | (832) |
| Operating profit | (1, 2) | 11,280 | 10,098 |
| Finance costs |  | (40) | (38) |
| Profit before taxation |  | 11,240 | 10,060 |
| Taxation | (4) | (440) | (412) |
| **Profit for the year** |  | **10,800** | **8,648** |

## Greatline Group
### Consolidated Statement of Changes in Equity for the year ended 31 March 2015

|  | Share capital $m | Share premium $m | Retained earnings $m | Total $m |
|---|---|---|---|---|
| Opening capital | 2,000 | 1,000 | 4,227 | 7,227 |
| Profit for year | – | – | 10,800 | 10,800 |
| Dividend | – | – | (10,506) | (10,506) |
| Closing balance | 2,000 | 1,000 | 4,521 | 7,521 |

## Greatline Group
### Consolidated Statement of Cash flows for the year ended 31 March 2015

|  | $m | 2014 $m |
|---|---|---|
| **Cash flows from operating activities** |  |  |
| Cash receipts from customers | 61,237 | 55,087 |
| Cash paid to suppliers and employees | (49,374) | (42,461) |
| Cash generated from operations | 11,863 | 12,626 |
| Income taxes paid | (418) | (414) |
| Net cash from operating activities | 11,445 | 12,212 |
| **Cash flows from investing activities** |  |  |
| Purchase of property, plant and equipment | (2,261) | (1,970) |
| Proceeds from disposal of property, plant and equipment | 1,175 | 867 |
| Purchase of non-current intangibles | (8) | (7) |
| Net cash used in investing activities | (1,094) | (1,110) |

**Cash flows from financing activities**

| | | | |
|---|---|---|---|
| Interest paid | | (40) | (38) |
| Dividend paid | | (10,506) | (11,057) |
| Proceeds from issuing debentures | | 200 | – |
| Net cash from financing activities | | (10,346) | (11,095) |
| | | | |
| Net increase/(decrease) in cash and cash equivalents | | 5 | 7 |
| Cash and cash equivalents at beginning of period | | 36 | 29 |
| **Cash and cash equivalents at end of period** | | 41 | 36 |

**Greatline Group**
**Consolidated Statement of Financial Position as at 31 March 2015**

| | Notes | $m | 2014 $m |
|---|---|---|---|
| **ASSETS** | | | |
| Non-current assets | | | |
| Intangible | (5) | 190 | 186 |
| Property, plant and equipment | (6) | 7,978 | 7,584 |
| | | | |
| Current assets | | | |
| Inventories | | 5,814 | 5,628 |
| Table receivables | | 2,417 | 2,380 |
| Cash and short term deposits | | 41 | 36 |
| | | 8,272 | 8,044 |
| **TOTAL ASSETS** | | 16,440 | 15,814 |

## EQUITY

| | | |
|---|---:|---:|
| Share capital | 2,000 | 2,000 |
| Share premium | 1,000 | 1,000 |
| Retained earnings | 4,521 | 4,227 |
| | 7,521 | 7,227 |

## LIABILITIES

Non-current liabilities

| | | |
|---|---:|---:|
| Deferred tax | 19 | 17 |
| Debentures loans | 4,500 | 4,300 |
| | 4,519 | 4,317 |

Current liabilities

| | | |
|---|---:|---:|
| Trade payables | 3,970 | 3,860 |
| Current tax | 430 | 410 |
| | 4,400 | 4,270 |

| | | |
|---|---:|---:|
| **TOTAL EQUITY + LIABILITIES** | **16,440** | **15,814** |

### Note 1 – Segmental analysis

**Geographical**

*Revenue*

| America $m | Europe $m | Asia $m | Total $m |
|---:|---:|---:|---:|
| 24,600 | 18,200 | 18,400 | 61,200 |

*Operating profit*

| America $m | Europe $m | Asia $m | Total $m |
|---:|---:|---:|---:|
| 4,200 | 3,620 | 3,460 | 11,280 |

**Line of business**

*Revenue*

|  | Media $m | Electronics $m | Other $m | Total $m |
|---|---|---|---|---|
|  | 38,800 | 21,700 | 5,700 | 61,200 |

*Operating profit*

|  | Media $m | Electronics $m | Other $m | Total $m |
|---|---|---|---|---|
|  | 5,760 | 4,490 | 1,030 | 11,280 |

**Note 2 – Operating profit**

|  | Year ended 31 March 2015 $m | Year ended 31 March 2014 $m |
|---|---|---|
| Operating profit is stated after charging: |  |  |
| • Depreciation of property, plant and equipment | 645 | 621 |
| • Loss on disposal of property, plant and equipment | 47 | 38 |
| • Amortisation of intangible non-current assets | 4 | 3 |
| • Cost of inventory recognised as an expense | 28,768 | 26,768 |
| • Operating leases | 86 | 79 |
| • External auditor's remuneration | 22 | 21 |

## Note 3 – Staff costs including directors' remuneration

|  | Year ended 31 March 2015 | Year ended 31 March 2014 |
|---|---|---|
|  | Number of employees | Number of employees |
|  | $m | $m |
| By activity: |  |  |
| • Customer order fulfilment | 10,500 | 10,220 |
| • Information technology | 2,500 | 2,500 |
| • Administrative and managerial staff | 1,000 | 980 |
|  | 14,000 | 13,700 |

Employee costs, including directors' remuneration:

|  | Year ended 31 March 2015 | Year ended 31 March 2015 |
|---|---|---|
|  | $m | $m |
| • Wages and salaries | 390 | 363 |
| • Pension costs | 40 | 36 |
| • Total | 430 | 399 |

Aggregate compensation paid to board members, including pension costs:

|  | Year ended 31 March 2015 | Year ended 31 March 2015 |
|---|---|---|
|  | $m | $m |
| • Total | 40 | 39 |

**Note 4 – Tax expense**

|  | Year ended 31 March 2015 Number of employees $m | Year ended 31 March 2014 Number of employees $m |
|---|---|---|
| Tax on current year's profit | 435 | 407 |
| Adjustment in respect of prior year | 3 | 1 |
|  | 438 | 408 |
| Increase/(decrease) in deferred tax | | |
| Tax on profit | 2 | 4 |
|  | 440 | 412 |

**Note 5 – Intangible non-current assets**

|  | Goodwill $m | Software $m | Total $m |
|---|---|---|---|
| Cost at 1 April 2014 | 165 | 32 | 197 |
| Additions | – | 8 | 8 |
| Cost at 31 March 2015 | 165 | 40 | 205 |
| Accumulated amortisation at 1 April 2014 | – | 11 | 11 |
| Charge for year | – | 4 | 4 |
| Accumulated amortisation at 31 March 2015 | – | 15 | 15 |
| Net book value at 31 March 2015 | 165 | 25 | 190 |
| Net book value at 1 April 2014 | 165 | 21 | 186 |

**Note 6 – Property, plant and equipment**

|  | Property $m | Plant and equipment $m | Total $m |
| --- | --- | --- | --- |
| Cost at 1 April 2014 | 2,800 | 6,753 | 9,553 |
| Additions | – | 2,261 | 2,261 |
| Disposals | – | (1,349) | (1,349) |
| Cost at 31 March 2015 | 2,800 | 7,665 | 10,465 |
| Accumulated depreciation at 1 April 2014 | 768 | 1,201 | 1,969 |
| Charge for year | 56 | 589 | 645 |
| Disposals | – | (127) | (127) |
| Accumulated depreciation at 31 March 2015 | 824 | 1,663 | 2,487 |
| Net book value at 31 March 2015 | 1,976 | 6,002 | 7,978 |
| Net book value at 1 April 2014 | 2,032 | 5,552 | 7,584 |

## 14 Reference material 14 – Fashionstore's financial statements

**Fashionstore Group**
**Extracts from financial statements**

**Fashionstore Group**
**Consolidated Statement of Profit or Loss for the year ended 31 March 2015**

|  | Notes | $m | 2014 $m |
|---|---|---|---|
| Revenue |  | 8,788 | 7,489 |
| Cost of sales |  | (6,480) | (5,677) |
| Gross profit |  | 2,308 | 1,812 |
| Distribution costs |  | (587) | (496) |
| Administration expenses |  | (613) | (518) |
| Operating profit | (1) | 1,108 | 798 |
| Finance cost |  | (4) | (4) |
| Profit before taxation |  | 1,104 | 794 |
| Taxation | (4) | (257) | (248) |
| Profit for the year |  | 847 | 546 |

## Fashionstore Group
## Consolidated Statement of Changes in Equity for the year ended 31 March 2015

|  | Share capital $m | Share premium $m | Reatined earnings $m | Total $m |
|---|---|---|---|---|
| Opening balance | 300 | 350 | 237 | 887 |
| Profit for year | – | – | 847 | 847 |
| Dividend | – | – | (819) | (819) |
|  | 300 | 350 | 265 | 915 |

## Fashionstore Group
## Consolidated Statement of Cash flows
## For the year ended 31 March 2015

|  |  | 2014 |
|---|---|---|
|  | $m | $m |
| **Cash flows from operating activities** |  |  |
| Cash receipts from customers | 8,819 | 7,568 |
| Cash paid to suppliers and employees | (7,626) | (6,325) |
| Cash generated from operations | 1,173 | 1,243 |
| Income taxes paid | (245) | (242) |
| Net cash from operating activities | 928 | 1,001 |
| **Cash flows from investing activities** |  |  |
| Purchase of property, plant and equipment | (109) | (87) |
| Proceeds from disposal of property, plant and equipment | 17 | 12 |
| Purchase of non-current intangibles | (10) | – |
| Net cash used in investing activities | (102) | (75) |

**Cash flows from financing activities**

|  |  |  |
|---|---|---|
| Interest paid | (4) | (4) |
| Dividend paid | (819) | (920) |
| Net cash from financing activities | (823) | (924) |
| Net increase/(decrease) in cash and cash equivalents | 3 | 2 |
| Cash and cash equivalent at beginning of period | 4 | 2 |
| Cash and cash equivalents at end of period | 7 | 4 |

**Fashionstore Group**
**Consolidated Statement of Financial Position as at 31 March 2015**

|  | Notes | $m | 2014 $m |
|---|---|---|---|
| **ASSETS** |  |  |  |
| Non-current assets |  |  |  |
| Intangible | (4) | 250 | 245 |
| Property, plant and equipment | (5) | 787 | 897 |
| Current assets |  |  |  |
| Inventories |  | 612 | 497 |
| Trade receivables |  | 343 | 312 |
| Cash and short term deposits |  | 7 | 4 |
|  |  | 962 | 813 |
| **TOTAL ASSETS** |  | 1,999 | 1,955 |
| **EQUITY** |  |  |  |
| Share capital |  | 300 | 300 |
| Share premium |  | 350 | 350 |
| Retained earnings |  | 265 | 237 |
|  |  | 915 | 887 |

**LIABILITIES**

Non-current liabilities

|  |  |  |
|---|---|---|
| Deferred tax | 9 | 7 |
| Debenture loans | 300 | 300 |
|  | 309 | 307 |

Current liabilities

|  |  |  |
|---|---|---|
| Trade payables | 521 | 517 |
| Current tax | 254 | 244 |
|  | 775 | 761 |

**TOTAL EQUITY + LIABILITIES**      **1,999**    **1,955**

## Note 1 – Operating profit

| | Year ended 31 March 2015 $m | Year ended 31 March 2014 $m |
|---|---|---|
| Operating profit is stated after charging: | | |
| • Depreciation of property, plant and equipment | 195 | 164 |
| • Loss on disposal of property, plant and equipment | 7 | 4 |
| • Amortisation of intangible non-current assets | 5 | 5 |
| • Cost of inventory recognised as an expense | 3,740 | 3,260 |
| • Operating leases | 8 | 7 |
| • External auditor's remuneration | 2 | 2 |

## Note 2 – Staff costs including directors' remuneration

|  | Year ended 31 March 2015 $m | Year ended 31 March 2014 $m |
|---|---|---|
| By activity: | | |
| • Distribution | 1,006 | 953 |
| • Information technology | 247 | 238 |
| • Administration | 209 | 206 |
| | 1,462 | 1,397 |

Employee costs, including directors' remuneration:

|  | Year ended 31 March 2015 $m | Year ended 31 March 2014 $m |
|---|---|---|
| • Wages and salaries | 51 | 45 |
| • Pension costs | 6 | 5 |
| • Total | 57 | 50 |

Aggregate compensation paid to board members, including pension costs:

|  | Year ended 31 March 2015 $m | Year ended 31 March 2014 $m |
|---|---|---|
| • Total | 12 | 10 |

## Note 3 – Tax expense

|  | Year ended 31 March 2015 $m | Year ended 31 March 2014 $m |
|---|---|---|
| Tax on current year's profit | 251 | 239 |
| Adjustment in respect of prior year | 4 | 6 |
|  | 255 | 245 |
| Increase/(decrease) in deferred tax | 2 | 3 |
| Tax on profit |  |  |
|  | 257 | 248 |

## Note 4 – Intangible non-current assets

|  | Goodwill $m | Software $m | Total $m |
|---|---|---|---|
| Cost at 1 April 2014 | 50 | 288 | 338 |
| Additions | – | 10 | 10 |
| Cost at 31 March 2015 | 50 | 298 | 348 |
| Accumulated amortisation at 1 April 2014 | – | 93 | 93 |
| Charge for year | – | 5 | 5 |
| Accumulated amortisation at 31 March 2015 | – | 98 | 98 |
| Net book value at 31 March 2015 | 50 | 200 | 250 |
| Net book value at 1 April 2014 | 50 | 195 | 245 |

**Note 5 – Property, plant and equipment**

|  | Property $m | Plant and equipment $m | Total $m |
|---|---|---|---|
| Cost at 1 April 2014 | 400 | 792 | 1,192 |
| Additions | – | 109 | 109 |
| Disposals | – | (36) | (36) |
| Cost at 31 March 2015 | 400 | 865 | 1,265 |
| Accumulated depreciation at 1 April 2014 | 60 | 235 | 295 |
| Charge for year | 8 | 187 | 195 |
| Disposals | – | (12) | (12) |
| Accumulated depreciation at 31 March 2015 | 68 | 410 | 478 |
| Net book value at 31 March 2015 | 332 | 455 | 787 |
| Net book value at 1 April 2014 | 340 | 557 | 897 |

## 15 Summary

We are now working through the Pilot exam from beginning to end so you can see all of the skills and techniques which may be required in this exam. This chapter simply reproduces the pre-seen information for the Pilot exam and we will work through this in more detail in the next two chapters.

**Next steps:**

(1) Make sure you have at least skim read the pre-seen before moving on to Chapter Five where we will consider how to do further analysis.

(2) It might be useful to make a list at this point of what you think some of the relevant technical areas might be – are you comfortable with these areas?

# Preseen information for the pilot case

chapter
5

# Analysing the pre-seen

**Chapter learning objectives**

- to understand various techniques and models that can help familiarisation with the pre-seen.

# Analysing the pre-seen

## 1 The importance of familiarisation

The pre-seen material is released approximately seven weeks before you sit the exam and one of your first tasks will be to analyse the context within which the case is set. Although your responses in the exam will be driven by the unseen material, you will only be able to fully assess the impact of each event on the organisation if you have a sufficient depth of knowledge and awareness of both the organisation and the industry in which it operates.

The purpose of the pre-seen material is to allow you to gain that knowledge and awareness. Remember, you will be acting in the position of a management accountant who works for the organisation in the early stages of a senior manager role. It will therefore be expected that you will have the same level of familiarisation as someone fulfilling that role.

It is extremely important that you study the pre-seen material thoroughly before you go into the examination. There are two main reasons for this:

- It will save time in the examination itself if you are already familiar with the pre-seen material.
- It enables you to develop a view of the situation facing the organisation in the case study.

You will not be able to respond to the examination tasks from the pre-seen material alone; the unseen material given to you in the examination will present significant new information that may alter the situation substantially. Even so, a major step towards success in the examination is a careful study, exploration and understanding of the pre-seen material.

Each set of pre-seen material is different but as a general rule, you can expect the following at the strategic level:

- Industry background
- History of the business
- Key personnel
- Current business/industry issues
- Financial Statements

In addition you may have information presented on

- Risk profile
- Competitor analysis
- CSR Policy

Each of these areas will need reviewing in detail.

You should question what each piece of information tells you, and why the examiner may have given it to you.

## 2 Exhibit by exhibit analysis

The purpose of this initial stage is to lay a foundation for further analysis. It's more about asking questions than finding solutions. Before you do anything else, you should read the pre-seen material from beginning to end without making any notes, simply to familiarise yourself with the scenario.

Read the material again, as many times as you think necessary, without making notes. You can do this over a period of several days, if you wish.

When you think you are reasonably familiar with the situation described by the material, you should start to make notes. By making notes, you will become more familiar with the detail of the scenario.

- Try to make notes on each paragraph (or each group of short paragraphs) in the pre-seen material.
- Think about what the paragraph is telling you, and consider why this information might be of interest or relevance.
- Ask yourself "why might the examiner have told me this?".
- Try to make your questions as broad as possible; consider as many different stakeholders as possible and try to put yourself in different positions (say the CEO, a key customer, a franchise operator etc) to consider the information from different perspectives.

# Analysing the pre-seen

### Illustration 1 – The CAST Group: Introductory overview

Given below is an example of some questions you could ask yourself relating to the first exhibit of the Strategic case Study pilot exam pre-seen information.

| Question | Potential Response |
|---|---|
| Why are we told that the initial strategic response of "holding the middle ground" and "retain their existing customer base" failed? | • Some reasons for the failure of this strategic approach are offered in the introductory overview e.g. younger customers moving to low cost suppliers and older customers moving upmarket.<br><br>• There is however a very significant hint that the company should pay closer attention to market trends. The E3 element of the syllabus indicates that students should understand *'the evaluation and prioritisation of environmental drivers specific to the organisation'*.<br><br>• It would therefore be wise to consider the other categories of PESTEL analysis and Porter's Five Forces when analysing the material to establish how these have been treated by CAST and the effect of these on the current and future plans. |

# chapter 5

| | |
|---|---|
| What is the significance of being told that "Cast's retailing model is supported by a complex logistical operation" | • This should prompt the student to research how other on-line retailers are structured and how they control the distribution of merchandise and associated costs.<br><br>• For example in terms of efficiency, there is one part of the rise of online retailing that almost inevitably generates problems i.e. returns.<br><br>• Conventional retailers and mail order firms have laboured to cope with them for decades. For example, British mail order fashion were swamped with racks of returned items, all needing individual – human – attention before they could be resold. Are these costs being taken into consideration?<br><br>• In a similar context the syllabus for E3 specifically request that students consider *strategic supply chain management in the context of building and managing strategic relationships with stakeholders e.g. customers, suppliers etc* |
| We are told that " a single server" supports the company websites and "provides all of the associated services such as processing of customer credit and debit card payments" | • CAST sales are exclusively online and as such they have an obligation to ensure that customers will be confident in their dealings with CAST and that their personal information is protected.<br><br>• Similarly CAST need to be sure that the risks of disruption of service caused by hardware or software failure are removed given the effect that this would have on sales processing and profitability. Any drive to increase volume of sales would need take this into account.<br><br>• The syllabus for E3 specifically asks students to *consider the impact of IT and IS on an organisation and its strategy* |

## 3 Note Taking

When you're making notes, try to be as creative as possible. Psychologists tell us that using conventional linear notes on their own use only a small part of our mental capacity. They are hard to remember and prevent us from drawing connections between topics. This is because they seek to classify things under hierarchical headings.

Here are some techniques that candidates find useful. See which ones work for you as you practise on the pilot case in this text.

### Spider diagrams

Spider diagrams (or clustering diagrams) are a quick graphic way of summarising connections between subjects.

You cannot put much detail into a spider diagram, just a few key words. However, it does help you to 'visualise' the information in the case material.

You must expect to update your spider diagram as you go along and to redraft it when it starts to get too messy. It is all part of the learning process.

### Timelines

Timelines are valuable to make sense of the sequence of events in the pre-seen and to understand where the company in the case study presently stands. The case study exam takes place in real time, so you need to be clear how long is likely to elapse between the data in the pre-seen and the actual exam. This is the time period during which the issues facing the company can be incorporated into the unseen material.

The case writer is not trying to trick you or spring something entirely unexpected on you, but you need to be aware of the timeframe and the changes that have already occurred in the company's history, so that you can offer realistic advice for the company's future.

### Organisation charts

Preparing an organisation chart will familiarise you with the roles and the overlaps, and also help you to identify gaps or ambiguities in roles, as well as helping you to remember the names and roles of the key people in the case. In some cases this will be provided for you; where it isn't, you may want to draw one out.

## Post-it-notes

Post-it-notes can be used to stick onto each page of the printed pre-seen material and to jot key points on. Additionally, you may want to keep a post-it-note for each person, and as you work through the pre-seen material. You could even stick the notes on your desk, a notice board or wall so that you can keep glancing at them to remember who's who in the case and what issues and problems have been identified. You could also jot down your ideas for alternative directions that the company could take, to prepare you for exam day.

## Colours

Colours help you remember things you may want to draw upon in the exam room. You could write down all your financial calculations and observations in green whilst having red for organisational and blue for strategic. Some candidates use different colour highlighter pens to emphasise different aspects of the pre-seen material perhaps using the same colour coding suggestion.

Additionally, sometimes making notes in different colours helps you to remember key facts and some of the preparation that you have done using the pre-seen material.

Use whatever colours work for you – but it does help to make notes on both the pre-seen material and the research you do. DO NOT just read the material – you must take notes (in whatever format) and if colours help you to understand and link your research together then use colours.

## 4 Technical Analysis

Now you're reasonably familiar with the material it's time to carry out some technical analysis to help you identify and understand the issues facing the company.

A good starting point is to revise any 'technical' topics that might be relevant. The pre-seen material might make a reference to a particular 'technical' issue, such as the application of value chain analysis, corporate governance requirements, internal controls, the use of hedging techniques, company valuations, and so on. If you have forgotten about any topic that might be relevant, go back to your previous study materials and revise it.

# 5 Financial Analysis

You will almost certainly be given some figures in the pre-seen material. These might relate to the company's profits or losses, or product profitability. There might be statements of profit and loss and statements of financial position for previous years, future business plans, cash flow statements, capital expenditure plans, EPS and share price information and so on.

A key part of your initial analysis will be to perform some simple financial analysis, such as financial ratio calculations or a cash flow analysis. These might give you a picture of changes in profitability, liquidity, working capital management, return on capital, financial structure or cash flows over time, and will help ensure you have a rounded picture of the organisation's current position.

If a cash flow statement is not provided, it may be worth preparing a summary of cash flows. You may have to make some assumptions if the detailed information isn't provided but even with these, there is great value in appreciating where the money has come from, and where it is being spent.

## Profitability ratios

You might find useful information from an analysis of profit/sales ratios, for:

- the company as a whole
- each division, or
- each product or service.

Profit margins can be measured as a net profit percentage and as a gross profit percentage. You can then look at trends in the ratios over time, or consider whether the margins are good or disappointing.

Analysing the ratio of certain expenses to sales might also be useful, such as the ratio of administration costs to sales, sales and marketing costs to sales or R&D costs to sales. Have there been any noticeable changes in these ratios over time and, if so, is it clear why the changes have happened?

## Liquidity ratios

The two main measures of liquidity are:

- the current ratio (= ratio of current assets: current liabilities)
- the quick ratio or acid test ratio (= ratio of current assets excluding inventory: current liabilities).

The purpose of a liquidity ratio is to assess whether the organisation is likely to be able to pay its liabilities, when they fall due for payment, out of its operational cash flows. The current ratio is probably more useful when inventory is fairly liquid and inventory turnover is fast. The quick ratio or acid test ratio is a better measure of liquidity when inventory turnover is slow.

Check these ratios for any significant change over time, or for the possibility of poor liquidity. As a very rough guide, a current ratio below 2:1 and a quick ratio below 1:1 might be low. However, the liquidity ratios are only likely to be of significance for the case study when the ratios get very low, or the deterioration in the ratios is very large. For example, if a company has current liabilities in excess of its current assets, a liquidity problem would seem likely.

### Working capital ratios

Working capital ratios can be calculated to assess the efficiency of working capital management (= management of inventory, trade receivables and trade payables). They can also be useful for assessing liquidity, because excessive investment in working capital ties up cash and slows the receipt of cash.

The main working capital ratios are:

- average turnover period for inventory: a longer period might indicate poor inventory management
- 'receivables days' or the average time that customers take to pay: a long period could indicate issues with the collection of cash, although would need to consider this in light of the entity's credit terms and industry averages.
- 'payables days' or the average time to pay suppliers: a long period could indicate cash flow difficulties for the entity, although would need to consider in light of credit terms.

You should be familiar with these ratios and how to calculate the length of the cash cycle or operating cycle.

### Financial structure ratios

You might be required to consider methods of funding in your case study examination. If a company plans to expand in the future, where will the funds come from?

- Additional debt finance might only be possible if the current debt levels are not high, and financial gearing is fairly low. (The interest cover ratio is also a useful measure of debt capacity. It is the ratio of profit before interest and tax to interest costs. When the ratio is low, possibly less than 3, this could indicate that the company already has as much debt capital as it can safely afford.)

- If a company will need additional equity finding, will internally generated profits be a sufficient source of funds or will a new share issue be necessary?

You should be able to accurately prepare gearing ratios, which is debt: debt + equity.

**Cash flow analysis or funding analysis**

If the main objective of a company is to maximise the wealth of its shareholders, the most important financial issues will be profitability and returns to shareholders. However, other significant issues in financial strategy are often:

- cash flows and liquidity, and
- funding

A possible cash flow problem occurs whenever the cash flows from operations do not appear to be sufficient to cover all the non-operational cash payments that the company has to make, such as spending on capital expenditure items.

An analysis of future funding can be carried out by looking at the history of changes in the statement of financial position. It is a relatively simple task to look at the growth in the company's assets over time, and at how the asset growth has been funded – by equity, long-term debt or shorter-term liabilities. If equity has funded much of the growth in assets, it might be possible to see how much of the new equity has been provided by retained profits, and how much has come from new issues of shares (indicated by an increase in the allotted share capital and share premium reserve).

It is crucial that you are able to accurately calculate and interpret the key ratios such as margins, ROCE, P/E ratios and gearing.

## Recap of key ratio calculations

### Key ratios:

| Ratio | Formula |
|---|---|
| Gross profit margin (GPM) | (Gross profit/Revenue) × 100% |
| Net profit margin (NPM) | (Net profit/Revenue) × 100% |
| Operating profit margin | (Operating profit/Revenue) × 100% |
| Profit before tax margin | (Profit before tax/Revenue) × 100% |
| Return on Capital Employed (ROCE) | (Operating profit/Capital Employed) × 100% |
| Asset turnover | Revenue/Capital Employed |
| Current ratio | Current assets/Current liabilities |
| Quick ratio | (Current assets – Inventory)/Current liabilities |
| Receivables days | (Trade Receivables/Credit sales) × 365 days |
| Inventory days | (Inventory/Cost of Sales) × 365 days |
| Payables days | (Trade Payables/Cost of Sales) × 365 days |
| Gearing (variant 1) | Debt/Equity |
| Gearing (variant 2) | Debt/(Debt + Equity) |
| Interest cover | Operating Profit/Finance Cost |

# Analysing the pre-seen

### Exercise 1 – Basic Financial Analysis

Complete the following table using the information in Chapter four. Commentary on the results can be found in Chapter six.

| Ratio | 2015 | *Working* | 2014 | *Working* |
|---|---|---|---|---|
| Revenue growth | | | | |
| Gross profit margin | | | | |
| Operating profit margin | | | | |
| Return on Capital Employed (ROCE) | | | | |
| Current ratio | | | | |
| Receivables days | | | | |
| Inventory days | | | | |
| Payables days | | | | |
| Gearing | | | | |

## 6 Industry analysis and research

**Why is industry research important?**

Remember, part of your preparatory work is to analyse the context within which the case is set. A full analysis is not possible without an understanding of the industry and research may support the information provided in the pre-seen. From this analysis, you may be better able to understand the key issues and address the requirements.

The pre-seen material usually contains a good summary of relevant information about the industry. This can be relied on as accurate at the time it is published.

You could further research the industry setting for the case you are working on so that you can develop a better understanding of the problems (and opportunities) facing companies in this industry. Hopefully, it will also stop you from making unrealistic comments in your answer on the day of the exam. Finally, there will be a strong linkage between your research of the industry and the technical analysis you will be carrying out. Industry research will allow you to add further comments in terms of:

- identifying industry lifecycle stage and the factors driving it;
- identifying whether any of the five forces are strong or strengthening and the factors causing this;
- considering the competitive strategies being followed by companies operating in the real world and how they are achieved (e.g. special technologies, use of brands) and whether they could be adopted by the company in the pre-seen
- identifying real world issues against the PEST framework (this may involve some basic research into the laws and technologies of the industry);
- considering the impact of globalisation on the future of the industry and on the firm in the pre-seen.

Don't think that your preparation should be limited to just looking at the industry. A wider understanding of the way business is conducted and the influence of the economic and political environments on business could be just as useful. For example, an additional factor to consider is the state of the investment markets, which will affect costs of capital and share prices.

One of the best ways to achieve this wider appreciation is to regularly read the business pages of a good national newspaper.

**How to conduct industry research**

One of the big problems with conducting industry research is knowing where to stop. In today's technology driven society, a wealth of information is available at your fingertips so perhaps the most important aspect when performing research is to focus on reliable sources. In order to help direct your research, think about the following sources of information:

*Personal networks*

Some candidates have been lucky enough to find themselves facing a set of pre seen material describing the industry they work in. In this situation, they have plenty of colleagues they can talk to about the case.

# Analysing the pre-seen

Alternatively, and depending on the industry in the Case Study, it is possible that you know someone in the business from whom you can get information. Likely contacts include:

- people who work in the industry or who have worked in it;
- family members or their friends;
- contacts at work who have dealings with the industry in the case;
- other people sitting the case study exam, either via your tuition provider or using online forums, such as CIMAsphere.

Discussing the case and your analysis of the situation of the business with an expert will help you to test out your understanding of what is important.

*Trade media and news media*

A journalist is a paid professional who searches out and presents information about an industry. If you can find a trade journal for the industry in the case, it will save you a lot of searching for yourself.

Trade journals can be located in four ways:

- Visit a good newsagent. The difficulty here is that only very large industries such as accounting, financial advising, computing, music and construction provide enough customers for a newsagent to consider stocking the magazine.
- Visit a library. As well as public libraries, most universities and better colleges will permit you a reader's ticket to consult their journals on a read only basis. However, such libraries will not let you borrow journals and may place restrictions on photocopying them. Good librarians will also be able to locate relevant journals for you.
- Ask someone who works in the industry for the name of the journals for the industry.
- Use the Internet. Many trade journals now have websites and, in many cases, the journals can be downloaded as PDFs. Naturally there will be restrictions on logging in if you have not paid a fee, but there is a surprising amount of free media available. The best approach is to go to a search engine and type in a search inquiry such as: 'trade magazine for [name of industry] industry' or 'articles on [name of industry or real world firm]'.

News media is more general although some quality business newspapers may carry special supplements on particular industries from time to time.

It is also very important to spend time reading the financial pages of any good newspaper, not necessarily the Financial Times. It is relevant to understand what is happening in the real world with acquisitions, mergers, down-sizing, boardroom conflicts, etc. The more widely that you read the financial press, the more it will help you to understand and fully appreciate all of the many complex factors that affect companies and the selection and implementation of their strategies.

It is also recommended that you should keep yourself updated with latest information on exchange rates, interest rates, government policies, the state of the economy, and particularly what is happening in the business sectors concerning mergers and acquisitions. The acquisition of a competitor, or a hostile takeover bid is a very important strategic move. Acquisitions happen everyday in the real world and you can familiarise yourself with how these work by reading the business press.

Obviously, news media is available in hard copy from shops but also most good newspapers have websites that give you the day's stories and also have searchable archives on past stories about the industry or specific firms within it.

*Using the Internet*

This is the most convenient and commonly used method of researching the industry, but as noted above, try to target the information you're looking for in order to avoid wasting time. Generally, you will be looking for the following sorts of information:

- Websites of firms similar to the one(s) in the pre-seen material. This can help you learn about the sorts of products and competitive strategies they follow and may also yield financial information that can be compared with the data in the pre-seen material.
- Trade journals of the industry in the pre-seen. This will provide information on real world environmental issues facing the business.
- Articles on the industry in journals and newspapers. These will keep you up to date on developments.
- Stock market information on the real firms.
- Financial statements of real firms (often these can be downloaded from companies' websites free of charge).
- Industry reports produced by organisations such as the DTI and the large accountancy firms, which are surprisingly common, and often available for free on the Internet, if you search well.

## Analysing the pre-seen

You could review the accounts and establish:

- typical industry working capital ratios,
- typical ratios of noncurrent
- assets to sales,
- margins,
- growth rates.

You could then compare the accounts with the current share price and compare the market capitalisation with the asset value, and review all the normal investment ratios. You may provide yourself with some 'normal' industry figures as a basis for any comparisons you may wish to make of the unseen material in due course. You should also review all the non-financial information provided, looking in particular for:

- new technological developments, new products;
- the competitive situation

If companies can be identified that are in the same or similar industries to the industry in the case, then it is possible to gain much information from these websites.

It is not helpful, as some candidates have done, to concentrate on any one single company, however similar you believe that is to the case. The examination team have made it clear that cases are not likely to be based exclusively on just one real world company and hence data will differ from any sets of accounts that you may consider the case is based on.

Company websites of public companies in similar industries can provide the annual report and accounts, any press releases, publicity material and product descriptions, and detailed documentation on such matters as rights issues and share option schemes. Often they contain specially commissioned pieces of market research that you can download. However, it's worth remembering that this research is there to encourage investors to anticipate higher returns in the future and will tend to put an optimistic gloss on events. One very efficient way to use the internet for research is to set up Google alerts for the topics you're interested in. This will provide you with daily emails containing links to new information on your specified areas.

## 7 Risk Analysis

It can be a good idea to prepare a risk analysis to aid your understanding of the pre-seen. When carrying out risk analysis it is good to consider the risk, the potential impact and any possible mitigation.

A good example of a risk analysis can be seen in Exhibit 3 of the CAST strategic level pre-seen detailing the potential risks and their impact. It does not however suggest how you may mitigate any of those risks noted..

This type of document won't always be provided and you may need to prepare it yourself.

## 8 Position Audit

Once you've analysed all of the above you're ready to carry out a position audit.

CIMA defines a position audit as:

Part of the planning process which examines the current state of the entity in respect of:

- resources of tangible and intangible assets and finance,
- products brands and markets,
- operating systems such as production and distribution,
- internal organisation,
- current results,
- returns to stockholders.

What you should be attempting to do is stand back so you can appreciate the bigger picture of the organisation. Within your SWOT analysis you should look for:

- Threat homing in upon weakness – the potential extinction event.
- Threat to a strength – should be able to defend against it but remember competencies slip.
- Opportunity on a strength – areas they should be able to exploit.
- Opportunity on a weakness – areas where they could exploit in the future if they can change.

In addition to preparing a SWOT analysis, it is useful to prepare a two-three page summary of your analysis. Try not to simply repeat information from the pre-seen but add value by including your thoughts on the analysis you've performed.

## 9 Main issues and précis

Once you've prepared your summary you are finally able to consider the key issues facing the organisation. Your conclusion on the main issues arising from the pre-seen will direct your focus and aid your understanding of issues in the exam.

Once you've got a list of the main issues, give yourself more time to think. Spend some time thinking about the case study, as much as you can. You don't have to be sitting at a desk or table to do this. You can think about the case study when you travel to work or in any spare time that you have for thinking.

- When new ideas come to you, jot them down.
- If you think of a new approach to financial analysis, carry out any calculations you think might be useful.

Remember, all of the above preparatory work enables you to feel as if you really are a management accountant working for this organisation. Without the prep, you're unlikely to be convincing in this role.

## 10 Summary

You should now understand what you need to do in order to familiarise yourself with the pre-seen sufficiently. Working through this chapter will produce quite detailed analysis. Chapter Six will attempt to summarise this into key conclusions.

### Next steps:

(1) Ensure you have applied each stage of analysis to the CAST pre-seen

(2) Produce a brief summary of the key issues facing CAST. We will give you our opinion in the following chapter but you should write your own notes on this first.

# chapter 5

## Test your understanding answers

### Exercise 1 – Basic Financial Analysis

| Ratio | 2015 | Working | 2014 | Working |
|---|---|---|---|---|
| Revenue growth | 11% | (2,985 – 2,687)/2,687 | – | n/a |
| Gross profit margin | 30.0% | 895/2,985 | 33.9% | 910/2,687 |
| Operating profit margin | 17.6% | 524/2,985 × 100% | 20.4% | 547/2,687 |
| Return on Capital Employed (ROCE) | 64% | 524/(712 + 100) | 81% | 547/(667 + 100) |
| Current ratio | 2.09 :1 | 657/314 | 2.29:1 | 599/261 |
| Receivables days | 14 days | (117/2,985) × 365 | 14 days | (105/2,687) × 365 |
| Inventory days | 51 days | (297/2,090) × 365 | 53 days | (256/1,777) × 365 |
| Payables days | 33 days | (190/2,090) × 365 | 28 days | (138/1,777) × 365 |
| Gearing – using Debt/(Debt + Equity) | 12% | 100/(100 + 712) | 13% | 100/(100 + 667) |

# Analysing the pre-seen

# chapter 6

# Summary of the pre-seen

**Chapter learning objectives**

- To apply the techniques covered in the previous chapter to the pilot pre-seen

Summary of the pre-seen

# 1 Introduction

In the previous chapter we showed you some techniques to help you in your analysis of the pre-seen.

Once you have completed your analysis of the pre-seen for the pilot paper you can review this chapter to ensure you have identified the key points. We will take you through each exhibit highlighting the key conclusions before bringing this together into a summary using the SWOT framework.

# 2 Exhibit by exhibit analysis

The key issues and conclusions that could have been brought out of the pre-seen exhibits are as follows:

**Reference material 1 – Company history, the present strategy, products, organisation and structure.**

*History and development*

- The Cast Group began life in 1920 as a single shop formed by Frank Smith, to sell men's clothing. By 1952, when Frank Smith retired as CEO, the company comprised of eleven stores trading as *Frank Smith and Sons* having diversified into women's clothing and household goods.

- The company was now managed by the former CEO's four sons who, in addition to changing the brand name to *WoodVale*, embarked on a nationwide expansion policy taking the total number of stores to 65.

- All sites were purchased by mortgages, serviced by trading income and paid off by 1990. They aimed at the mass market with low prices but reasonable quality. The company remained unquoted with the shares being held throughout the founder's extended family.

- Despite being a major presence on most high streets, sales started to decline largely as a result of changing consumer tastes, supermarkets and new retail chains selling inexpensive clothes and the development of retail parks on the outskirts of major towns.

- The reaction to these changes was to rebrand and introduce new lines such as CD's, cosmetics and books. In addition WoodVale also purchased a small cosmetic retailer with a presence in most town centres creating a "shop within a shop".

- By 2010, with rapid declines in revenue and increasing pressure from internet retailers, it was unanimously agreed on a major shift in strategy which resulted in the sale of all its traditional stores by 2011 and pursuance of a new online retailing strategy.

Cast was formed. It remains unquoted and operates as a single entity trading through six main trading names which each of those having their own website.

## *Present strategy*

Current trading names and products are:

- Cast Disk – DVD's; Blue-ray disks and music downloads, computer games and other entertainment media
- Papercut – Books
- Childsplay – Branded toys and games
- Smile – Cosmetics
- Warm – Fashion clothes
- Zap – Consumer electronics

## *Organisation*

- CAST's retail model seems standard when drawing comparisons with real-world online retailers.
- However, mention of a "complex logistical operation" seems to contradict the earlier inference of the "single logistics centre". Three distribution centres hold stock as well as some lines which are held by manufacturers or other online retailers. Sales of the latter items of merchandise earning a commission for orders received via websites.
- Each website has its own team, again raising the issue of duplication, and there appears to be a confusion over the roles of the marketing and buying both of which seem to operate in unison. There are benefits from this relationship, however, particularly in the sourcing of additional discounts from the supplier should a product prove to be a good seller
- There is significant emphasis on the use of search algorithms to both market goods and maximise profitability by product positioning in the home page. Website teams are evaluated on the sales revenue and contribution figures.
- The IT function is obviously of critical importance to the success of Cast and it is surprising that a single server supports all the sites. A "remote location" houses a recovery site which maintains a full back up of files and can act as a primary site in the event of the server going offline. No further detail is given in this context.

# Summary of the pre-seen

- Repetition in the pre-seen of the complexity of the logistics arrangements with sophisticated technology combining with unskilled labour highlights the potential for error. The latter are predominantly involved with routine "picking and packing" operations. In addition to Cast's own personnel, there are representatives of courier companies and postal service employees on site as a result of the volume of business.

## *Conclusion*

- Cast remains a significant presence in the marketpalce being the largest unquoted company in its home country. It has however been beset by change, particularly driven by the external environment to which it has not always reacted realistically.

- Sensible early financial management gave Cast the benefit of significant cash to develop an online presence. Despite this sound financial base, questions would be asked at this point given the history of the business as to the skills and competences of Cast to compete in the online retail world. Of particular concern would be the duplication of effort in the maintenance of six different websites and products ranging from fashion clothes to DVD's.

- In addition the complexity of the IT system and the "mix" of sophisticated technology with unskilled manual labour does raise concerns over the accuracy of the final customer order.

**Note:** The E3 syllabus emphasises the importance of IT in achieving the organisation's strategic and competitive position. It would be prudent at this stage in your familiarisation to draw comparisons with the operations of real world online retailers such as John Lewis, ASOS, Amazon etc.

## Reference material 2 – Industry analysis

- Online retailing has grown rapidly and continuously over the last decade. Despite the rate of growth slowing, there is still room for expansion.

- A wider range of products are bought as the attraction of lower prices becomes a reality.

- Average values per sale are increasing as the retailers offer "bigger ticket" items and a larger range of products are being sold on line. Growth of comparison sites, M-commerce (purchasing and comparison of goods and prices via smart phones and tablets) and social media are all influencing buying decisions.

- The impact on traditional retailers is huge – either reduction in store capacity and/or the entry of this retailer into the online market.

*Conclusion*

- The analysis of the industry provides a range of both threats e.g. new entrants and opportunities e.g. new product ranges for Cast.

**Note:** It would be prudent at this stage of your familiarisation to research the industry and apply some of the strategic analysis tools recommended in the syllabus – e.g. PEST, Porter's Five Forces, Product Lifecycle, BCG Matrix – drawing your own conclusions as a consequence.

**Reference material 3 – Risk factors**

The information presents a host of threats and weaknesses for the Cast group, examples of which are provided below.

- Sales forecasting problems due to uncertainty over consumer spend
- Increased competition
- Economic decline
- Seasonality
- Lost sales due to IT problems
- Product liability and legal claims
- Purchase of unproven products
- Inefficiency in distribution centres
- Inventory control
- Costs associated with delivery
- Control of customer personal information
- Exposure to fraud via new payment methods
- Failure of card issuers

*Conclusion*

- A major risk which has increased since the adoption of an online internet selling strategy is the reliance on IT systems. It is intriguing that there is currently no IT director on the Board (there is an IT Manager reporting to the Retail Services Director.)

**Note:** At the strategic level and acting in the early stages of a senior manager role, you are expected to identify, assess and suggest risk mitigation strategies for the business. Reference material 3 provides you with the opportunity to do exactly that by presenting information obtained from a comparative company (albeit a quoted company) in the industry rather than the business depicted in the pre-seen.

# Summary of the pre-seen

### Reference material 4 – Cast mission statement and strategy

- The mission statement depicts the over-riding purpose of an organisation. Other than emphasising the domestic market and customer-focus, Cast's mission statement says very little.
- Cast's strategy emphasises volume growth, this being justified in terms of gaining economies of scale to gain cost advantages, deter new entrants and create switching costs for customers. It is interesting than any thoughts of competing via differentiation have been dismissed.
- There is no comment on whether some product lines might deserve greater focus than others (for example, if you do the calculations, then cosmetics have much higher operating margins than toys)
- The main cost advantage highlighted is gaining discounts through bulk purchasing. However, most of the threats relate to Cast's relationship with its suppliers suggesting that this is a key area to be aware of in possible tasks and triggers
- This strategy is not without its challenges – for example, larger retailers have entered the market (e.g. supermarkets) that have the wherewithal to benefit from even greater economies of scale and more easily absorb the costs of distribution logistics.

### *Conclusion*

- Despite the fact that the industry is not yet saturated and volume growth opportunities still exist, the reality of the Cast strategy needs to be questioned.
- In the SWOT the threats seem to outweigh the opportunities, suggesting the need to rethink future plans. In particular Cast's strategy regarding suppliers may need developing.

**Note:** you may wish to consider possible sources of competitive advantage for an online retailer by using, for example, Porter's Value Chain.

### Reference material 5 – Cast Directors' biographies

- The directors have a wide range of previous business experience which ranges from television production to manufacturing.
- They are all comparatively new to Cast, with the longest serving director having been appointed in 2006 (who incidentally is the only director with previous experience within Cast having worked for the organisation since 1997)
- None of the directors are shown as having any previous experience in online retailing, which could be seen as a major weakness.

- There is only one non-executive director as Cast remains unquoted. Obviously this could become a problem were Cast to seek a listing but you could also argue that Cast should adopt the principles and guidelines of good governance, even if it remains unquoted.

*Conclusion*

- For an organisation that wishes to expand in online retailing, there appears to be a significant lack of experience in the specialist knowledge associated with that market.
- The retail services director also has a potential conflict of interest given that she also holds a non-executive director position with an internet service provider.

**Reference material 6 – Cast Internal Audit department**

- The internal audit department is well staffed and has a good mix of qualified and unqualified personnel.
- Planning and reporting maintain a suitable level of independence with the non-executive Chairman being the main contact for both aspects – although it is not clear what "administrative purposes" means.
- The main area of concern is that, despite the results of investigations being documented, audit reports being made available to and discussed by the board, there is no mention absence of subsequent action taken once the reports re produced.

*Conclusion*

- There is a danger that although the IA department may be planning and carrying out work diligently, the lack of a prescribed course of action, followed by a review of progress on completion of their planned work may detract from any perceived benefit.

## Reference material 7 – Financial statement extracts

Ratio analysis was previously performed in Chapter Five. The results are shown here:

| Ratio | 2015 | Working | 2014 | Working |
|---|---|---|---|---|
| Revenue growth | 11% | (2,985 – 2,687)/2,687 | – | n/a |
| Gross profit margin | 30.0% | 895/2,985 | 33.9% | 910/2,687 |
| Operating profit margin | 17.5% | 524/2,985 × 100% | 20% | 547/2,687 |
| Return on Capital Employed (ROCE) | 64% | 524/(712 + 100) | 81% | 547/(667 + 100) |
| Current ratio | 2.09 :1 | 657/314 | 2.29:1 | 599/261 |
| Receivables days | 14 days | (117/2,985) × 365 | 14 days | (105/2,687) × 365 |
| Inventory days | 51 days | (297/2,090) × 365 | 53 days | (256/1,777) × 365 |
| Payables days | 33 days | (190/2,090) × 365 | 28 days | (138/1,777) × 365 |
| Gearing – using Debt/(Debt + Equity) | 12% | 100/(100 + 712) | 13% | 100/(100 + 667) |

### Comments:

- Cast has achieved strong revenue growth of 11% in a competitive market but this appears to be at the expense of profitability.

- Further information is required to determine whether the fall in gross margin is due to price-cutting to win business, a fall in purchasing discounts achieved, other cost rises or a change in mix towards lower margin products.

- These factors then have a knock-on effect on why the operating margin has fallen. For example, changes in mix may be highly significant, given the variation in operating margins between different lines:
    - Film and music – 22%
    - Toys – 11%
    - Cosmetics – 29%
    - Books – 12%
    - Clothing – 14%
    - Electronics – 17%

- The working capital position has changed over the year, particularly payables and inventory days. Higher overall payables have impacted the current ratio with the cash position remaining positive and the cash balance increasing slightly over the year.
- The gearing ratio has improved with the level of debt has reducing over the year.
- In isolation these numbers are difficult to interpret due to the lack of direct comparison with the range of products sold. Nevertheless, the additional financial information provided on two companies Greatline and Fashionstore is useful to indicate trends within the industry.

**Note:** Refer section 13 and 14 below for comparative ratios and commentary.

**Reference material 8 – Corporate Social Responsibility Report**

- *We buy and sell our products responsibly*

    An honest, fair and ethical treatment of everyone in the supply chain. This ensures that CAST policy is in line with customer expectations.

    To facilitate this approach, partnerships with suppliers are created for responsible sourcing of products. This is monitored by a manager who reports directly to the board on the maintenance of these standards. In addition suppliers must demonstrate their commitment to a safe working environment for employees, fair treatment of staff and no employment of child labour.

    The development of long-term relationships with key suppliers similarly allows CAST to influence their key suppliers to modify their product and/or packaging for the benefit of the environment. In this way CAST has committed to reducing carbon emissions by some 20% by 2020 and is "sell on its way to achieving this target" although no detail of performance is given.

- *We care for the environment*

    With energy efficient facilities, the use of solar and wind power, packaging designed to minimise waste and be easily recycled, collections which are organised to be fuel efficient and the encouragement of staff to generate energy saving ideas, Cast is committed to minimising the impact of its operations on the environment.

## Summary of the pre-seen

- **We offer local communities our active support**

    The acknowledgement from CAST that they are major employers and consequently have an impact on the lives of the local residents where they operate, helps a great deal to facilitate their involvement in local activities, initiatives and charities.

    The creation of local focus groups ensures that direct feedback is obtained on issues affecting the local community and, as a result, swift, direct and relevant action can be taken.

    In the context of supporting local communities the reference to the non aggressive pursuance of tax avoidance schemes is confusing and perhaps worthy of further investigation.

- **We offer our employees good jobs and genuine career prospects**

    The overall perception here is that CAST are determined to create an atmosphere for their employees toward the creation of a better working environment for all.

    Clear commitments are stated where employers and employees work closely together where views are shared openly and frankly around working practices, wage rates, working patterns, on-going training, equal opportunities and in particular the health and safety of employees.

### Conclusion:

- CSR seems to be a significant part of Cast's strategic planning. We are not told whether this is because of a wish to be a good global citizen or because of the impact on customers in a highly competitive market place.
- Cast's CSR policy addresses key stakeholders of customers, suppliers, the environment, local communities and employees. Targets are set and performance measured against which managers are evaluated

### Reference material 9 and 10 – Cast Group Press Release and press cutting

- The new CEO is put forward as someone who will assist the Cast group in "future strategies" indicating that new developments are on the way. The existing internet retailing strategy has been successful and cash is available to invest in new products or markets. The reference to the new CEO's experience with "quoted companies" could suggest that flotation is something that the board are aiming toward.
- The press cutting is the first indication of conflict on the board in terms of decision making plus a large "unproductive cash mountain" resulting from the move to internet retailing.

*Conclusion:*

- The references to board conflict, the unproductive cash "mountain" and the lack of direction as to the future is indicative that considerable change is on the way.

**Reference material 11 – Competitor analysis**

- The aforementioned problem of finding a suitable competitor against which comparison can be drawn is a least partly resolved by the directors of Cast choosing to benchmark themselves against two quoted companies.
    - Greatline sells a wide range of products in several different countries
    - Fashionstore operates internationally but focusses on the sale of fashionable clothes.

*Conclusion:*

- Whilst accurate comparisons are difficult, the companies chosen at least reflect the mood of the home based customers.

**Reference material 12 – Share price**

- The market capitalisation of Greatline is greater, they have almost seven times the revenue of Fashionstore and are more profitable.
- However, Fashionstore has a higher but more volatile share price. The higher level of risk is also indicated by a higher beta factor.
- The P/E ratio reflects market expectations and confidence in a company so would incorporate both growth prospects and perceived risk. The fact that Greatline has a higher P/E ratio is due to its lower risk but possibly also due to pessimistic views on Fashionstore's growth prospects given recent problems.

*Conclusion*

- On balance, the steady growth and profitability of Greatline makes it a more useful benchmark than the fluctuating success of Fashionstore who are likely to have been hit by the introduction of new competitors such as ASOS.

# Summary of the pre-seen

## Reference material 13 and 14 – Financial statement extracts for competitors

Additional information is presented on the two companies Cast considers to be the best comparators as competitors.

The information is best presented in tabular format for ease of comparison.

| Ratio | Cast 2015 | Cast 2014 | Greatline 2015 | Greatline 2014 | Fashionstore 2015 | Fashionstore 2014 |
|---|---|---|---|---|---|---|
| Revenue growth | 11% | – | 11% | – | 17% | – |
| Gross margin | 30.0% | 33.9% | 24.2% | 24.3% | 26.3% | 24.2% |
| Operating margin | 17.6% | 20.4% | 18% | 18% | 13% | 24% |
| ROCE | 64% | 81% | 94% | 87% | 91% | 67% |
| Current ratio | 2.09 :1 | 2.29:1 | 1.88:1 | 1.88:1 | 1.24:1 | 1.07:1 |
| Receivables days | 14 days | 14 days | 14 days | 16 days | 14 days | 15 days |
| Inventory days | 51 days | 53 days | 45 days | 49 days | 34 days | 32 days |
| Payables days | 33 days | 28 days | 31 days | 34 days | 29 days | 33 days |
| Gearing | 12% | 13% | 37% | 37% | 25% | 25% |

*Conclusions*

- Based on the analysis above, Cast appears to be holding its own in highly competitive and difficult trading circumstances. The ROCE however does indicate the potential for future growth.

- Cast has the highest gross margin of the three companies, which is very encouraging, but we do not have sufficient information to explain why.

- Revenue growth has been achieved and despite a decrease in profitability Cast are in strong position when compared with the most similar company Greatline (Fashionstore being too specific to fashion rather than the range of merchandise which Greatline offers)

- There is little to say when drawing comparisons with the working capital position of the three companies other than Cast seem to have the highest inventory days which could mean a risk of obsolescence. This situation is however improving but is worthy of further investigation.

- The gearing ratio for Cast indicates a good position which reflects the strong cash position for the Cast group

## 3 SWOT analysis

A SWOT analysis is a useful tool to summarise the current position of the company. It is simply a listing of the following:

- The STRENGTHS of the organisation. These are internal factors that give the organisation a distinct advantage.

- The WEAKNESSES of the organisation. These are internal factors that affect performance adversely, and so might put the organisation at a disadvantage.

- The OPPORTUNITIES available. These are circumstances or developments in the environment that the organisation might be in a position to exploit to its advantage.

- The THREATS or potential threats. These are factors in the environment that present risks or potential risks to the organisation and its competitive position.

Strengths and weaknesses are internal to the organisation, whereas opportunities and threats are external factors.

A SWOT analysis can be presented simply as a list of strengths, followed by weaknesses, then opportunities and finally threats. It would be useful to indicate within each category which factors seem more significant than others, perhaps by listing them in descending order of priority. Alternatively a SWOT analysis, if it is not too long and excludes minor factors, can be presented in the form of a 2 × 2 table, as follows:

# Summary of the pre-seen

| Strengths | Weaknesses |
|---|---|
| | |

| Opportunities | Threats |
|---|---|
| | |

With this method of presentation, the positive factors (strengths and opportunities) are listed on the left and the negative factors (weaknesses and threats) are on the right.

### Test your Understanding 1

Prepare a SWOT analysis of Cast based on the summary of each exhibit and the guidance above.

| Strengths | Weaknesses |
|---|---|
| | |

| Opportunities | Threats |
|---|---|
| | |

132

## 4 Summary

You should now be comfortable with all the key issues identified in the Cast pre-seen and ready to start thinking about the exam.

**Next steps:**

(1) It is a good idea, once you have analysed the pre-seen for the live exam, to brainstorm a list of possible triggers (what might happen) and tasks (what you have to do) which you may face in the exam.

This is NOT an exercise in question spotting as you cannot hope to simply guess the requirements and only study a limited amount of topics. However this brainstorm will help you to think about how the pre-seen may relate to the competencies and may mean fewer complete surprises on the day of the exam.

Warning: In the past some candidates seem to have been a little guilty of drafting "pre-fabricated" answers based on pre-seen material and then simply writing these out in the exam. It is vital that you address the new information in the unseen material and reflect the specifics of the requirements.

# Summary of the pre-seen

## Test your understanding answers

### Test your Understanding 1

| Strengths | Weaknesses |
|---|---|
| • Profitable<br>• Cash rich<br>• Strong customer focus<br>• Diversified product range<br>• CSR policy | • Dependent on supply chain<br>• Potential stock obsolescence<br>• Inexperienced board<br>• Lack of IT representation at board level<br>• Board conflict<br>• Lack of strategy<br>• Sales forecasting problems due to uncertainty over consumer spend<br>• Purchase of unproven products<br>• Inefficiency in distribution centres<br>• Inventory control<br>• Control of costs associated with delivery<br>• Control of customer personal information |
| **Opportunities** | **Threats** |
| • Acquisition of competitor<br>• New product ranges offered for sale<br>• International expansion<br>• Flotation on stock market | • Prices undercut by competition<br>• Increased competition<br>• Economic decline<br>• Seasonality<br>• Lost sales due to IT problems<br>• Product liability and legal claims<br>• Exposure to fraud via new payment methods<br>• Failure of card issuers<br>• Acquisition of competitor |

chapter 7

# Practice triggers and tasks

**Chapter learning objectives**

- To understand how underlying knowledge from E3, P3 and F3 could be applied within the case study

# Practice triggers and tasks

## 1 Introduction

In previous chapters you have been introduced to the concept of triggers and tasks and in Chapter Six we have helped you to prepare and analyse the pre-seen information for the pilot exam – Cast. Before we think about the exam day itself we will do some practice exercises which will help you prepare for as many different scenarios as possible arising in the exam. This will also give you an opportunity to revise some key aspects of the syllabus and consider how they may be applied to the scenario. It is crucial that you go through this process to fully prepare yourself for the exam.

However, you need to be careful – this is NOT an exercise in question spotting. We are aiming to revise the knowledge required and practise the skills needed to perform well in any exam rather than guess what may come up. Any set of pre-seen exhibits can give rise to a huge range of possible tasks – we have only provided a sample here.

Once you understand the competencies by which this exam will be marked, are completely comfortable with the syllabus diagnostics at the beginning of Chapter Three and have thoroughly prepared the pre-seen information produced in Chapter Four then you are ready to continue with these exercises. Each task begins with a small scenario (or trigger) to introduce the topic and set the scene. You should be using the skills discussed in Chapter Eight to work through these tasks. These tasks are discrete – i.e. they do not follow on from each other but stand alone as sample exercises. Later on in this book we will consider how the tasks will flow into a complete exam.

**Note:** These task exercises are not related to each other. All you need to attempt this task is the pre-seen material and the additional material provided below. You should not make reference to any material provided for other practice tasks.

## 2 E3 – Strategic Management

### Exercise 1

*Trigger:*

**Newspaper Article**

> **Will Papercut turn septic?**
>
> Papercut, the online book retail arm of Cast Group, is starting to look a little infected.
>
> With its rather conventional website, and product range limited to conventional 'hard copy' books, Papercut's business model is starting to look very 'last century'.
>
> With twenty per cent of all book purchases now being electronic downloads, and a further ten per cent estimated to be illegally downloaded, the book retail industry has changed greatly over the last twenty years. Admittedly, Papercut no longer tries to retail books through high street stores, but it still sticks rigidly to the old hardback and paperback products.
>
> Readers are becoming less and less willing to wait for the delivery of their next book. With e-books, of course, delivery takes a matter of seconds. Buy a book from Papercut, however, and you're left sitting at home waiting for a courier to call. By far the most common complaint about Papercut relates to late delivery. Ironically, this is one key part of the service that Papercut doesn't provide.
>
> Ironically, the last ten years have seen a steady increase in the high street sale of conventional books, but this growth has been seen in the supermarket sector, where many stores offer a limited range of fiction and non-fiction titles, at substantial discounts.
>
> Papercut also needs to watch its suppliers. Several publishers are known to be looking at the idea of forming a conglomerate, to e-retail books direct to the reader. Papercut might just find itself cut out altogether.
>
> So, let's just hope that the Cast management sort out the problem, before it becomes necessary to amputate the infected digit.
>
> *The Retailer*

# Practice triggers and tasks

### Task

**You are a Senior Finance Manager, advising Judith, the new CEO.**

As you arrive at work, Judith calls you into her office…

"Have you seen the latest edition of 'The Retailer' magazine? There's an article in it (see attached) that mentions Papercut. The article seems to suggest that Papercut is suffering increased threats from competitors, but it also mentions suppliers and customers. I think that the article must be referring to some theoretical model that I'm not familiar with.

Can you prepare me a briefing note? I have a meeting with the rest of the Board in an hour, and I know some of them will have seen the article. I need to be able to provide the Directors with a detailed analysis of our competitive environment. Include a brief overview of any theoretical model(s) that you refer to."

## Exercise 2

*Triggers:*

**Extract from Board Meeting Minutes**

**4.3 RSD briefly outlined issues relating to Fastrack.**

On-time delivery performance continues to fall, and has reached critical levels in some regions. Drastic action is required, as this failure is starting to affect our reputation.

Action: RSD to identify and evaluate strategic options.
Recommendation to CEO required by 10.30 am tomorrow.

**Extract from Distribution Manager's report to the Board**

**Fastrack Logistics Services Ltd**

Fastrack is our largest logistics provider. Across the Group, approximately 40% of all deliveries are contracted with Fastrack. We spent $85m with Fastrack, in 2014, equivalent to 62% of their turnover. We are, by far, their largest customer.

As far as we can establish, as Fastrack is a private company, they made net profit of about $23m on turnover of $140m in their last financial year. They reported net assets of $43m, and employ just over 300 staff, 30 of whom are based in our distribution centres.

We have always had a good relationship with Fastrack. I meet regularly with Eric White, their Managing Director. We signed a contract with Fastrack in 2013, which is due for renewal later this year. In the contract, we specified a minimum of 80% 'next day' delivery, for items handed to Fastrack personnel by 5pm. The latest analytics show that their delivery performance has fallen each month for the last eight, and is currently at 76.3% next day delivery. We are about to file our first monthly performance penalty claim, as specified in the contract, and expect this to be for about $0.9m. Eric White has already agreed the statistics, so Fastrack will not be in a position to dispute the claim.

My last meeting with Eric wasn't very pleasant. I presented the performance analytics, and Eric became very distressed. He told me that Fastrack has major problems with its staff, and motivation levels are low. Apparently, there are rumours circulating within Fastrack that the company is to be sold, although Eric denies this. He did, however, express a desire to retire next year (when he reaches the age of 65) and said that there is no suitable successor in Fastrack. I think he might be forced to sell, and I know a couple of our other logistics suppliers are likely to be interested. I believe that Eric owns most of the shares in Fastrack, with the rest shared among his family and the senior management.

Eric seems completely unable to address the staff issues, and I know Fastrack has been looking for a Head of HR for the last year, without success. The senior management team are not 'professional managers', having all worked for Fastrack for many years and risen through the organisation structure. Two of them are ex-drivers.

*Distribution Manager*

## Practice triggers and tasks

*Task:*

**You are a Senior Finance Manager, advising the Board of Cast, and have just received the following email:**

To: sfm@cast.net
From: rsd@cast.net
Subject: Fastrack
Date: <DATE>
Time: 09.00

Hi

We've been having some issues with Fastrack, our largest courier partner. You'll find the background in the attached extract from the minutes of yesterday's Board meeting. There's also a report from my Distribution Manager, including some information about Fastrack.

I need to report back to Judith at 10.30 today. Can you put together a report by then? Sorry for the rush.

Regards
Brenda
Retail Services Director

# chapter 7

### Exercise 3

*Trigger*

**Extract from Post-implementation review of a project by an external consultant:**

> **Management of change**
>
> Overall, the organisation structure resulting from the project was excellent (see earlier in this report). However, that failure by staff to adopt the new structure, and the resulting motivation and productivity issues, were a result of weak leadership in the management of change.
>
> The project manager fulfilled his responsibilities, and delivered a solution which was fit for purpose. The new organisation structure, and job descriptions, were in line with best practice. The confusion within the department, following the reorganisation, can be attributed to a failure (on behalf of the project sponsor) to recognise the key role of leadership in the change management process. The new organisation structure should have become effective within a very short period after implementation. Instead, poor communication and a lack of clear 'top management buy-in' resulted in a six month period of disruption and unrest. Staff turnover, during this period, was also much higher than normal.

# Practice triggers and tasks

*Task*

**You are a Senior Finance Manager, advising the Board of Cast.**

You find the following email in your inbox:

> To: sfm@cast.net
> From: rsd@cast.net
> Subject: Change Management
> Date: <DATE>
> Time: 09.00
>
> Hi
>
> The IT department recently went through a reorganisation, and it didn't go well. As sponsor of the project, I feel responsible. I didn't really have much to do with the project, as I'm not an IT specialist, but the post-implementation review criticised me for 'lack of leadership'. I'd assumed that it was the project manager's role to lead the project?
>
> The post-implementation review was carried out by a consultant, and I've attached the relevant section of her report. I need to understand "the role of leadership in the change management process" – I think that's the phrase the consultant used. I would also like some clarification on the role of a project sponsor.
>
> I have a meeting with the IT Manager, who managed the project, at 10.00 today. Can you put together a briefing note by then? Sorry for the rush.
>
> Regards
> Brenda
> Retail Services Director

# chapter 7

### Exercise 4

**You are a Senior Finance Manager, advising the Board of Cast.**

*Trigger:*

**Extract from Cast strategic plan, 2015-20**

> **Market penetration**
>
> From our stated strategic goals:
>
> "Cast's most immediate strategic priority is to build sales volume. The company aims to dominate the markets that it serves. That is partly to make the best possible use of any economies of scale that it might exploit and also to deter competitors from entering the market segments that the company has chosen to serve."
>
> This leads to the following strategic objectives:
>
> (1) Increase market share, in all markets
>
> (2) Widen the range of products available
>
> (3) Negotiate better discounts with suppliers, as a result of increased sales volumes
>
> (4) Improve margins, as a result of lower purchase costs.

143

# Practice triggers and tasks

*Task:*

**Judith (the CEO) calls you into her office.**

"I was talking to a friend of mine, who works for a big electronics company. She says that they use the Balanced Scorecard to control and monitor the implementation of their strategy. I know what the Balanced Scorecard is, but I thought it was only used for setting objectives. We've never bothered with it at Cast, because our strategic planning process is very good at turning our mission into objectives, but now I'm starting to think that maybe we should look again.

Can you prepare me a short PowerPoint presentation, that I can use at this afternoon's Board meeting? No more than ten slides, please. I've put a page from the strategic plan on your desk. It's about the market penetration aspect of our strategy. Can you use that to illustrate how we might use the Balanced Scorecard to monitor and control strategy implementation?

I'll need the presentation in about an hour, so I can look through it before the Board meeting."

# chapter 7

## 3 P3 – Risk Management

### Exercise 5

*Trigger*

No further information is associated with this task. You should base your answer on the pre-seen material and exhibits.

*Task*

You are a Senior Finance Manager, advising Arthur, the non-executive Chairman.

Arthur telephones you…

> "As you know, the Head of Internal Audit reports to me, as Chairman. That is to preserve the independence of the function from any undue influence.
>
> I had a discussion with the Head of Internal Audit, and he tells me that we are taking a 'risk-based approach' to internal audit, but it is based on a 'risk map' prepared by a consultant, several years ago. Now, I know we don't do risk analysis as a Group, but I think it's something we should consider. I've spoken to Judith, and she agrees. Judith also said that I could have a couple of hours of your time.
>
> Could you provide me with a risk analysis, please? I'd like you to include all the major financial and non-financial risks, and perhaps you might find some sort of framework to prioritise the risks? That will help me, when I next speak to the Head of Internal Audit."

# Practice triggers and tasks

### Exercise 6

**You are a Senior Finance Manager, advising the Board.**

You find the following email in your inbox:

> To: sfm@cast.net
> From: rsd@cast.net
> Subject: Big data
> Date: <DATE>
> Time: 09.00
>
> Hi
>
> At yesterday's Board meeting, we were discussing risk management. Arthur mentioned something about 'big data', but none of us had the nerve to tell him that we had no idea what he was talking about. Arthur seemed to think that this 'big data' thing might help us to manage some of the risks facing Cast. I seem to remember he specifically mentioned a couple of risks. I'll ask my PA to send you the relevant Board minute.
>
> Can you prepare a briefing note that explains what big data is, and how it might be used in the management of risks, please? If you could relate it to the risks mentioned by Arthur, that would be perfect.
>
> I need to report back to Judith at 10.00 today. Can you put together something by then?
>
> Regards
> Brenda
> Retail Services Director

**Subsequent email:**

To: patosfm@cast.net
From: rsd@cast.net
Subject: Board minute
Date: <DATE>
Time: 09.05

Hi

Brenda asked me to copy this to you:

**3.9 Risk management**

Chairman mentioned that the charity he works with, as a trustee, uses big data to improve its risk management process. It was suggested that Cast might find this approach useful, for example in the management of risks relating to customers ceasing to use Cast Group, and to predicting inventory obsolescence.

Action: RSD to investigate

Regards
Alice
*PA to Retail Services Director*

# Practice triggers and tasks

### Exercise 7

**You are a Senior Finance Manager, advising the Board.**

**You find the following email in your inbox:**

> To: sfm@cast.net
> From: hia@cast.net
> Subject: Risk identification
> Date: <DATE>
> Time: 09.00
>
> Hi
>
> Judith said she'd lend me your services this morning. Sorry if that's a shock, but I only spoke to her last night.
>
> Last year, we did an audit of the internal control systems here at Cast. My report was quite critical, particularly about the way we identify risks (or don't).
>
> Arthur and Judith felt that I'd been unreasonable, so they suggested that you might give them a 'second opinion'. You don't need to do any research – I've attached the relevant section from my internal audit report. Take a look at it, and do a brief report to Judith and Arthur, with your conclusions as to whether you believe the current control system adequately identifies risks, and a few obvious recommendations (assuming you feel changes are necessary).
>
> I promised Judith a report by 10.30 today, as she has a meeting with Arthur at 11.
>
> Thanks for your help.
> Regards
> Sam
> *Head of Internal Audit*

**Accompanying excerpt from Internal Audit report:**

### 4 AUDIT FINDINGS

### 4.3 Risk identification

The current risk identification processes are as follows:

(1) During the annual strategic planning process, the planning team (the Board, minus Chairman) reviews the risks mentioned in the previous strategic plan, and discusses whether any changes are required. These risks were identified from a 'risk factors' report taken from the published report and accounts of a rival.

(2) Any new risks, or changes to those included in the strategic plan, are identified by individual members of staff and discussed with the CEO. There is no formal procedure (or standard form) for reporting new or changed risks.

(3) Risks are NOT considered during monthly performance reporting, nor are they included (other than as 'threats') in the SWOT analysis prepared by each Director, on a quarterly basis.

This aspect of the control system was discussed with the CEO. The response was "we are not a listed company, so there is no requirement to have a formal risk management process or a documented internal control system. All the Directors and Managers know what the risks are, and I trust them to come to me with any issues."

During interviews with Directors and department heads, none could give an example of having discussed or reported a risk issue, other than during the annual strategic planning process.

**Excerpt from Internal Audit report HIA11/2014 – 'Internal Control Systems' March 2014**

**Note:** The 'risk factors' report referred to above is Reference Material 3 of the pre-seen material

# Practice triggers and tasks

### Exercise 8

You have received the following email:

**STRICTLY CONFIDENTIAL**

To: sfm@cast.net
From: ceo@cast.net
Subject: Risk management of the Diamante acquisition
Date: <DATE>Time: 09.00

Hi
Firstly – this is NOT public knowledge outside the Board. Keep it to yourself.

We've been approached by the Managing Director (and majority – 52% – shareholder) of a jewellery retailer, Diamante Ltd (not its real name). It's a private company, and he wishes to retire. He doesn't have any family to take over the running of the business, and the other shareholders (his mother and brother – 24% each) have no interest in running the business. He hasn't spoken to them, but feels sure that they would sell, for an appropriate price. I made some notes (attached) at a meeting with the MD, and they're attached.

I want to brief the Board this afternoon, but I need to know what might go wrong with the acquisition, both before and after we buy it (if we do). I don't expect you to identify and manage the risks, as I'd have to give you far too much confidential information. We can do everything within the Board, for now. I do, however, need to know what sort of things we should be doing.

Could you prepare a short presentation, for me to use at the Board meeting, suggesting a suitable risk management framework to use for the acquisition? Make it specific, and use lots of relevant examples to illustrate your points. It's important that the Board members understand, as you won't be there to explain it. Aim to produce a maximum of 10-15 slides, please.

Let me have your slideshow by 10am, please. I may need to discuss it with you, before I see the Board.
Thanks
Judith

The following meeting notes were attached to the email:

### Castle Gems – Diamante Ltd

- Owned by Mr Jones (52%), his mother (24%) and brother (24%). He hasn't spoken to them yet.
- Net assets of $3m, turnover $12m, operating profit last year $3.4m
- Has one store in Manchester, but also trades online. Online now represents 62% of turnover.
- Owns freehold of store, estimated to be worth about $1m.
- Employs 23 staff, 11 in store, rest in purchasing, marketing, admin, IT.
- Looking to retire – no interested successor
- Sales are 89% domestic, 11% overseas
- Wide product range, from cheap fashion jewellery to precious gems

# Practice triggers and tasks

## 4 F3 – Financial Strategy

### Exercise 9

**Trigger**

No further information is associated with this task. You should base your answer on the pre-seen material and exhibits.

**Task**

You find the following email in your inbox:

> To: sfm@cast.net
> From: cfo@cast.net
> Subject: Financial structure of Cast Group
> Date: <DATE>
> Time: 09.00
>
> Hi
>
> We had a Board meeting last night, and Arthur expressed an opinion that we are holding too much cash. Judith said she wanted a second opinion about our capital structure, from someone who hasn't been directly involved in our financial strategy or reporting. As you're the only (almost) qualified accountant outside the Finance department, I guess that means you.
>
> Can you prepare a briefing note that analyses our current financial structure, please? I guess you should also express an opinion as to whether you think we're holding too much cash.
>
> I need to report back to Judith at 10.00 today. Can you put together something by then? Sorry for the rush.
>
> Regards
> Dana
> *Chief Financial Officer*

### Exercise 10

**Trigger – updated financial position:**

Financial position as at <DATE>

- Cash in hand and at bank: $128m
- Short term (demand) deposits $100m
- Current liabilities $301m
- Trade receivables $131m
- Inventories $332m

No major (over $10m) investments are scheduled for the remainder of the financial year.

You have received the following e-mail from Judith:

To: sfm@cast.net
From: ceo@cast.net
Subject: Financing 'X'
Date: <DATE>
Time: 13.00

STRICTLY CONFIDENTIAL

Hi

We're in the middle of a Board meeting, which looks like it may take all afternoon.

One of the items for discussion is a very major investment. I can't tell you what it is, but we would need about $300m to finance it: $250m immediately, and the rest over the first year. I can't ask the finance department, because it's too confidential.

Can you prepare a briefing note that evaluates the financing options, please? I've attached a brief summary of today's financial position.

The Board is back from lunch at 14.00 today. Can you put together something by then?

Regards
Judith
*Chief Executive Office*

# Practice triggers and tasks

### Exercise 11

*Trigger:*

**Cast Group – Extract from share register**
**STRICTLY PRIVATE AND CONFIDENTIAL**

| Name | Holding |
|---|---|
| **Family members** | |
| Trustees of F Smith discretionary trust | 7,430,000 |
| A Smith | 250,000 |
| F Smith | 140,000 |
| P Smith | 1,200,000 |
| K Knowles | 200,000 |
| D Peters | 320,000 |
| F Singh | 1,240,000 |
| J Simonetti | 400,000 |
| Trustees of F & P Smith children's' trust | 2, 300,000 |
| Trustees of Cast pension fund | 1,280,000 |
| R Waller | 90,000 |
| D Rodrigues | 90,000 |
| **Senior staff** | |
| J Anderson | 20,000 |
| B Carroll | 10,000 |
| C Denning | 10,000 |
| D Elliot | 10,000 |
| E Fletcher | 10,000 |
| **TOTAL** | **15,000,000** |

**Note: No options have been granted for future purchase**

# chapter 7

**Task**

As you return from lunch, Judith calls you into her office:

> "As you know, we have a large cash balance. At the last Board meeting, we were discussing our investment plans, and it seems that we've run out of ideas. Other than acquiring competitors, which we don't want to do, it seems that the only option is to accept the general growth rate in the market, and try to steal small percentages of market share.
>
> That gives us a problem. What should we do with the cash? It's not earning much return, as interest rates are low. We don't want to pay it out as an additional interim dividend, as the shareholders might expect the same every year. There would also be tax implications, for the shareholders, of such a big windfall.
>
> Dana suggested a share repurchase, but she doesn't know anything about the process as she trained in the public sector. Could you produce me a briefing note, looking at the advantages and disadvantages of share repurchase, compared with paying a one-off dividend, please? Include an explanation of the steps involved in a share repurchase, and an evaluation of any financial consequences, too.
>
> Here's a summary of our share register.
>
> Let me have the briefing note in a couple of hours. We have another Board meeting this evening, and I'd like to update the rest of the Board."

# Practice triggers and tasks

## Exercise 12

*Trigger*

No further information is associated with this task. You should base your answer on the pre-seen material and exhibits.

*Task*

You find the following email in your inbox:

> To: sfm@cast.net
> From: ceo@cast.net
> Subject: Flotation?
> Date: <DATE>
> Time: 13.00
>
> STRICTLY PRIVATE AND CONFIDENTIAL
>
> Hi
> As you know, we're under pressure (from some shareholders) to turn Cast into a public company and obtain a stock exchange listing.
>
> At the Board, we've already discussed the strategic implications, but we're unsure about the detailed accounting implications. Dana is on holiday, and we can't ask anyone in the Finance Department due to the confidentiality issue.
>
> Could you prepare me a brief (no more than ten slides) presentation, that I can show the Board this afternoon? We need to know the impact of flotation on the financial statements, with particular attention to our interaction with society.
>
> The Board is back from lunch at 14.00 today. Can you put together something by then?
>
> Regards
> Judith
> *Chief Executive Officer*

## 5 Summary

You should better understand the wide range of possible tasks which you may encounter in the exam. You should also have a better appreciation of the level of detail required in your answers to score a high mark in the exam.

**Next steps:**

(1) Have you attempted all of the tasks in this chapter? Don't be tempted to look at the answers until you have, at the very least, made detailed notes on your response.

(2) If you struggled with any of these tasks, this may indicate a knowledge gap which you need to revisit.

# Practice triggers and tasks

## Test your understanding answers

### Exercise 1

**Note:** These suggested answers are indicative of what could be produced by a very competent student, in the time allowed, and would earn a good pass. They are not 'reference', or 'model', answers. Other, equally valid, points would receive credit. It is important that you attempt to produce your own answers and then reflect on whether you have addressed the requirement BEFORE reviewing these suggested solutions.

To: CEO
From: Senior Finance Manager
Briefing note: The Competitive Environment of Papercut

The article in The Retailer references the 'Five Forces' model developed by Professor Michael Porter of the Harvard Business School. This analyses the competitive environment of a business unit or SBU under five headings, as follows.

### Competitive Rivalry

This competitive force looks at what we would conventionally refer to as competitors – other organisations, operating in our industry, selling similar products to similar customers.

- Many of its rivals are larger (such as Greatline), and therefore have greater bargaining power with suppliers and are probably able to offer lower prices due to lower purchase costs and economies of scale.

Conclusion: Papercut suffers a high degree of Competitive Rivalry.

### Bargaining Power of Suppliers

Porter suggests that a firm competes with its suppliers, through the exercise of bargaining power over the price and quality of supplies. This directly affects the ability of the firm to make profits.

- Papercut, in common with the rest of the Group, has good relationships with its suppliers.
- However, there is a threat that publishers may form a conglomerate, to sell directly to readers. This would eliminate the need for intermediaries such as Papercut.

- Papercut relies, to a great extent, on the service quality of logistics (courier) companies to deliver books to customers. Any failure to deliver reflects badly on Papercut.

Conclusion: Papercut suffers a moderate degree of Supplier Power.

**Bargaining Power of Customers/Buyers**

Porter suggests that a firm competes with its customers, through the exercise of bargaining power over the price and quality of supplies. This directly affects the ability of the firm to make profits.

- Customers experience low switching costs when buying online, as the rivals of Papercut are 'only one click away'.
- Customers can shop around for the best price.
- Papercut cannot differentiate its product, as the books it sells are identical to those sold by rivals.
- Papercut finds it difficult to differentiate service levels, as all online book retailers offer similar service levels such as delivery and website navigation.

Conclusion: Papercut suffers a high degree of Buyer Power.

**Threat of New Entrants**

Porter suggests that the Threat of New Entrants represents competitive force, as firms have to waste valuable resources erecting and maintaining barriers to entry. Those resources could, otherwise, be taken as additional profit.

- The business model of Papercut is highly automated, with major investment in IT systems required in order to enter the industry. However, the cost of IT is continually falling, and suppliers of other online products can easily expand into books.
- Papercut exploits some economies of scale, but is too small for this to represent a significant barrier to entry.
- As global business becomes easier, and worldwide logistics improve, geography becomes much less of a barrier to entry. Papercut, in common with other Cast businesses, is vulnerable to foreign entrants to its market.

Conclusion: Papercut suffers a high degree of New Entry Threat.

### Threat of Substitutes

According to Porter, a substitute can use a different technology, originate in a different industry, or simply be an alternative use for the same disposable income.

- The main technological substitute to Papercut is e-books. Electronic book readers are growing in popularity, and e-books represent 20% of the market. Papercut does not supply e-books. Nor does Cast Disk.

- There is a growing trend towards the illegal (in many countries) download of e-books. This represents a threat to all book retailers, whether they provide e-books or not.

- Other Cast businesses, such as Cast Disk and Zap, offer substitutes to books. Leisure time is scarce, and customers must choose whether to spend it reading a book, listening to music, or playing a video game or app. All of these businesses compete for the same part of the customer's disposable income.

Conclusion: Papercut suffers a high degree of Substitution Threat.

### Overall conclusion

The article in *The Retailer* is correct in its conclusion that the competitive environment of Papercut is hostile.

# chapter 7

### Exercise 2

## Strategic Options Relating to Fastrack

To: RSD
From: SFM
Date: <DATE>

### Contents

- Terms of reference
- Introduction
- Strategic option 1 – do nothing
- Strategic option 2 – change supplier
- Strategic option 3 – offer support and assistance
- Strategic option 4 – acquisition
- Conclusions
- Recommendations

### Terms of reference

This report identifies and evaluates the strategic options relating to Fastrack. Each of the strategic options will be evaluated in terms of its suitability, feasibility and acceptability. The report ends with a recommendation for further action.

Disclaimer: This report has been prepared very quickly, and is based only on the information provided. Further analysis is required, to verify the conclusions reached.

### Introduction

Fastrack is in trouble. Motivation levels are low, due to rumours that the company is to be sold. As a result, performance is falling. On-time delivery is at a critical level, and Fastrack is now liable to penalty charges of $0.9m. The MD is unable to deal with the issues, and has expressed a desire to retire. Fastrack has no successor.

As Fastrack is our largest logistics provider, responsible for about 40% of our goods, any failure by Fastrack reflects badly on us. Our reputation will suffer, and reliable delivery is a CSF. Urgent action is required.

### Strategic option 1 – do nothing

- *Suitability:*

    The risk of reputational damage is too high. We cannot allow on-time delivery rates to fall, and we cannot rely on Fastrack to resolve the problem. There is also a serious risk that one of our rivals, or another logistics company, will acquire Fastrack. While this might resolve the delivery issue, it could put us in a position where the new owner does not wish Fastrack to continue to do business with us. We rely on Fastrack for 40% of our deliveries.

- *Acceptability:*

    Customers will not accept delivery failure.

- *Feasibility:*

    This option requires no resource.

### Strategic option 2 – change supplier

- *Suitability:*

    The Fastrack contract is due for renewal soon, so it will be possible to terminate the relationship. Finding an alternative supplier should not be too difficult, as there are very many alternatives available.

- *Acceptability:*

    Simply terminating the contract is not in line with our CSR statement, as we strive for partnership with suppliers. Other suppliers may respond negatively.

- *Feasibility:*

    Finding an alternative logistics provider, with sufficient capacity to take on 40% of our deliveries, may prove difficult and time-consuming.

### Strategic option 3 – offer support and assistance

- *Suitability:*

    Offering support to Fastrack is in line with our stated policy of vendor partnership.

- *Acceptability:*

    Deliveries should improve, which would please customers. Being proactive in our dealings with Fastrack is in line with our CSR statement, and should reinforce the view among our other suppliers that we are a good customer.

- *Feasibility:*

    It should be possible to place Earnest Fletcher or one of his subordinates with Fastrack, as interim Head of HR, in return for a fee.

**Strategic option 4 – acquisition**

- *Suitability:*

    Cast has no stated strategy to diversify into logistics. However, owning a logistics company would mitigate risk. There may also be a conflict of interest, assuming that Fastrack also serves other online retailers. This may lead to a loss of customers, post-acquisition.

- *Acceptability:*

    Other suppliers may perceive a threat that Cast might also acquire them. Returns from the new business may not be acceptable to Cast shareholders, though Fastrack's profitability (at 16%) is roughly comparable to that of Cast (17%). Opportunities for synergies should exist, which would improve the profitability further.

- *Feasibility:*

    It appears that Eric White might welcome an approach. Cast has significant cash, which could fund the purchase. This would also put the funds to better use, as returns on the acquisition are likely to exceed those received on the cash balance. The available cash (about $240m) would allow an acquisition price up to a multiple of ten times Fastrack's profits – a very high multiple for a company in difficulties. Payment of penalties (at a rate of 4% of annual net profit, per month) will deteriorate Fastrack's profits very quickly. This will reduce the value of Fastrack, and make it more attractive as an acquisition.

# Practice triggers and tasks

### Conclusions

The only strategic option which passes all three tests is Option 3 – to offer immediate support and assistance to Fastrack in the form of an interim HR manager.

### Recommendations

HRD should identify a suitable candidate to be offered to Fastrack as Interim Head of HR. An appropriate fee should be determined. RSD and Distribution Manager should meet with Eric White, immediately, to offer assistance.

Option 4 should be investigated further, as a possible longer-term strategy.

### Exercise 3

**Notes:** Project management organisation structures (and the role of the Project Sponsor) are in E2, so you should be familiar with this material from your earlier studies.

To: Retail Services Director
From: Senior Finance Manager
Briefing note: The role of leadership in change management, and the role of a project sponsor

### Introduction

The purpose of this briefing note is to clarify and evaluate the role of leadership in the management of change, following the comments made in the post-implementation review report on the recent IT Department re-organisation. There is also a clarification of the role of 'project sponsor' in a project management structure.

### The management of change

A three stage model of change was proposed by Kurt Lewin in the1950's. He argued that, in order for change to occur successfully, organisations need to progress through three stages. This process is:

(1) unfreezing habits or standard operating procedures,

(2) changing to new patterns, and

(3) refreezing to ensure lasting effects.

In the unfreezing stage, managers need to make the need for change so obvious that most people can easily understand and accept it. Unfreezing also involves creating the initial motivation to change by convincing staff of the undesirability of the present situation.

The change process itself is mainly concerned with identifying what the new behaviour or norm should be. It is vital that new information is communicated concerning the new attitudes, culture and concepts that the organisation wants to be adopted, so that these are internalised by employees.

Refreezing or stabilising the change involves ensuring that people do not slip back into old ways. As such it involves reinforcement of the new pattern of work or behaviour.

**Leadership and change**

In order to successfully implement change, someone must take overall control of the change process. This person is referred to as the change leader.

The change leader is a key figure within the organisation who takes overall responsibility and control for the proposed change within the organisation.

For a major, organisation-wide change this role may well be best filled by the CEO, but it can be taken on by anyone with the appropriate power and leadership skills within the organisation. For more limited change, it should be a senior manager with well-developed leadership skills and a high profile within the organisation.

The change leader is responsible for articulating what change is needed and why, acting as a figurehead for the change process, as well as helping to deal with any problems or conflicts that arise during the change process.

**The change leadership process**

Kotter (Leading Change, 1996) suggested that leading change is an 8-step process:

(1) Establish a sense of urgency – the change leader needs to help others see the need for change and convince them that it must be implemented promptly.

(2) Creating the guiding coalition – the change leader is unlikely to be able to control the entire change process by themselves. They must therefore assemble a group with enough power to lead the change process and ensure that they are able to act as a team.

(3) Developing a change vision – the change leader needs to create an overall vision of the future, illustrating what the change is designed to accomplish as well as its benefits. Strategies will be developed to achieve the proposed changes.

(4) Communicating the vision – the leader needs to communicate the vision and strategies identified in the previous stage to as many stakeholders as possible. This will maximise buy-in.

(5) Empowering broad-based action – the change leader needs to remove obstacles to change (restraining forces) and encourage staff to get involved in generating ideas.

(6) Generating short-term wins – plan for interim achievements that can easily be made visible, then publicise and reward staff members involved.

(7) Never letting up – maintain the change process, hiring, promoting and developing employees who support and implement the required changes.

(8) Incorporating changes into the culture – continually reinforce the change and communicate and reward achievement. This stage looks at ways of ensuring that the new change a standard part of everyday work and to prevent staff slipping back into their old habits.

### Critical success factors

Change is likely to succeed if there are:

- clearly understandable goals,
- realistic time frames, rather than merely looking for a 'quick fix',
- clear guidance as to how each individual's behaviour needs to change,
- clear, unified leadership with no conflict between managers, and
- management support for training and other necessary investment.

### The role of a project sponsor

The sponsor is the person providing the resources for the project. That is, the person ensuring that the project is successful at the business level. It is the project sponsor who will take responsibility for the project budget and will ensure that the project does not go over budget.

The sponsor will have formal authority and will oversee the project. The sponsor acts as a liaison between the Board of Cast and the project manager. The sponsor provides authority, guidance and maintains project priority.

While the project manager is responsible for delivering a successful project, the sponsor is responsible for ensuring that the organisation's objectives are achieved.

**Conclusions**

The consultant may have been a little unfair in criticising the project sponsor for failing to lead the change process.

The key question is "did the project manager have the necessary status within the organisation, and the required leadership skills, to successfully lead the change process?" If yes, then the responsibility for any failure lies with the project manager. If no, then the project sponsor should have fulfilled the role of change leader.

**Exercise 4**

**Slide show:**

**Slide 1**

- Using The Balanced Scorecard to monitor and control strategy implementation
- (Example – Market Penetration)

Judith Anderson
<DATE>

**Slide 2**

OVERVIEW

What is The Balanced Scorecard

- 4 perspectives
- Mission – goals – CSFs – KPIs
- Monitoring and control
- Illustration – Market Penetration
- Conclusions
- Questions?

## Practice triggers and tasks

**Slide 3**

WHAT IS THE BALANCED SCORECARD

- 'An approach to the provision of information to management to assist strategic policy formulation and achievement.
- It emphasises the need to provide the user with a set of information which addresses all relevant issues of performance in an objective and unbiased fashion.
- The information provided may include both financial and non-financial elements and cover areas such as profitability, customer satisfaction, internal efficiency and innovation' Kaplan & Norton

**Slide 4**

4 PERSPECTIVES

- Financial
- Customer
- Internal business process
- Learning and growth

**Slide 5**

MISSION – GOALS – CSFs – KPIs

(1) From the mission, generate goals in each perspective
(2) For each goal, identify a CSF
(3) For each CSF, identify one or more KPIs
(4) Allocate KPIs to those who can control performance in that area

**Slide 6**

MONITORING AND CONTROL

- Use KPIs generated, as on previous slide
- For each KPI, compare 'actual' to 'target' level
- Change activity levels or behaviours, to achieve KPIs
- Achieving KPIs should lead to achievement of the goals and mission
- Periodically, review CSFs and KPIs

**Slide 7**

ILLUSTRATION – MARKET PENETRATION

- Financial: Improve margins > 'Increase gross margin to X% by Y date'
- Customer: Increase market share > 'Increase repeat purchases by x%'
- Internal business process: Negotiate discounts with suppliers > 'reduce supplier prices by x%'
- Learning and growth: Widen range of products > 'add X new product lines per month'

**Slide 8**

CONCLUSIONS

- The Balanced Scorecard can be used to monitor and control strategy implementation

**Slide 9**

ANY QUESTIONS?

## Practice triggers and tasks

### Exercise 5

**Notes:** Establishing the probability and likelihood of risks is a matter of judgement – you may disagree with the following analysis. Marks would be awarded for any reasonable interpretation of the material. You should also take into account any actions already taken, by Cast, to mitigate risks. Your analysis should therefore be based on 'residual' or 'net' risk.

**Cast Group**

**Risk Analysis**

**Introduction**

The following analysis categorises risks according to their probability (how likely the event is to occur) and impact (the financial or non-financial consequences of the event). Internal audit should find this analysis useful, as the risks have been, to some extent, prioritised.

**High probability, high impact**

- Rivals use their bargaining power to secure better supply prices
- Loss of market share to a rival
- Development of new, Internet-related, technologies

**High probability, low impact**

- Competition between Cast trading names (stocking the same product, at different prices)
- Fraud or theft by employees
- Failure to deliver to promise
- Adverse publicity on social media
- Injury to, or death of, an employee (at work)
- Online (customer) fraud
- Inventory obsolescence
- Product liability (injury to customer)
- Loss of a customer

**Low probability, high impact**

- Hacking of customer or supplier data, via website
- Unexpected resignation, illness or death of a senior staff member
- Significant deterioration in overall delivery performance
- Server crash
- Database failure
- Telecommunications failure
- Breakdown in relationship with a logistics supplier
- Fire or flood at a distribution centre
- Suppliers develop their own sales channel(s)
- Foreign competitor enters the market
- Recession (economic slump)
- Failure of financial institution

**Low probability, low impact**

- Incorrect input of product details or price, to website
- Inaccurate inventory records
- Breakdown in relationship with a product supplier

# Practice triggers and tasks

### Exercise 6

**Briefing note: Big Data and Risk Management**

To: RSD
From: SFM
Date: <DATE>

**Introduction**

The Chairman of Cast has suggested that 'Big Data' might be used to improve 'risk management'. This briefing note defines those two terms, explores the relationship between them, and relates big data to two specific risks that affect Cast.

**What is 'Big Data'?**

- There are several definitions of Big Data, the most commonly used referring to large volumes of data beyond the normal processing, storage and analysis capacity of typical database application tools.

- The definition can be extended to incorporate the types of data involved. Big Data will often include much more than simply financial information and can involve other organisational data which is operational in nature along with other internal and external data which is often unstructured in form.

- One of the key challenges of dealing with Big Data is to identify repeatable business patterns in this unstructured data, significant quantities of which is in text format.

- Managing such data can lead to significant business benefits such as greater competitive advantage, improved productivity and increasing levels of innovation.

**What is 'Risk Management'?**

- Risk management should be a proactive process that is an integral part of strategic management.

- This perspective is summarised in CIMA's risk management cycle, illustrated below:

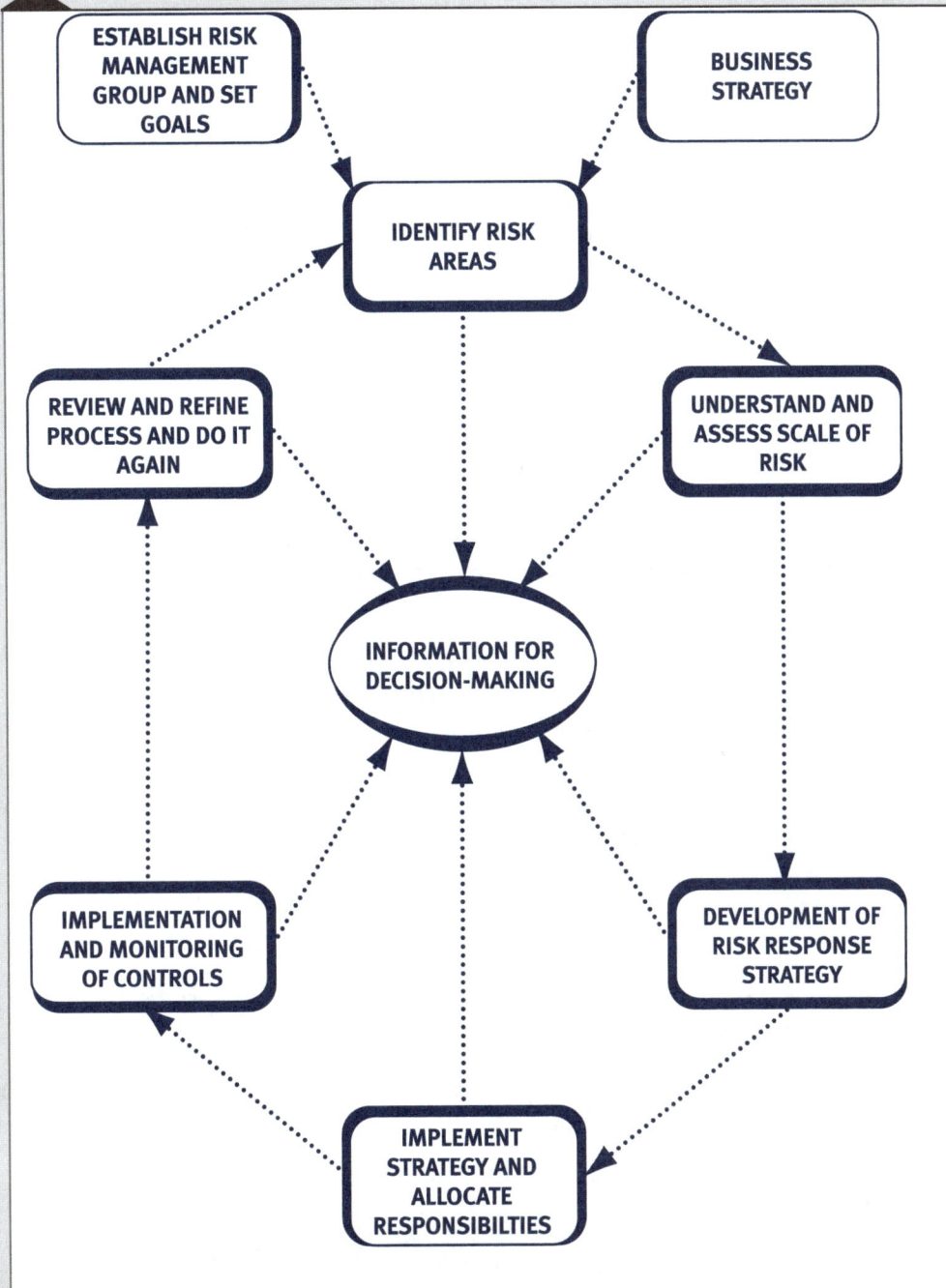

**How might big data be used to improve risk management?**

- Big Data can be used in two specific stages of the risk management cycle:
    (1) Assessment of the scale of the risk
    (2) Monitoring of controls

- In the assessment of the scale of the risk, Big Data analytics can improve assessment of the probability of an event

- In the monitoring of controls, Big Data can be used to compare the probability of an event before mitigation, with the probability after mitigation

### Customer loss

- A customer loss occurs when a customer ceases using one or more of the Cast Group trading platforms
- Big Data could be used, not just to estimate the probability of an individual customer leaving, but also to identify 'symptoms' that might indicate that a particular customer is at risk (for example, a slowing in the rate of visit or purchase, posting an adverse review, or deleting emails without 'clicking' on links)

### Inventory obsolescence

- An inventory item becomes obsolete when it is no longer purchased, or when the inventory level exceeds the predicted demand over a reasonable period
- Big Data could be used, not just to estimate the probability of an individual inventory item becoming obsolete, but also to identify 'symptoms' that might indicate that a particular item is at risk (for example, a slowing in the rate of purchase, an increasing number of adverse product reviews, or historical data relating to the 'life cycles' of similar products)

### Conclusions

- A Big Data approach is complex to use, and requires sophisticated analytical software
- The Chairman is correct in his assertion that a Big Data approach can improve risk management
- A feasibility study should be prepared.

# chapter 7

## Exercise 7

**Internal Control and Risk Identification**

To: CEO/Chairman
From: SFM
Date: <DATE>

**Contents**

(1) Terms of reference

(2) Introduction

(3) Current risk identification processes

(4) Weaknesses of current processes

(5) Best practice

(6) Conclusions

(7) Recommendations

(1) **Terms of reference**

This report examines the adequacy of the processes currently in place to identify risks. It concludes as to the adequacy of those processes, in the context of internal control, and makes appropriate recommendations.

Disclaimer: No research has been carried out in order to prepare this report, other than a general overview of Cast's position and environment. This report relies on the findings of Internal Audit report HIA11/2014, and assumes those findings to be correct. It further assumes that processes have not changed since the date of that report.

(2) **Introduction**

Cast is a private limited company. As such, it is not bound by the corporate governance regime, nor does it have to report on internal control or risk management.

Nevertheless, Cast is a large organisation, and perhaps aspires to stock exchange listing. Internal processes are compared against a model of best practice for a company of similar size, and suitable for any organisation considering becoming public.

## Practice triggers and tasks

### (3) Current risk identification processes

Internal Audit report HIA11/2014 states that the risk identification process is as follows:

(1) During the annual strategic planning process, the planning team (the Board, minus Chairman) reviews the risks mentioned in the previous strategic plan, and discusses whether any changes are required. These risks were identified from a 'risk factors' report taken from the published report and accounts of a rival

(2) Any new risks, or changes to those included in the strategic plan, are identified by individual members of staff and discussed with the CEO. There is no formal procedure (or standard form) for reporting new or changed risks.

(3) Risks are NOT considered during monthly performance reporting, nor are they included (other than as 'threats') in the SWOT analysis prepared by each Director, on a quarterly basis.

There are assumed to be no other processes in place.

To summarise:

- The risks incorporated in the strategic plan were taken from the published report of a rival.
- The risks in the strategic plan are discussed annually, by the board.
- The reporting of new and changed risks is informal, and relies on reactive action by individuals.

Such processes are typical of a smaller organisation, operating in a relatively static business environment. The competence of the management team is not in doubt.

### (4) Weaknesses of current processes

Several relevant points are worth reiterating:

- Cast is no longer a small organisation. It is the largest unquoted company in the country.
- Cast employs over 500 staff, has turnover approaching $3bn and assets in excess of $1bn.
- The retail sector is very dynamic, and online retailing particularly so.
- The Cast Board benchmarks performance against that of listed companies, and follows their share prices.
- There may be an aspiration to move to stock market listing.

# chapter 7

(5) **Best practice**

- Risk management should be a proactive process that is an integral part of strategic management.

- This perspective is summarised in CIMA's risk management cycle, illustrated below:.

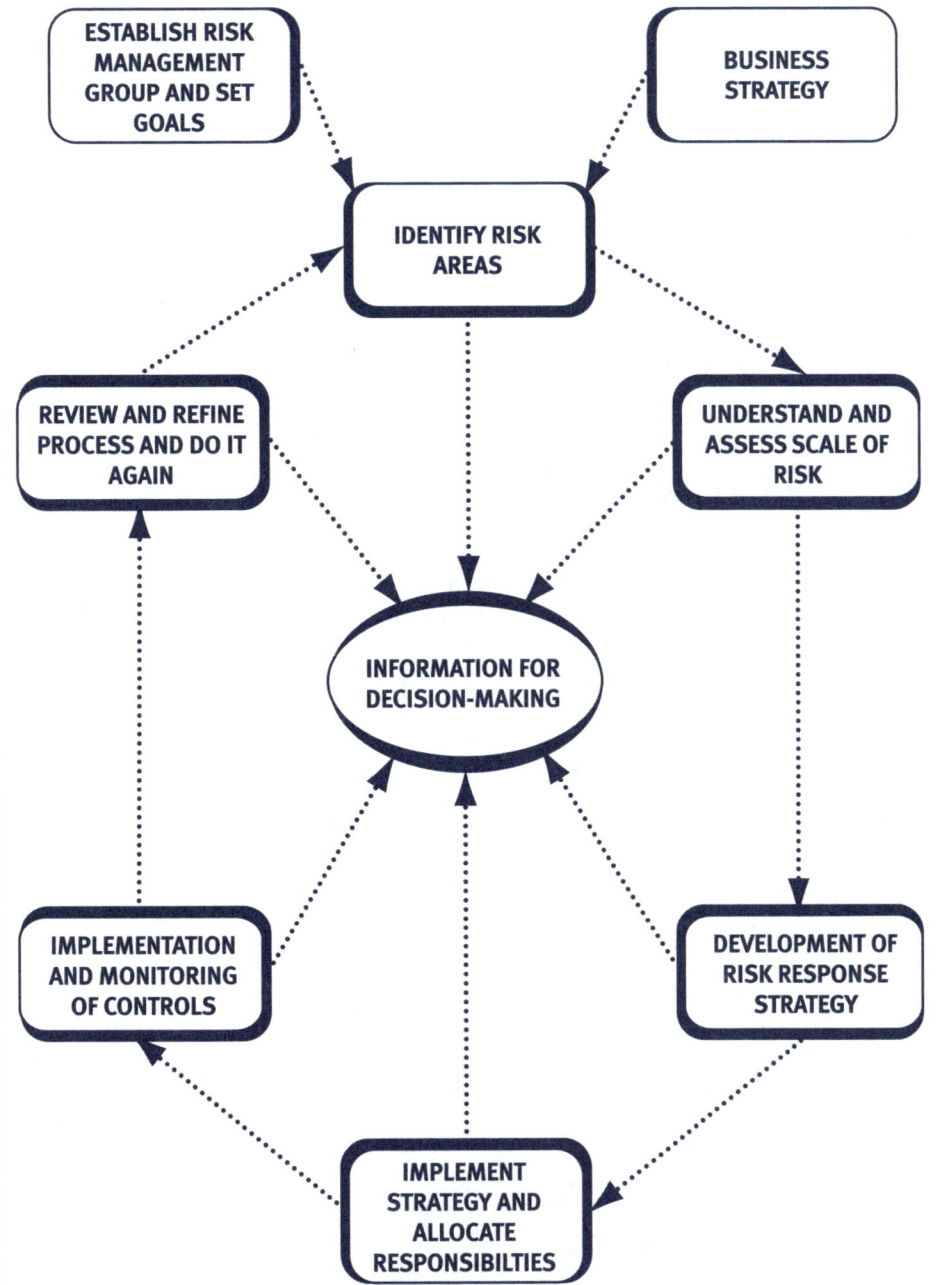

For a company the size of Cast, and bearing in mind the comments in section 4 of this report, a typical risk identification process (the first few stages of the risk management cycle illustrated above) might consist of:

(1) A Board discussion of the organisation's risk appetite – what is seen as a reasonable or acceptable amount of residual/net risk (after actions to mitigate risk)?

(2) Establishment of a risk management group (senior managers)

(3) Identification of risk management objectives

(4) Identification of risk areas relevant to the strategic plan

(5) Identification, categorisation and evaluation of risks

Further processes, not covered by the terms of reference of this report would include formulating risk responses, creating a risk register, implementing risk responses, and reporting on risk.

Items 4 and 5 above would be carried out on an ongoing basis, due to the dynamic nature of modern business environments. This may well require full time staff (such as a risk manager).

The Board would review risk appetite, and discuss risk objectives, on an annual basis. The Board would receive regular (quarterly or monthly) risk management reports, from the risk manager or risk management group.

(6) **Conclusions**

The current risk identification processes (indeed, the whole risk management processes) of Cast fall some way short of best practice for a company of this size.

(7) **Recommendations**

A risk management process, such as that outlined in Section 5 of this report, should be implemented.

### Exercise 8

**Slide 1**

- Managing the Risks of Acquisition
- (Example – Diamante)

Judith Anderson
<DATE>

**Slide 2**

OVERVIEW

- What is risk
- Overview of process
- What is our risk appetite
- Nominate a risk manager
- Identify risk areas
- Identify and evaluate risks
- Decide on risk mitigation activities
- Implement strategy
- Control and report
- Questions?

**Slide 3**

WHAT IS RISK?

- Risk in business is the chance that future events or results may not be as expected.
- Risk is often thought of as purely bad (pure or 'downside' risk), but it must be considered that risk can also be good – the results may be better than expected as well as worse (speculative or 'upside' risk).

**Slide 4**

OVERVIEW OF PROCESS

- Determine our risk appetite
- Nominate a risk manager
- Identify risk areas
- Identify and evaluate risks
- Decide on risk mitigation activities
- Implement strategy
- Control and report

**Slide 5**

WHAT IS OUR RISK APPETITE?

- What is seen as a reasonable or acceptable amount of residual/net risk (after actions to mitigate risk), to expose Cast to, both before and after the acquisition of Diamante?
- Are we risk takers, or risk averse?
- The amounts are relatively small, in comparison to our cash balances, so do we care about risk (in this case)?

**Slide 6**

NOMINATE A RISK MANAGER

- One of us should be responsible for making sure that risk is managed
- We may need some help (an acquisition team?)
- Do we have anyone with experience in
  - acquisitions?
  - risk management?
  - jewellery retail?

**Slide 7**

IDENTIFY RISK AREAS

Risks relating to (for example):

- Process – might the acquisition fail?
- Ownership – might the owners not all agree?
- Price – might the owners' valuation be higher than ours?
- Asset value – might the store sell for less than we expect?
- Staff – might their staff resist change?
- Realising value and synergies – might the expected savings/benefits not arise?
- Our stakeholders – might our shareholders not support us
- Reputation – what if it all went wrong?

**Slide 8**

IDENTIFY AND EVALUATE RISKS

- What are the risks?
- How likely is each risk (probability)?
- What would be the impact, should the thing happen (in terms of lost revenue, increased cost, time, disruption, reputation…)?

**Slide 9**

DECIDE ON RISK MITIGATION ACTIVITIES

- Avoid – change the strategy, or just abandon the bid
- Share – agree warranties with the sellers
- Transfer – could we insure some risks?
- Reduce – better management, analysis
- Accept – do nothing to mitigate

**Slide 10**

IMPLEMENT STRATEGY

- Do what we planned to do

**Slide 11**

CONTROL AND REPORT

- Regular reports, from the risk manager
- Monitor risks, in case probability and/or impact changes
- Look out for new risks

**Slide 12**

ANY QUESTIONS?

### Exercise 9

**Notes:** Evaluating financial structure is, to some extent, a matter of judgement – you may disagree with the following analysis. Marks would be awarded for any reasonable interpretation of the material.

**Briefing note: Cast Group financial structure**
To: CFO/CEO
From: SFM
Date: <DATE>

**Introduction**

The capital structure, and cash balance, of Cast have been queried by the Chairman.

Disclaimers: this report is based on the information provided, which was very limited. I am not aware of the detail of Cast's strategy. The cash balance may already be earmarked for some major investment(s).

**Equity**

- In common with most private companies, Cast has a relatively low share capital compared to its turnover and profit.

- Equity has a value of $15m, at par. This clearly includes shares issued after Cast/Woodvale had been trading for a period, as there is also $18m in the Share Premium account, showing that some shares have been issued at above par.

- Despite very significant dividend payouts, of approximately $350m a year, the equity has also accumulated retained earnings of $679m (as at 31 March 2015).

- This gives a total for shareholders' funds of $712m (15 + 18 + 679).

**Debt**

- The only debt is the debenture loans, valued in the Statement of Financial Position at $100m.
- It is not known when this debt was incurred, nor the terms on which it was issued (coupon rate, repayment…).
- Assuming that the 'finance costs' in the Profit and Loss statement all relate to interest on these debentures, the coupon rate appears to be only 1%. This is extremely low, so the finance costs may be a net figure, taking into account all interest (payable and receivable) and charges.
- It is known that Cast has 'short term deposits'. It is possible that the reason why the debentures have not been redeemed is the low coupon rate?

**Gearing**

- Taking the above figures, Cast has gearing ratios of 14.7% (debt:equity) and 12.8% (debt:debt+equity).
- Due to the fact that Cast is a unique organisation, and unquoted, it is not possible to express an opinion as to whether these figures are high or low.

**Cash**

- At 31 March 2015, Cast had a cash (or near-cash) balance of $243m.
- This is a very significant amount, equivalent to 8% of turnover, 17.6% of operating profit, 4% of total assets, or 31.1% of the debt + equity figure referred to above.
- Advantages of a large cash balance
  - The risk of a fall in business activity levels is reduced. Cast can cover liabilities when due, even if revenues are reduced or income delayed.
  - Cash can earn interest, although interest rates are low and shareholders could rightly claim that the company is not delivering value.
  - Cash is always available for a large investment, or acquisition. Cast could avoid having to approach providers of finance, and just implement strategy immediately.

## Practice triggers and tasks

- Disadvantages of a large cash balance
- Shareholders expect Cast to invest their funds in its business, to add shareholder value, not to leave them as cash or earning low interest rates.
- Were Cast a listed company, a large cash balance might make it a more attractive acquisition target.
- How could the cash balance be reduced?
- The cash balance could be reduced in a number of ways:
  - By financing expansion, either through the purchase of assets or making an acquisition
  - By paying a much larger than normal dividend (effectively returning 'surplus; cash to shareholders).
  - By buying back shares, or repaying debentures (again, returning surplus cash to investors)
  - By placing cash on long term deposit, or into less marketable investments, to earn a better return

### Conclusions

- The capital structure of Cast 'is what it is'. It cannot be compared to that of other companies, nor is it possible to express an opinion as to whether it is good or bad, as Cast is unique and cannot be compared with any other company.
- Cast only has 'too much cash' if the shareholders are unhappy with the return on their investment, and the cash is not 'earmarked' for future investment or acquisition.

# chapter 7

### Exercise 10

**Briefing note: Financing 'X'**
To: CEO
From: SFM
Date: <DATE>

**Introduction**

- To invest in 'X', $250m is required immediately, and $50m over the next 12 months.
- Disclaimer: The following is based on information available, and I have assumed no material change to the pattern of our business.

**Cash**

- We have available cash and near-cash of $228m
- It would be a mistake to use all of this to finance X, as some may be required to cover short term operational requirements (and contingency)
- $200m might reasonably be available, to invest in 'X'?

**Operating cashflow**

- We generate operating cashflow at a rate of about $30m per month (average for last two years $400m a year). This may be seasonal, but information is not available.
- Some of this can be used to finance the year 1 operating requirement of $50m
- There would be little risk to dividend payout ($350 – 375m?)
- We can improve operating cashflow, for a short period, by improving working capital management. For example:
    - Assuming that our trade payables are still at the March 2015 level of $190m, an extra $50m could be generated by increasing our payables days from 33 (based on cost of sales) to 42.
    - Similarly, we could aggressively chase receivables (although they only represent 16 days sales).
    - Reducing inventories might increase risk too much, as goods may not be available for customers. However, it may be possible to stock fewer items and, instead, 'call off' stock from manufacturers.
- This ignores any additional operating cashflow, generated as a result of 'X', and any opportunities to free up cash from 'X'

### New finance Required

- This leaves a shortfall of $50m immediately ($250m required – £200m cash used)

### Debt

- We could borrow from a commercial bank, either on overdraft or short term loan
- A bank may not require security, bearing in mind our historically healthy finances
- Operating cashflows (possibly with a dividend payout unchanged from last year) should be sufficient to repay this within 12 months, and we may never actually need the full facility (see Cash section, above)
- This ignores any additional operating cashflow, as a result of 'X'
- We could issue further debentures, but this could not happen 'immediately'
- Debenture terms would probably be worse than at present, and may be worse than those for bank borrowing
- The cash requirement is not long term, so debentures are inappropriate

### Equity

- We could ask our shareholders to purchase additional shares
- This would be a major increase in share capital, but shares could be issued at a significant premium
- You may not wish to trouble the shareholders, and an equity issue could not happen 'immediately'
- The cash requirement is not long term, so a share issue is inappropriate

### Conclusions

- Use $200m of cash, and borrow the rest on overdraft
- Finance operating (year 1) costs out of operating cashflow

# chapter 7

### Exercise 11

*Be careful – the task DID NOT require the advantages and disadvantages of returning cash to shareholders. It asked specifically for a comparison between repurchase and one-off dividend.*

**SHARE REPURCHASE**

To: CEO
From: SFM
Date: <DATE>

**Introduction**

- Cast is considering returning a significant surplus cash balance to its shareholders. A share repurchase has been suggested.

- Disclaimer: This note is based on information provided

**Advantages of repurchase vs dividend**

- Shareholders can choose who receives the return of cash, whereas a dividend is paid to all

- Shareholders will view it as a 'one-off' exercise, and not expect it every year

- Shareholders may get tax benefits, but this depends on their Income Tax and Capital Gains Tax positions

- Future dividend cost will be reduced (as there will be fewer shares in issue) without reducing dividend per share

- Some shareholders might become extremely wealthy (if they are not already). For example, P Smith might be the only shareholder choosing to sell, and would receive $200m.

**Disadvantages of repurchase vs dividend**

- Some shareholders may perceive it as unfair, if the repurchase does not apply to all

- Shareholders may suffer tax penalties, but this depends on their Income Tax and Capital Gains Tax positions

- Some shareholders (for example, trusts and pension fund) may not be permitted, by their rules, to sell shares in Cast

- The repurchase might lead to shareholders offering shares for sale, as they realise just how much their shareholdings are worth. They could, of course, only offer shares to other existing shareholders
- If the repurchase were to apply to all shareholders, NONE of them would be eligible to vote in favour of the repurchase (see below). I have no idea what would happen, in this case.

**Process**

(1) Decide how much cash you wish to return to shareholders (for example, $200m)

(2) Value Cast as a going concern (for example, Post after Tax $395m × P/E ratio of Greatline 4.9 = $1,935m)

(3) Value the shares ($1,935m/15m = $129 per share)

(4) Calculate how many shares to repurchase ($200m/129 = 1.55m, or 10.3%)

(5) Decide whether to repurchase equally from all shareholders, or from selected individuals. The former is more equitable, though there may be some shareholders who wish to liquidate their entire holding, and others who do not want to sell any. (see advantages, above)

(6) As there are sufficient distributable profits, the purchase can be made out of reserves. This is referred to as an off-market purchase and the rules are set out in sections 690 to 708 of the Companies Act 2006.

A summary of these sections is as follows:

- There is no longer a requirement for a company's Articles to specifically permit a buy back (this was removed by the Companies Act 2006), but the company must not have any restriction or prohibition in its Articles. [s 690]

- The shares being purchased must be fully paid-up, and the shares must be paid for on purchase. [s 691]

- The purchase must be approved by a special resolution. This means that 75% must vote in favour

- The person(s) whose shares are being purchased cannot vote on this resolution. [s 695]

- A copy of the contract or memorandum setting out the terms of the share purchase must be made available to all members. [s 696]

- A purchase of a company's own shares may be subject to stamp duty.
- Any purchase of the company's shares must be disclosed in the Directors' Report for the relevant year.

**The accounting entries**

It should be noted that there are two stages to the process. First, the payment for the shares must be recorded. Then an amount equivalent to the nominal value of the shares purchased must be transferred to the capital redemption reserve. This second part is required in order to maintain the company's capital

*Purchase of shares:*

- DR Share capital with nominal value
- DR P&L reserves with premium
- CR Bank with proceeds

*Maintenance of capital (as required by s733 of the Companies Act):*

- DR P&L reserves with nominal value
- CR Capital redemption reserve with nominal value

**Financial consequences**

- Cast might reduce cash balances, only to experience liquidity problems due to economic downturn or a new investment opportunity
- Cast will lose the (small) return on the cash invested, however the dividend yield far exceeds the likely return on short term investments.

**Practice triggers and tasks**

### Exercise 12

**Slide 1**

TITLE

The implications of flotation on the financial statements and our interaction with society

Judith Anderson
<DATE>

**Slide 2**

OVERVIEW

- Assumptions
- Statement of Profit or Loss
- Statement of Financial Position
- Statement of Cash flows
- Stakeholders
- Corporate governance
- Social responsibility
- Any questions?

**Slide 3**

ASSUMPTIONS

- Shares offered to the public will be additional to those owned by current shareholders
- Issue will be by 'Initial Public Offering' (IPO)
- Shares will be sold to a merchant bank, which will sell them on at a fixed price
- Existing shareholders will be prohibited from selling for a set period after the IPO

**Slide 4**

STATEMENT OF PROFIT OR LOSS

- Profit will reduce by the issue costs, which could be substantial, in the year of issue
- A dividend may be payable, at the end of the current financial year, depending on the issue terms

**Slide 5**

STATEMENT OF FINANCIAL POSITION

- Cash will increase by the net issue receipts (issue price × number of shares, minus issue costs)
- Share capital will increase by the par value of the shares issued
- Share premium will increase by the remainder of the gross issue receipts

**Slide 6**

STATEMENT OF CASH FLOWS

- Cash flows from financing activities will increase by the net issue receipts

**Slide 7**

STAKEHOLDERS

- New stakeholders will include:
    - Merchant bank
    - Professional advisors
    - Institutional investors
    - New shareholders
    - Financial media
    - The stock exchange
    - Potential future shareholder
- All must be considered, in future discussions relating to strategy
- Strategy-making will become far more complex

**Slide 8**

CORPORATE GOVERNANCE

- Cast will become subject to the Corporate Governance regime
- There will/may need to be changes to the following:
    - Annual reporting
    - Board membership (particularly non-executives)
    - Committees
    - Directors' and managers' remuneration
    - External audit
    - Internal audit
    - Remuneration
    - Employee share transactions
    - Shareholder meetings and communication

**Slide 9**

SOCIAL RESPONSIBILITY

- Stakeholder expectations, regarding Cast's social responsibility, will increase
- Social responsibility reporting may be necessary

**Slide 10**

ANY QUESTIONS?

(Note: I am happy to attend the Board meeting, in Dana's absence, to answer any questions)

# chapter 8

# Exam day techniques

**Chapter learning objectives**

- To develop a carefully planned and thought through strategy to cope with the three hours of exam time

# Exam day techniques

## 1 Exam Day strategy

Once you have studied the pre-seen, learnt the three subject syllabi thoroughly and practised lots of exercises and mocks, you should be well prepared for the exam.

However, it is still important to have a carefully planned and thought through strategy to cope with those three hours of exam time.

This chapter takes you through some of the key skills to master to ensure all your careful preparation does not go to waste.

## 2 Importance of time management

Someone once referred to case study exams as "the race against time" and it's difficult to imagine a more accurate description. Being able to do what the examiner is wanting is only half of the battle; being able to deliver it in the time available is another matter altogether. This is even more important than in previous exams you may have faced because each section in the real exam is now timed and once that time is up you will be moved on. Case study is not like a traditional exam where you can go back to a question if you get extra inspiration or feel you have some time left over. You have to complete each task within the time stated.

For this reason, time management is a key skill required to pass the Case Study Examination.

Successful time management requires two things:

1. A tailored time plan – one that plays to your personal strengths and weaknesses; and
2. Discipline in order to stick to it!

### Time robbers

There are a number of ways in which time can be wasted or not used effectively in the Case Study Examination. An awareness of these will help to ensure you don't waste time in your exam.

*Inactive reading*

The first part of each task must be spent actively reading, processing the information and considering the impact on the organisation, how the issues link together and what could be done to resolve them. You will not have time to have a second detailed read and so these thoughts must be captured first time around.

*Too much time spent on presentation*

You will be writing your answer in software with some similarities to Microsoft Word however the only functions available are

- Cut
- Copy
- Paste
- Undo
- Redo
- Bold
- Italic
- Underline

The temptation to make various words bold or italics or underlined, is very hard to resist. But, resist you must! There are very few marks available for having a response that is well presented, and these finer details will be worth nothing at all.

*Being a perfectionist*

Students can often spend such a long time pondering about what to write that over the course of a 3 hour exam, over half of it is spent staring into space.

As you are sitting a computer exam you not only spend time pondering, but also have the ability to delete so can change your mind several times before settling on the right word combinations. Just focus on getting your points down and don't worry about whether they could have been phrased better.

*Too much detail on earlier parts of the requirement*

As we've said earlier, not finishing answers is a key reason for failing the Case Study Examination. One of the main reasons why students fail to finish a section is a lack of discipline when writing about an issue. They feel they have to get all of their points down rather than selecting the better points and moving on. If a task requires you to discuss three different areas it is vital that you cover all parts adequately.

# Exam day techniques

*Too much correction*

Often students can reread paragraphs three or more times before they move on to writing the next part of their answer. Instead, try to leave the read through until the final few minutes of the task and try to correct as many obvious errors as possible. The CIMA marker will be reading and marking your script on screen and it is harder to read and understand the points you are making if there are many typing errors.

## 3 Assimilation of information

One of the most challenging things to deal with in a case study examination is the volume of information which you have available. This is particularly difficult when you have both pre-seen and unseen information to manage and draw from. It is important that you refer to relevant pre-seen information in your responses as well as incorporating the unseen information. The key things that you need to do to assimilate the information effectively and efficiently are:

- Read about and identify each event
- Consider what the issue is
- Evaluate the impact of the issue. Who is affected, by how much are they affected and what would happen if no action was taken?
- Determine the most useful and relevant exhibits from the pre-seen

Capturing all of your thoughts and ideas at this stage can be difficult and time consuming. The following section on planning your answer will show you how to do this effectively without wasting time or effort.

## 4 Planning your answers

In section 2 of this chapter we saw how important it was to manage your time in the exam to ensure you're able to complete all of the necessary stages in the preparation of your answer.

One important aspect of your exam is planning your answer. Sitting the Case Study Exam is not as straight forward as turning up, reading the requirements, and then writing your answer.

If you do attempt to write without any form of content plan, your response will lack direction and a logical flow, it won't fully address the key points required and any recommendations will lack solid justification. It is for this reason that time should be specifically allocated to planning the content of your answers.

Given the preparation you've done before the exam, reading the unseen can often feel like a firework display is happening in your brain; each new piece of information you read about triggers a series of thoughts and ideas.

The planning process must therefore begin as soon as you start reading the unseen information. Every second counts within the case study exam and so it's important to use all of your time effectively by capturing the thoughts as they come to you.

To make sure the time spent now is of use to you throughout the task, you will need consider carefully how best to document your thoughts. You will be provided with an on-screen notes page ('scratchpad') as well as a wipe-clean laminated notes page and marker pen. Any method you adopt to plan must be concise whilst still allowing you to capture all of your ideas and see the bigger picture in terms of how the issues interrelate with one another (see additional guidance below). Furthermore, the method must suit you! Everyone is different and what might work for one person could be a disaster for another. For example, some people prefer to work with lists, others with mind maps.

Most people find that some form of central planning sheet (to enable the bigger picture to be seen) is best. How you prepare the central planning sheet is a matter of personal preference and we've given illustrations of two different methods below. Practise each one to find out which you prefer and then tailor it further to settle on something that works for you.

### Method 1 – The ordered list

This process is ideally suited to people who prefer lists and structure.

### Step 1:

- Begin by reading everything in the task exhibit
- Ensure you have identified all aspects of the task and then write this on the left hand side of your planning sheet

### Step 2:

- Read everything in the trigger exhibit, making notes next to the relevant task

### Step 3:

- Review your list to identify any linkages to information provided in the pre-seen and note next to the task on your planning sheet

### Step 4:

- Brainstorm any technical knowledge you can use in responding to the task and note this on your planning sheet

# Exam day techniques

### Illustration 1 – Planning

On Monday morning your boss arrived in work full of enthusiasm for a new business venture he had thought of over the weekend. This was in response to a conversation that had taken place at Friday night drinks when the CEO expressed concern that she felt the business was stagnating and needed some new products to rekindle customer interest.

Your boss needed to harness his ideas and put together an outline plan for a mid-morning coffee meeting with the CEO. Typically, the idea had germinated without sufficient thought and you were asked to consider the critical factors that needed to be considered in launching the new product and write a briefing document for the meeting.

**Requirement:**

Prepare a plan for your briefing document.

**Solution**

| *Critical Factors* | *Goals and objectives* | *Skills and experience* | *Finance* | *Marketing and sales* |
|---|---|---|---|---|
| New Product | Matches objectives? | Experience in manufacturing? | Available finance? | Advertising |
|  | Strengths? | Available labour? | Investment? | Social media |
|  |  |  | Working capital? | Website? |
| Technical content? | SFA |  | NPV | 4Ps |

**Method 2 – The extended mind map**

This process is ideally suited to those who prefer pictures and diagrams to trigger their thoughts.

**Step 1:**

- Read the unseen information and identify the key tasks required
- As you read, write each task in a "bubble" on your planning sheet.

## chapter 8

**Step 2:**

- Keep adding each new part of the task you identify to your sheet. At the end you should have a page with a number of bubbles dotted about.

**Step 3:**

- Review your bubbles to identify any linkages to the trigger information or pre-seen exhibits. Add any relevant information to your planning sheet in a bubble attached the appropriate part of the task.

**Step 4:**

- Review the task bubbles and brainstorm any relevant knowledge which you can use in responding to the task. Add this to bubbles attached to the task

With detailed information provided in the exam it would be very likely that your brain would think of a wide range of ideas which, if left uncaptured, would be forgotten as quickly as you thought of them.

This is where mind mapping comes in handy. You would not of course need to draw one as neat as this and feel free to add colours or graphics to help your thought processes.

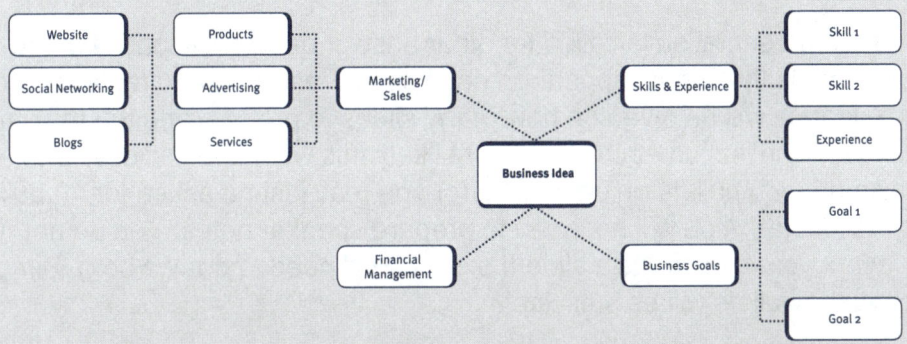

Have a go!

Why not try putting your thoughts on an exercise from the previous chapter into a mind map like the one above?

Some additional guidance

(1) This is perhaps the hardest part of the exam; as soon as you tell your brain it needs to come up with some ideas, it very often refuses to cooperate! Practice makes perfect so working through the exercises in Chapter 7 and attempting mock exams will really help your brain to deliver ideas when you need it to.

(2) Don't simply view technical models as something that must be included to tick a box if explicitly requested in the requirements. Instead use the models to help analyse the issues, suggest solutions or generate ideas. They were developed to be useful!

(3) If you start looking at one of the task requirements and are stuck for ideas, don't waste time staring into space. Move on to the next part of the task (but not onto the next task itself as you won't be able to return) and you'll find the creative juices soon start flowing.

## 5 Communication skills

The Case Study examinations aim to test a wide range of skills and you may be required to communicate in many different formats to various different audiences, each with different information needs. How well you communicate will be awarded as both part of the integration mark but also as part of the people skills, because communication skills is a subset of people skills.

Clearly the content of what you write is far more important than the chosen format, so you needn't spend more than a few seconds on the most basic elements of presentation – there won't, for example, be a mark for inserting the date in a letter or email.

Some of the formats you may need to use are shown below.

### Slide presentation

If a slide presentation is called for, your answer need only consist of the bullet points that would appear on each slide. Read the requirement carefully as guidance will be given on how many slides to prepare and the maximum number of bullets on each slide. Most likely this would be 2 slides, with a maximum of 5 bullets on each slide (or you may just be asked for 10 bullet points in total). You will not need to prepare speaker notes. You do not need to layout your answer as a slide (i.e. you don't need to draw a box). Simply noting the bullets will be sufficient.

# chapter 8

### Illustration 2 – Slides

A typical layout for the presentation of slides should be:

---

Slide 1

Title

- XX
- XX
- XX
- XX
- XX

---

Slide 2

Title

- XX
- XX
- XX
- XX
- XX

---

## An email

A requirement to draft an email may be in response to a specific question raised by an individual within the unseen information, or perhaps even in response to an email that is presented within the unseen.

You will need to ensure you give your email a title and make it clear who it is to and who it is from.

# Exam day techniques

### Illustration 3 – E-mail

A typical layout for the presentation of an email should be:

---

**To:** XX
**From:** XX
**Date:** XX

**Subject: XX**

Your answer to the requirement using short sentences as instructed

---

If you are asked to write an email, then you should write short sentences (the number of which may well be specified in the requirement) and NOT brief bullet points. The headings shown in the above illustration (who the email is to, from etc) may well be given as a proforma in the exam.

## A letter

Exactly the same as for an email but laid out in letter format. That means you should include a space for an address, a date, state to whom the letter is addressed and a summary of what the letter is regarding.

The letter should be signed off in the normal business fashion, unless you are told otherwise.

### Illustration 4 – Letter

A typical layout for the presentation of a letter should be:

---

**Address**

**Date**

**Dear X**

**Title**

Content of your answer to the requirement using short sentences or bullet points as instructed.

Yours sincerely,

A Management Accountant

---

## A report

In the pilot exam a commonly requested format is a report. This is likely to be an internal report but should still follow an appropriate and formal structure. The exact headings in your report will needed to be tailored to the exact task requirements but the following example is a good start:

### Illustration 5 – Report

A typical layout for a report should be:

> **Title: A report on the implementation of Total Quality Management**
>
> Introduction
>
> Brief background/context for requirement
>
> Main report content broken down using further sub-headings
>
> Conclusion
>
> Key conclusions and recommendations

## 6 Writing style

### Introduction

Writing style is something that develops over time. It is influenced by your education and experiences. To some it comes easily, they enjoy words – but remember, you are not looking to win any prizes in literature. It's about putting facts, ideas and opinions in a clear, concise, logical fashion. Some students get very worried about their writing styles. As a general rule you should try to write as you would talk.

### Logical flow

A typical point starts with a statement of fact, either given in the case or derived from analysis – 'what?'

This can then be followed by an interpretation – 'so what?'

This can then lead to an implication – 'now what?', or 'what next?'

*For example:*

(1) What? – The NPV is positive.

(2) So what? – Suggesting we should go ahead with the project.

(3) Now what? – Arrange board meeting to discuss strategic implications.

A similar structure can be obtained using the Socratic approach – what, why, how?

- So what?
- Why should we use it?
- How does it work?

### Who is reading the response?

Failure to pitch the level correctly will inevitably result in failure to communicate your ideas effectively, since the reader will either be swamped with complexity, or bored with blandness. The recipients of the report should also dictate the level of tact required.

| Tactless | Tactful |
| --- | --- |
| The directors have clearly made errors | There were other options open to the board that, with hindsight, would have been beneficial |
| The marketing director is responsible for this disastrous change in strategy. | The board should consider where this went wrong? It would appear that the marketing department may have made some mistakes |

Making your response easy to read

To ensure that the marker finds your answers accessible and easy to read, you should try to do the following:

- Use short words, short sentences, short phrases and short paragraphs. If you are adopting the 'what, so what, what now' approach, then you could have a paragraph containing three sentences. The next point can then be a new paragraph, also containing three sentences.

- Use the correct words to explain what you mean! For example, students often get confused between:
    - recommendations (what they should do – actions) and options (what they could do – possibilities).
    - objectives (what we want to achieve – the destination) and strategies (how we intend to achieve them – the route).
- Avoid using vague generalisations. Too often students will comment that an issue will "impact" on profit rather than being specific about whether profit will increase or decrease (or even better still, trying to quantify by how much). Other common phrases which are too vague include "communicate with" (you need to say specifically what should be discussed) and "look in to" (how should an option be looked in to?)
- Avoid unnecessary repetition. This can either be of information from the exam paper (pre-seen or unseen), of discussion within the report (in particular between what is said in one section and another) or can relate to the words that you use. Some students fall into the trap of thinking that writing a professional report means simply writing more words to say the same thing! The issue is quality not quantity.

    For example, compare the following:

    - 'I, myself, personally'    OR    'I'
    - 'export overseas'    OR    'export'
    - 'green in colour'    OR    'green'

- Watch your spelling – this may seem a small and unimportant point, but poor spelling makes a document seem sloppy and may convey an impression that the content is as loose as the general appearance! Poor spelling interrupts the marker as they read your report, so there is the danger that they conclude that it did not have a logical flow.

- Recommendations – be decisive – do not 'sit on the fence' or ask for more information. Make a clear recommendation based on the information you have and justify why you have chosen that course of action.

# Exam day techniques

### Exercise – 1

This exercise will get you thinking about what makes a well written script. The technical content of the requirement is not relevant – we are focusing on writing style and flow.

> The risk committee of Xplc met to discuss a report by its risk manager. The report focused on a number of risks that applied to a chemicals factory recently acquired in another country.
>
> She explained that the new risks related to the security of the new factory in respect of burglary, the supply of one of the key raw materials that experienced fluctuations in world supply and also an environmental risk.
>
> The environmental risk was with respect to the possibility of poisonous emissions from the new factory. The CEO who chaired the risk committee, said that the factory was important to him for two reasons. First, he said it was strategically important to the company. Second, it was important because his own bonuses depended upon it. He said that he knew from the report what the risks were, but that he wanted somebody to explain to him what strategies they could use to manage the risks. 'I don't get any bonus at all until we reach a high level of output from the factory,' he said. 'So I don't care what the risks are, we will have to manage them.'

You have been asked to outline strategies that can be used to manage risk and identify, with reasons, an appropriate strategy for each of the three risks facing the new venture.

### Required:

Consider these two responses and note the positive and negative aspects of each.

## Answer 1

Risk can be managed using the TARA strategies.

- **Transfer** the risk to another organisation for example by buying insurance. This is usually cost effective where the probability of the risk is low but the impact is potentially high.
- **Avoid** the risk altogether by withdrawing completely from the risky activity. This is done where the risk is high probability and high frequency and so it is too costly to reduce the risk sufficiently.
- **Reduce** the risk by implementing controls or by diversification.
- **Accept** the risk without taking any further steps to mitigate it. For this to be acceptable the frequency and the impact of the risk must place the risk within the risk appetite of the company.

### Risk of burglary

It is usual to insure against burglary an example of the transfer strategy. This is because of the high impact of burglary.

It is also usual to put safeguards in place such as security guards because of the probability of burglary. This is an example of risk reduction.

### Raw Materials Supply Fluctuation

Depending on the cost benefit analysis the company could chose to transfer the risk by entering into forward contracts to purchase the materials.

There will be a cost associated with this and it will lower but not remove the risk associated with supply and price fluctuations. They may choose to accept the risk as part of the operational risk associated with their industry.

### Environmental Risk

The company should take reasonable steps to reduce the chance poisonous emissions. It should use appropriate technology and controls to reduce the risk.

Risks cannot be completely eliminated so if the poisonous emissions could give rise to significant costs it should also purchase insurance and transfer the risk.

# Exam day techniques

**Answer Two**

Risk is managed by this:

(1) Identify the risk. This is by brainstorming all the things that the risk can be.

(2) Risk assessment. We won't know this properly until afterwards

(3) Risk Profiling. This is decided on consequences and impact

(4) Risk quantification. This can be average loss or it can be largest loss.

(5) Risk consolidation which will depend on the risk appetite and diversification.

The risks at the factory are:

- The main risk at the factory is environmental risk. You can't do anything about this risk because global warming is because of everyone

- The big risk is that the CEO is "I don't care what the risks are" this will need to have the risk awareness embedded in and the tone at the top.

- The other risk is that the CEO could manipulate the output levels to get his bonus. This needs to be looked at seriously because he is also on the risk committee and the remuneration committee and he is not independent and that should be a NED.

## 7 Summary

You should have an appreciation of some of the issues you may encounter in the exam and some possible techniques to overcome these.

**Next steps:**

(1) In the next two chapters we will present the unseen and guide you through the process of producing an answer. It is worth ensuring you can log on to the Pearson Vue site now and make sure you have registered for the practice case study exam. It is advisable to familiarise yourself with the software as much as possible.

(2) As you are about to embark on a full attempt at the pilot paper it is a good time to revisit previous chapters and ensure you are comfortable with all of the material so far before proceeding.

# chapter 8

## Test your understanding answers

### Exercise – 1

The first solution has several positive aspects:

- Brief introduction linking to requirement
- Overview of model with explanation and clear examples
- Specific points from scenario addressed
- Headings clearly signpost the answer
- Appropriate language

There are some areas which could be improved:

- Specific reference to the company name
- More explicit use of the information from the scenario

The second solution is not as strong as the first. Some of the main criticisms:

- Main aspects of the TARA framework are not clearly explained
- No attempt to introduce the answer
- Inappropriate language for a formal report/response
- Lack of tact regarding the CEO – the intended audience!!

As a piece of writing there is not much to say from a positive perspective except:

- Clear structure
- Writing is concise (but probably a bit too brief)

# Exam day techniques

# chapter 9

# Unseen information for the pilot case

**Chapter learning objectives**

# 1 Pilot Case – unseen information

The pilot case study contained the following triggers and tasks.

Note that in the exam these are not labelled as "tasks" or "triggers" but are presented simply as exhibits, emails, articles and so on. Similarly exhibits are not numbered.

### Exhibit 1 – Trigger 1

**Today is 16th May 2015.**

**You are a senior manager advising Judith, the new Group CEO, on issues relating to shareholders.**

**The current position is as follows:**

Cast is a private company and so its shares are not freely traded. The company was established as a family business, but there are now 40 shareholders. There are no close family ties holding the shareholders together. Over the years the shares have changed hands because of inheritance. The present shareholders are not closely related.

The only significant shareholder is Arnold, who is the great grandson of the shopkeeper who founded the business. Arnold owns 30% of Cast's shares.

Cast's constitution forbids the sale of shares to anyone other than an existing shareholder. That creates two problems. First of all, shareholders cannot liquidate any of their shareholding unless they can find a willing buyer amongst the other shareholders. There is a feeling that the few sales that have occurred have tended to be for less than the real value of the company's shares. Secondly, there is a tax charge when shares change hands because of inheritance. This requires a fair value to be negotiated with the tax authorities and that has created significant problems over the past few years.

Several shareholders believe that Judith's appointment is an ideal time for Cast to seek a stock market quotation. The company is large enough to be in the top 250 companies in its national stock exchange in the event that it is quoted. These shareholders have written to the company with a formal request that the directors begin the process of seeking a quotation. Arnold is aware of this request and has spoken to Judith to express his reluctance to see the company seek a quotation.

**Judith has asked you to step into her office to discuss something important.**

### Exhibit 2 – Trigger 1 continued

**Judith hands you a copy of a letter which can be accessed in the reference material.**

**Reference material – letter**

To the board of Cast,

We write as the owners of more than 40% of Cast's equity.

Our company has had a long and distinguished history. It had humble beginnings, but through hard work and imaginative management it has grown from a single shop to one of the country's leading retailers.

In the past, we have prided ourselves on being one of the country's largest unquoted companies. We have valued our independence and the freedom to take decisions without being held accountable to a widespread and transient body of market participants. Unfortunately, we no longer feel that the advantages of our unquoted status outweigh the disadvantages. We believe that Cast cannot expand unless we seek a stock market quotation.

We urge the board to commence the process of registering the company with the stock exchange. Clearly, this will be a challenging and expensive process. We believe that the costs will be more than compensated by the benefits.

Yours sincerely,

Simon and eight other shareholders.

Unseen information for the pilot case

### Exhibit 3 – Task 1

**She goes on to say:**

"I hope that you slept well last night because today is going to be busy. The CEO has just sent me a copy of a letter and I have to brief the board on the most appropriate response this afternoon.

The only thing that surprises me about this letter is that it has taken so long for them to make a formal request. The shareholders have been talking about this for ages.

My big worry is just keeping everybody happy. I need you to work out who is going to be affected by this. I always think that identifying the stakeholders lets you know who will be affected and how. So I need you to give me a list of stakeholders, along with an explanation of why each is affected and how their interests will be affected.

While you are doing that, I also need you to think about Arnold. He owns so many shares that we need to keep him happy at all costs. I met with him recently and asked what he thought about a quotation, but he just gave me a sneaky smile and said that lots of people ask him that very question all the time, then he changed the subject.

I want to be ready because the board is bound to ask how we should deal with Arnold. He didn't sign the letter from the shareholder group, although I don't know if he was even asked to. I need you to think about a strategy for dealing with Arnold and to put your thoughts down on paper.

I know this doesn't leave you much time but I need all that within the hour."

## Exhibit 4 – Task 2

*Task 2 (also based on trigger 1)*

**A week later you receive the following email from Judith:**

**From:** Judith Anderson, ja@cast.co.uk

**Sent:** 22nd May 2015, 09:25 a.m.

**Subject:** Presentation

The directors are keen to know roughly how much the shares should be placed at if we go ahead with the quotation. They paid a consulting firm a lot of money and spent an afternoon learning about company valuation. None of the stuff that was covered was new to me, but it got me out of my office for a while.

I need you to prepare a note for me about the suitability of each of these four main valuation methods for our purposes. I'll have a think about it too and so I'll be able to check my opinions against yours.

Some of the board are starting to get a bit worried about all of this. They realise that there are some governance issues arising from the initial pricing, but they have very little idea of what they are. Could you have a think about that as well and put your thoughts in writing? If we both think about it separately then we will come up with more that I could working on my own.

I am sorry, but I need all of this very urgently.

**Judith Anderson**
Group CEO
Cast
E: ja@cast.co.uk
T: 0161 236 1234

chapter 9

215

# Unseen information for the pilot case

**Attachment to email:**

---

# Business Valuation models

A presentation by Val Consulting

VAL Consulting   1

---

- Val Consulting has considerable experience in the valuation of businesses.
- We can advise clients on the application of the principal valuation models in order to determine an approopriate asking price for the sale or the placing of a company.

# Our approach

VAL Consulting   2

---

**VAL Consulting**

- Using as asset-based valuation, the value of an entity is equal to the net assets attributable to the equity shares. Intangible assets are only included if they have a realisable value.

# Asset-based valuations

VAL Consulting   3

# chapter 9

Earnings-based valuations assume that the value of an entity is equal to the present value of the future earnings that will be generated by the business. This method is based on two elements, the price/earnings (P/E) ratio and the post-tax earnings per share (EPS) of a business, which when combined give the market price per share (MPS)

**Earnings-based valuations**

The dividend growth model assumes that the annual dividend payable by an entity will grow at a constant annual growth rate.
The equation for obtaining a market value, based on a shareholder's expected rate of return ($k_e$), the projected growth rate (g) and the company's dividend ($d_0$) is:
$$d_0(1 + g)/(k_e - g)$$

**Dividend-based valuations**

- Cash-based valuations assume that the value of an entity is equal to the present value of future cash flows to be generated by the business

**Cash-based valuations**

# Exhibit 5 – Trigger 2

## Trigger 2 – Article

# New Economy – Old Problems

Parcels in the Cast Group warehouse

The Cast Group has a long-established reputation as a "family" company. Founded several decades ago, its shops were a familiar sight in every major shopping centre. It has always specialised in the sale of treats and leisure goods and so the company has always had a reputation for being a cheerful place to shop.

Recent revelations about Cast's employment practices have tended to undermine the company's reputation. Tales of embittered and embattled staff at the company's distribution centres have emerged in the aftermath of a recently broadcast television documentary.

Cast is the country's largest unquoted company. It is a family business, with shares held tightly by the various members of the founder's extended family. The company's employment practices mirror its status as a family-owned company whose shareholders view every penny spent on staff welfare as a personal cost.

Cast has always insisted on dealing directly with its employees over matters such as pay and conditions. Staff are consulted through their department heads and supervisors. There is a staff consultation committee comprising a small group of long-serving employees that meets with senior management one every three months. The company refuses to speak to trade union officials. Employees who threaten industrial action for better pay and conditions are warned that strike action will be deemed a breach of contract and will lead to instant dismissal.

Most of Cast's staff are employed at the company's large distribution centres where goods are packed and shipped to customers. The pace of work is relentless, with employees required to pack and label 100 items per hour in order to keep pace with their daily quotas. The work is badly paid, but the centres are located in areas of high unemployment and employees who leave are replaced quickly and easily.

The documentary was shot secretly by a reporter who had been employed to work in the largest warehouse. The hidden camera showed men and women struggling to meet their hourly and daily quotas. One employee was caught complaining that she could not afford to leave because she had nowhere else to go, but she was concerned that her physical and mental health were deteriorating from the pressure of work.

Predictably, Cast's director of human resources responded to the concerns raised by saying that the employees were free to work wherever they wished and that Cast met all relevant rules concerning minimum wage and health and safety. Furthermore, the board meets regularly with the company's staff consultation committee, which gives all staff the means to identify any concerns.

# chapter 9

> **Exhibit 6 – Task 2**
>
> **Judith calls you into her office when you arrive at work the following morning.**
>
> "Have you seen this article on the internet? I always knew that our policy of refusing to recognise trade unions would get us into trouble one day. People think that we pay badly, but the law sets a statutory minimum wage and we pay a good 10% more than that to even our worst-paid staff.
>
> Anyway, the directors are furious that we have been portrayed like this. They want to argue that we are nice people really because we create jobs in an area of high unemployment and so we inject wealth into a deprived community. I think that we need a bit of a balanced debate inside the company before we start making rash statements to the press. You have always been an ethical sort of person. I want you to put together a discussion of the ethical implications of Cast's employment practices. If I like it then I'll give you full credit when I forward it to the board.
>
> You have been really busy lately, but one last thing. The CEO has asked me to indicate how Arnold's position as a 30% shareholder will affect our share price. I know that I am also about to be asked how the share price will be affected by these allegations. If you could give me one of your wonderful papers on the impact of these on our share price then I'll try and make sure you have an easier week soon."
>
> **The article that Judith refers to can be accessed using the reference materials above.**

## 2 Summary

This chapter has introduced you to the unseen information for the pilot exam.

### Next steps:

(1) You should work through this exam using the unseen information (ideally the online Pearson Vue version) and the following chapter, which contains lots of guidance to help you with your first attempt. The examiners consider it crucial that any practice you do, such as using the pilot paper, is treated like a real exam. You should therefore be writing out your own answers before reviewing the suggested solutions. Merely reading the requirements and then the suggested solutions has limited value.

# Unseen information for the pilot case

# chapter 10

# Walkthrough of the pilot exam

## Chapter learning objectives

- To understand the thought processes that will help you when working through the exam
- To have the opportunity to attempt the pilot paper with guidance

# Walkthrough of the pilot exam

## 1 The Aim of a Walkthrough

The aim of this chapter is to give you a chance to practise many of the techniques you have been shown in previous chapters of this study text. This should help you to understand the various thought processes needed to complete the full three hour examination. It is important that you work through this chapter at a steady pace.

Don't rush on to the next stage until you have properly digested the information, followed the guidance labelled 'Stop and Think!' and made your own notes. This will give you more confidence than simply reading the model solutions. You should refer to the unseen produced in the previous chapter as you proceed through these exercises.

The following chapter will then guide you through the suggested solutions and marking key.

## 2 Summary of trigger 1

The information presented in trigger one indicates the crystallisation of a theme which was developing throughout the pre-seen information i.e. the potential for CAST to become a listed company. This is in line with the appointment of a new CEO who has been recruited from a quoted company background which may increase the potential of a successful listing.

The former "family business" is now owned by a wider range of shareholders who have no close relationship. The main significant shareholder is Arnold (grandson of the owner) who holds 30% of the shares and is potentially a resisting force in the completion of the deal.

In addition, the trigger suggests that there are legal and taxation hurdles which become relevant should the flotation progress.

The unseen trigger information includes a letter from a group of shareholders in task 1a) holding some 40% of the total equity "urging" the board to commence the process of registering the company with the stock exchange.

Stop and think!

(1) Who will be affected should the flotation progress as requested?
(2) What do we know about the legal and taxation hurdles?
(3) How would we manage the resistance to the flotation being voiced by Arnold?
(4) What is the significance of Arnold's 30% shareholding?

## 3 Overview of task 1

The new CEO of Cast has received a letter from a group of shareholders who claim to represent 40% of the total shareholding, requesting that Cast begin the process of listing on the stock exchange. There is one clear pocket of resistance, namely Arnold, a family member with a 30% shareholding.

You are required to prepare a note for the CEO to brief the board covering:

- A list of stakeholders affected should the decision to float Cast be taken
- An explanation of why and how their interests will be affected
- A strategy for dealing with the major shareholder Arnold.

### Let's plan

We need to create a planning page that ensures you identify and respond to all parts of the requirement. You can use the techniques discussed in Chapter Eight or develop your own method. Here we will use the ordered list approach.

Split your planning sheet (use your wipe clean whiteboard) in three sections – one for each part of the task as follows.

For the strategy of dealing with Arnold for example, we will need to have clear structure to address the requirement – WHAT is the dilemma; WHY is it a dilemma and HOW would you recommend that CAST deal with the potential problem. Separate your answer plan into these three categories:

# Walkthrough of the pilot exam

| |
|---|
| *A list of stakeholders affected* |
| *An explanation of why and how their interests will be affected*<br><br>*Why?*<br><br><br><br>*How?* |
| *A strategy for dealing with the major stakeholder Arnold* |

Note that the second section is roughly twice the size of the other two as it is likely that the explanation of the effect on interests will take considerable thought. Remember the verb EXPLAIN = to make clear. It is likely therefore to be worth more marks rather than simply listing the stakeholders affected.

We have split down the second part of task 1a therefore to consider the "why and the how"

You now need to brainstorm all the relevant points you can think of under the above headings, making sure you are bringing together your knowledge from the relevant syllabus as well as your analysis of the pre-seen information.

Let's think a bit more about these requirements by breaking them down into the component parts.

# chapter 10

"I need you to give me a list of stakeholders", this is simply providing a list of those stakeholders likely to be affected by the proposal to seek a stock market quotation. There are unlikely to many marks available for this exercise alone.

"Along with an explanation of why each is affected and how their interests will be affected". The verb "to explain" is often skirted over by candidates. It does require detailed thought so that the recipient of the information is clear and fully understands the implications of any chosen action – in this case who is affected, why are they affected and how. This therefore likely to carry a significant chunk of the marks available for task 1.

"I need you to think about a strategy for dealing with Arnold and to put your thoughts down on paper". The request for a 'strategy' means that we need to consider how Arnold actions may affect WHAT we do (strategically) rather than HOW we do things (operationally). The answer therefore needs to be specific to CAST rather than a general answer and is likely to require significant thought.

As a rough rule of thumb you should spend about 15-20% of the time available for reading and planning. So for this section of the exam, where you are given 60 minutes, you should be spending approximately 10 minutes planning your answer before you complete the exercise below. This would leave you about 45 minutes to write your answer and ideally a few minutes spare to check through what you have written on completion of your answer. Based on the discussion above, the requirement to provide the list of stakeholders could take 5 minutes with the remainder of the time equally split between explaining why and how they affected and what to do about Arnold!

### Exercise 1

Prepare a response to the first task in the pilot exam.

## 4 Overview of task 2

Based on the information presented in trigger 1, we are requested to provide additional information to the board. Candidates need to be clear that the requirement centres on the suitability of each of the valuation methods for Cast. The methods have already been explained in detail, and at substantial cost, to the board by a firm of consultants.

You are required to prepare a note for the CEO to brief the board covering:

- The suitability of each of four different valuation methods for the purposes of Cast flotation
- An explanation of the governance issues associated with quotation

# Walkthrough of the pilot exam

**Let's plan**

Extending the planning process which we began earlier we need to think carefully here of the use of the term "suitability".

Each of the models referred to therefore should be considered in the light of the current financial position of Cast.

For evaluation we must consider the advantages and disadvantages of each of the valuation models for Cast clearly justifying why each would suitable or not.

The explanation of governance issues requires you to make clear to the board any problems which may occur in this context or changes required to the way the business is managed as a result of the quotation. Close attention needs to be paid to the comment "but they have very little idea of what they are" suggesting considerable detail is necessary.

| *Asset based* |
|---|
| |

| *Earnings based* |
|---|
| |

| *Dividend based* |
|---|
| |

| *Cash based* |
|---|
| |

| *Governance issues with flotation* |
|---|
| |

# chapter 10

> **Exercise 2**
>
> Prepare a response to the second task in the pilot exam.

## 5 Summary of trigger 2

Following on from the previous trigger and reinforcing the message that Cast was once a family business, this trigger introduces a press release about a documentary which challenges the working practices at the company's distribution centres. Shot secretly the film reveals employees of both genders struggling to cope with the pressure of work and having no trade union to represent their case.

Employees are threatened with "instant dismissal" if they take strike action. Despite being overworked the film depicts workers who are afraid to take any action for fear of losing their jobs. The response from the HR Director is merely compliant indicating that "all relevant rules re minimum wage and health and safety" are met, further suggesting that if the employees have a problem then the staff consultation committee allows employees to voice their concerns.

### Stop and think!

(1) Given the recent discussion surrounding the flotation of Cast what is the likely effect of these allegations on Cast's reputation?

(2) What is the effect on the share price of Cast should these allegations prove to be true?

(3) What is the ethical dilemma in this scenario? What are the implications for Cast?

(4) Is Cast taking advantage of unskilled workers with no alternative employment available?

## 6 Summary of task 3

You are required to do the following:

- Prepare a discussion document on the ethical implications of CAST's employment practices.

- Prepare a paper on how the share price maybe impacted by the allegations

- Include in the discussion document an analysis of how the 30% shareholding of Arnold could affect the share issue price on stock exchange listing.

# Walkthrough of the pilot exam

**Let's plan**

In the previous exercise we used an ordered list to plan the answer. We could easily use a mind map here to collect our thoughts and ensure all areas are covered. Draw an oval/circle on your whiteboard about a third of the way down the page and write in it 'effect on CAST reputation of allegations' repeat this approach for each of the requirements using the exact requirement.

Be careful not to paraphrase too much as you could end not properly planning your answer or addressing the requirement when you write it up. For example if you just wrote 'implications' it is very likely you would go off on a tangent and not fully answer the question as set.

The latter two requirements within task 2 are potentially challenging and require you to "stop and think".

Taking each in turn:

- "I want you to put together a discussion of the ethical implications of Cast's employment practices"

    What is needed here is a consideration of how the opinion of an ethical investor would be affected by allegations of poor working conditions. There is no evidence of abuse of workers but your answer should cover the potential impact of the publication of poor working conditions on the financial (reduced profits due to investment to improve conditions) and non financial (company reputation). In addition we need to be sure to address these in the light of the share price and, as such, it is important that Cast publicises its positive treatment of the workforce and therefore maintain its share price.

- "The CEO has asked me to indicate how Arnold's position as a 30% shareholder will affect our share price"

    Arnold's position is a little more specific and your answer would need to address how any actions taken by Arnold would affect Cast and his own reputation.

Your planning page would start off looking like this:

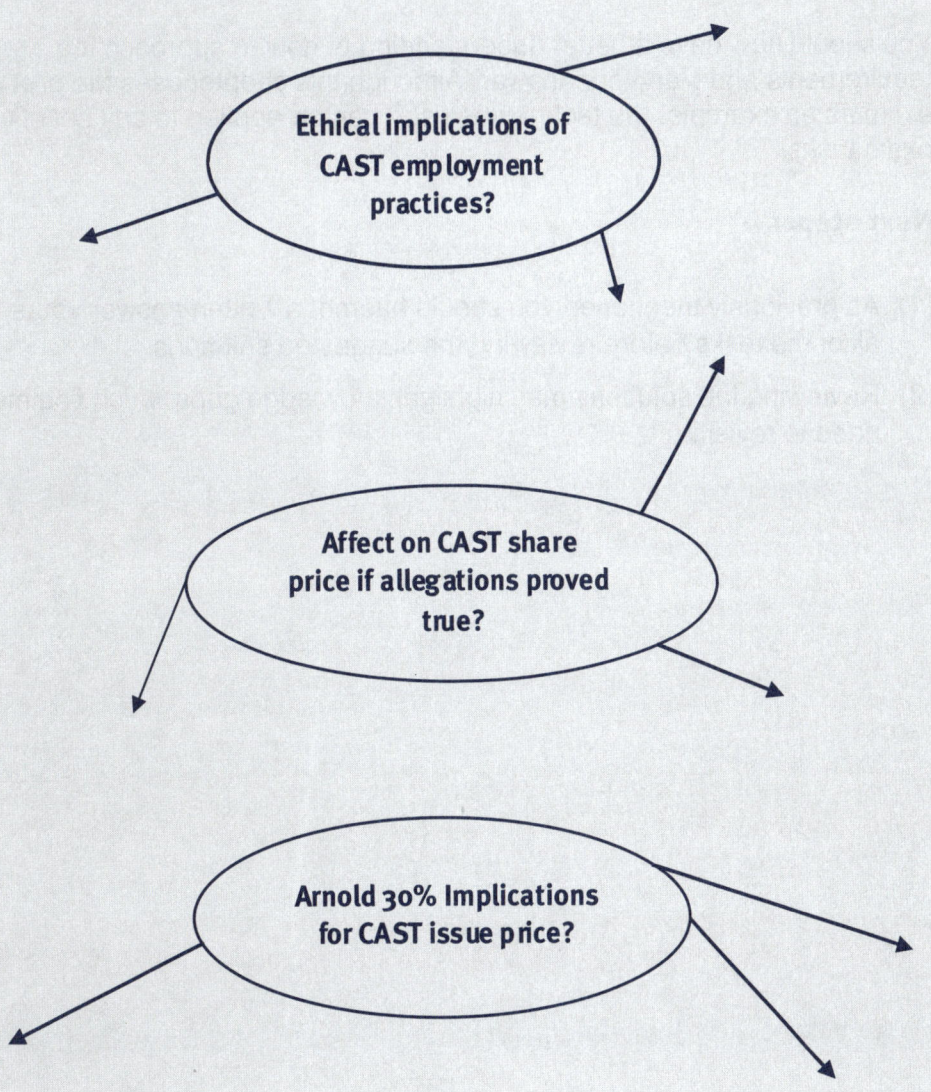

Now spend 10 minutes completing your plan before attempting Exercise 2. You would then have 45 minutes to write your answer and a few minutes to check through what you have written before reviewing the solution.

### Exercise 3

Prepare a response to the third task in the pilot exam.

# Walkthrough of the pilot exam

## 7 Summary

You should now have a better understanding of how to approach the exam requirements and plan your answer. Although this chapter uses the pilot exam as an example, the techniques used can be applied to any set of exam tasks.

**Next steps:**

(1) As previously mentioned you should attempt a written answer yourself to all of the tasks before reviewing the suggested solutions.

(2) Reviewing the solutions may highlight knowledge gaps which you may need to revisit.

# chapter 10

**Test your understanding answers**

## Exercise 1

*These answers have been provided by CIMA for information purposes only. The answers created are indicative of a response that could be given by a good candidate. They are not to be considered exhaustive, and other appropriate relevant responses would receive credit.*

*CIMA will not accept challenges to these answers on the basis of academic judgement.*

(a) Stakeholder analysis

**Briefing for presentation to Cast Board**

**High power low Interest** – Potential shareholders
**High power high interest** – Arnold, other existing shareholders
**Low power low interest** – Customers
**Low power high interest** – Suppliers, Employees

I have identified above six key stakeholders and have plotted their interest using a Mendelow matrix. Ironically, Cast's mission statement (see pre-seen) focuses on the company's customers and yet they are viewed as having little interest and lacking in power.

Our principal concern is Arnold. He owns a significant block of shares that gives him a degree of influence simply through his voting power. That ownership stake inevitably gives him an interest in Cast's direction, but he has the further interest arising from his family ties to the company. A quotation is unlikely to have any direct benefit for Arnold, if only because his annual dividend is sufficient to make him a very wealthy person.

The other shareholders have a different set of interests. None owns a sufficiently large block of shares to exert any significant power through votes. They have little to lose, therefore, in terms of dilution of voting rights in the event of a placement. Their primary interest in a quotation is that their stake in Cast will be far more readily realisable. They may, for example, decide to diversify their holdings by selling shares in Cast and using the proceeds to invest in other industries.

Potential shareholders are unlikely to have a significant interest in the newly quoted company because they can already invest in a range of online retailers. The only reason that Cast may be of any particular interest would be if the shares were introduced at a significant discount to their intrinsic value. Hopefully, Cast's management team will ensure that the shares are sold at an appropriate price and so there is unlikely to be a great deal of interest in subscribing. The markets will have to be willing to buy, though, or the placement will fail. The initial market price will be set by supply and demand by the market.

Cast's suppliers will have a moderate interest and relatively little power. If Cast is quoted then the group will possibly find it easier to raise funds for expansion and so suppliers may have an even more powerful customer to deal with. If Cast expands then suppliers will lose further bargaining power in dealing with the company. The business is not, however, particularly capital intensive and there is probably very little need for additional equity to fund expansion, so suppliers are unlikely to be greatly affected.

Cast's employees will have little power over anything that the company does because they are unskilled and can easily be replaced. These changes are also very unlikely to interest the employees. The company does not treat its staff particularly well. The pressures arising from a quote to report strong earnings will not lead to the company reducing staff benefits because they could not be much poorer. Also, the company is unlikely to introduce a share-based incentive scheme, so the employees will not have any direct interest in the share price.

Customers are generally regarded as stakeholders, but Cast's customers will not be particularly affected by this development. Cast's customers buy because of price and convenience. A stock market quote is unlikely to change the manner in which Cast conducts business with its customers.

To sum up, Arnold is the most important stakeholder in this matter. The board will have to consider his interests very carefully in order to ensure the success of the quotation.

## (b) Strategy for dealing with Arnold

**From:** Adviser
**To:** Judith
**Subject:** Arnold

Hi Judith,

I have been thinking ahead to the difficult problem of dealing with Arnold in the event that the proposal to pursue a stock market quotation goes ahead.

Our basic dilemma is that most of the shareholders are keen to seek a quotation, which means that Arnold could be unable to prevent this from going ahead even if he resists. His resistance could, however, prove both costly and disruptive. The market may be reluctant to pay a great deal for Cast's shares if Arnold threatens to, say, sell a large block of shares as a sign of his displeasure.

Any attempt to defeat Arnold is likely to harm Cast, even if it results in Arnold's influence reducing. We need to work towards persuading him to work with us willingly.

The first approach that we might pursue would be to persuade Arnold that pursuing a quotation is consistent with the company's underlying values. The business has grown successfully from humble origins as a small family business, but most large corporations started in the same way.

We should try to persuade him that a quotation is part of the natural process of development for a successful business. We should point out that Cast is a very different entity to the one that was created by its founders and that the changes in Cast's business model might be mirrored by changes in its governance and ownership.

Arnold's interest in the company's origins are due to his family connection to the founder. We could recognise that by offering him a non-executive directorship. Giving him a seat on the board would enable him to ensure that the company's values are maintained and pursued. His influence could be underpinned by having him chair at least one of the board committees. If Arnold had a place on the nominations committee then it would not be a particularly onerous responsibility, but he would be able to influence the appointment of board members and so he could affect Cast's ongoing management style.

# Walkthrough of the pilot exam

If Arnold could also be persuaded to accept some dilution of his influence then that would defuse the concerns that the markets might have concerning his intentions. It might be possible to persuade him to sell some of his shares as part of the placement on the stock exchange. Cast could persuade him to put the proceeds to some good use, such as the establishment of a charitable foundation, which Cast might also support as part of its ongoing development as a quoted company.

### Exercise 2

(a) **Valuation models**

Cast should avoid asset-based valuation models. Most entities that operate as going concerns are worth more than the sum of their asset values. It would be a little defeatist to value Cast as a collection of assets, particularly as the company is not particularly resource intensive. The company owns significant intellectual property in the form of intangibles such as brand recognition and customer databases. Those assets are extremely valuable, but they are impossible to value in a manner that lends itself to inclusion in the financial statements. This means that Cast's share price is likely to be undervalued. The fact that Cast's assets include a significant cash balance is also something that ought to be played down, rather than highlighted by a valuation model. It may be appropriate for an unquoted company to remain highly liquid so that its board can move quickly in order to pursue opportunities, but a quoted company cannot afford to tie up assets in such an unproductive manner.

Earnings-based valuations have greater potential because Cast is a profitable company that will generate returns for its shareholders. The company has not been operating in its present form for very long, but we could use that to our advantage by arguing that the historical earnings per share figure will grow. We could suggest some realistic forecasts for next year's EPS as a further discussion point.

234

Unfortunately, any valuation exercise is likely to create a tension between the interests of buyers and sellers and buyers will be naturally suspicious of any arguments that historical performance measures be replaced with more optimistic alternatives. This method also requires the identification of a suitable quoted company whose price/earnings ratio can be applied to the EPS. There are several companies that operate in a similar manner to Cast. Ideally, we should offer a range of P/E ratios and argue that Cast should be compared with the most successful of these businesses.

Dividend-based valuations are probably unsuitable in this case. Firstly, the company has been a family business since its creation. The dividends paid to date could reflect the interests of the family members rather than the company's ability to service dividends. The relationship between the company and its shareholders has been relatively close and so there has been very little need for the company to worry about signalling. For example, the company could afford to pay a healthy dividend in a good year without being unduly concerned that the shareholders will panic if the payment is not sustained in future years. In other words, the company's dividend history probably says little or nothing about the company's ability to service future dividends as a quoted company that is answerable to the shareholders. The dividend growth model essentially determines the net present value of future dividends on the basis of past observations of dividend payments and growth rates.

The fact that the company has created a substantial cash balance implies that the payment of dividends has not been a priority in the past and that attitude will almost certainly change once the company is quoted.

Cash-based models make perfect theoretical sense. The problem is that the cash flows and the associated discount rates do not lend themselves to defensible forecasts. Apart from the asset-based models, the approaches discussed above could be viewed as surrogates for the estimation and valuation of future cash flows. The fact that Cash has a relatively short history in its present form could be used to advantage in this case. The company's free cash flows since the revision to the basic business model can be determined. These will be more likely to lend themselves to realistic and defensible forecasts than the dividend models. The forecasts will not be any more contentious than those that are likely to appear in a prospectus or other offer document. The cost of capital could be based on the cost of equity for other retailers in a similar market.

The historical movements in share prices for both Greatline and Fashionstore provide something of a caveat in our analysis of these models (see pre-seen). We regard both as potential comparators and yet their share prices have tended to move in a fairly independent fashion. Greatline's price has crept up steadily while Fashionstore's has been somewhat volatile. Some of the models that we might apply would have produced very different results depending on whether we had selected Greatline or Fashionstore as our reference point.

(b) **Governance issues**

The first complication is the question of where the directors' allegiance lies. The directors clearly have a duty to the company and the present shareholders. There could be an argument that the directors' duty to the shareholders is a corporate responsibility to the shareholders as a whole rather than a particular group. In other words, it may not be appropriate for the directors to aim to maximise the share price in order to privilege the interests of the present shareholders over those of the incoming shareholders.

From an agency point of view, the directors may be motivated to develop a strong relationship with the incoming shareholders, because they will have a greater say in the directors' future. On that basis, the directors may be tempted to push the placement price down because that is likely to lead to the share price rising after the issue, which will reduce the risk of the disappointment associated with a subsequent fall in the share price.

The cash surplus creates a complicated stewardship dilemma for the shareholders. It was clearly acceptable to the original shareholders, but the market would expect the cash to be returned to the shareholders or invested. Either of those actions could occur before or after the placement. A decision has to be made and announced to avoid uncertainty, which could depress the issue price. If the directors invest the cash in the business then it may take some time for the return on that investment to be recognised. If the cash is invested in the business then it may take some time for a return to be recognised and so the directors may be tempted to disburse the cash. On the other hand, disbursing the cash will create the impression that the directors have no clear idea concerning the future growth of the company because they have elected not to expand the business.

The directors will have to ensure they are competent to manage this process. The issue is a complicated area that may be new to the directors because their recent experience is in the management of a private company (see pre-seen). Most have, however, worked for other businesses and some may have had some exposure to quoted companies. Furthermore, in the short term they can pay for professional advice from consultants, or they may even bring an additional executive director with a quoted company background on to the board.

It could be argued that Cast's board will require change in the event of a quotation, even if that change is only to increase the complement of non-executive directors (see pre-seen). Arthur Brown may well continue as non-executive chairman, given his experience in banking. But the company would almost certainly have to appoint additional non-executives to support him.

### Exercise 3

#### (a) Ethical implications

The basic problem arising from an ethical analysis of Cast's employment practices is that the employees' interests are in conflict with the shareholders. Resolving the dilemma can be assisted by expressing the dilemma in terms of positive and negative duties.

The directors have a negative duty to the shareholders to avoid spending more than necessary on running the company. Enhancing the employees' working conditions is a positive duty. It is generally accepted that negative duties are more compelling than positive duties. For example, the directors will definitely be responsible for an ethical breach of their duty to the shareholders if they overpay the employees. It is debatable whether the directors are responsible for the legal and economic conditions that make it possible to pay a low wage for working under quite difficult conditions.

There could be further dimensions to an ethical argument.

The refusal to recognise trade unions may be regarded as undemocratic. The employees are being denied the opportunity to be represented by a union that can consult and speak for the workforce. In many countries, trade unions are regarded as an important safeguard against exploitation of staff by greedy or uncaring employers. It appears that Cast's board is keen to force the employees to accept the terms and conditions laid down by the company and is unwilling to negotiate. Such behaviour will only work when the employees have no alternative but to accept such treatment. It could be argued that this is, in itself, evidence of abuse by Cast's board.

The pace of work is again a matter of balancing the shareholders' interests against the employees'. Slowing down the pace of work would require the employment of more staff and so the cost of labour would increase. The ethical question that has to be resolved is the extent to which the employees' complaints about stress and tiredness indicate excessive workload or simply tight deadlines. If the pace of work is abusive and sustained only because the employees have nowhere else to work then the company is being exploitative.

The payment of overtime rates is really a matter for market forces. If the employees were aware that this would be the arrangement when they signed their contracts then the company is within its rights.

It seems unfair to dismiss staff without attempting to rectify matters. It may be possible to assist staff by offering training or reassignment to a less demanding job. Dismissal does condemn staff to being left on the local jobs market and appears to be motivated by a desire to intimidate the remaining staff.

It is noticeable that the allegations against Cast are at odds with the statements made in the company's CSR report (see pre-seen). By claiming that the company offers employees "good jobs and genuine career prospects" it is committing itself to doing so even if it might be argued that an employer's duties are far more limited than that.

### (b) Implications for the issue price

It is unlikely that Arnold's shareholding will have a major impact on the issue price. The market will wish to know whether he intends to take an active role in the management of the company. He has not really done so in the past and we should indicate that he is unlikely to do so in the future.

He stands to lose a great deal if his behaviour impacts the share price and so the markets may not be unduly concerned that he has the power to undermine confidence by selling blocks of shares.

Arnold has had a life-long commitment to the company and we would expect that to continue. He would attract a great deal of bad personal publicity if he was seen to interfere with the smooth running of the company. He would be viewed as irresponsible.

There are ethical investors who might be a little unwilling to invest in a company that has a poor record in employee relations. They would probably not regard the claims made against Cast as sufficiently serious to warrant refusing to investing in the company. Cast is not abusing workers to any serious degree. It is not, for example, causing severe injury or employing child labour. Cast should ensure that it maintains acceptable working conditions for its staff so that the company can bear scrutiny. If Cast loses the support of these investors then it will be difficult to redeem matters.

Cast should take care to communicate and publicise its treatment of the workforce. The markets might be slightly nervous that bad publicity could cost the company sales and profits. There could also be concerns that the company will be forced to incur higher labour costs and that will also reduce profits. Cast could deal with those concerns by devising a strategy for addressing the complaints and making it clear that the strategy had been incorporated into the forecasts in the prospectus. The communication process will also help to ensure that the company does not run into problems with, say, appointing staff.

# Walkthrough of the pilot exam

# chapter 11

# Review of solution to pilot case and marking guide

**Chapter learning objectives**

- To gain a deeper understanding of the way case study is marked so that you can write your answer in the exam to score more highly.

# Review of solution to pilot case and marking guide

## 1 Introduction

As we have already explained in previous chapters the case study examinations are marked against a series of competencies. It is important that you understand this process to ensure you maximise your marks in the exam.

Once you have reviewed Chapter ten, attempted the exercises and reviewed the suggested solutions this chapter takes you through the detail of how these exercises would be marked. We have also a sample student script to show some possible strengths and weaknesses which you may recognise in your own answer.

**Note:** The CIMA official marking guide for the pilot case is given as follows:

| Competency | Section/task | Marks | Total marks available for competency |
|---|---|---|---|
| Technical skills | (1) Arnold | 4 | 27 |
| | (2) Valuation models | 16 | |
| | (3) Adverse publicity and share price | 5 | |
| | Integration | 2 | |
| Business skills | (1) Indentifying stakeholders | 13 | 26 |
| | (2) Valuation models | 4 | |
| | (2) Governance responsibilities | 6 | |
| | Integration | 3 | |
| People skills | (1) Arnold | 4 | 25 |
| | (3) Ethics | 13 | |
| | (3) Adverse publicity and share price | 6 | |
| | Integration | 2 | |

242

| Leadership skills | (1) Identifying stakeholders | 5 | 22 |
| --- | --- | --- | --- |
| | (1) Arnold | 5 | |
| | (2) Governance responsibilities | 5 | |
| | (3) Adverse publicity and share price | 5 | |
| | Integration | 2 | |

In this chapter we try to show how these marks could have been awarded/won.

## 2 Exam task 1

As we saw in the previous chapter the first section you were required to prepare a report covering:

- Analysis of stakeholders affected by a business decision
- Strategy for dealing with a major shareholder in the light of a business decision

Let's examine each of these areas in turn.

### Analysis of stakeholders affected by a business decision

It is important to recognise that such an analysis is largely testing your Business Skill and Leadership skills. You therefore need to consider your understanding of this organisation, the external environment in which it operates and any individuals or groups "who will be affected by or can affect" the business decision highlighted.

You may well have highlighted several relevant stakeholders when working through the pre-seen information but this requirement asks you to apply that knowledge to the circumstances depicted in the unseen detail provided on the day of the exam.

This part of the requirement is asking you to consider the implications of such an analysis and "why and how" each stakeholder group highlighted would be affected by the decision to list the company on the stock exchange and "how" it might affect what Cast does. This whole section is allocated 60 minutes so for this part of the exercise you have approximately 30 minutes.

Working on a rough ratio of 2 minutes for every point you make, this implies you need to make about 15 points. However this is not necessarily 15 separate discrete ideas. At this level a large part of the value of your answer is in explaining and justifying the implications of what you are saying.

## Review of solution to pilot case and marking guide

The initial response to the requirement is to demonstrate the use of Medelow's matrix and note down how each of the stakeholders affected could be positioned within this useful model. These are purely technical marks and you are likely to earn only ½ mark for each stakeholder identified

- The first sentence of the suggested solution introduces the context and topic of the briefing note. The second then links the pre-seen and unseen information together by introducing a conflict of opinion in terms of the classification of a stakeholder group (customers) and the mission statement of Cast i.e "I have identified above six key stakeholders and have plotted their interest using a Mendelow matrix. Ironically, Cast's mission statement (see pre-seen) focuses on the company's customers and yet they are viewed as having little interest and lacking in power"

    This is a good illustration of the application of theory to the circumstances depicted. It is true that customers are, and always will be, important to a retailer but in the light of a decision to float the company they are unlikely to be affected at all providing service levels and quality of merchandise are unaffected.

    This earns us our first marks; one for noting that customers are key to CAST and one for reflecting on their significance in the light of the business decision facing CAST i.e. addressing the competence "business skill" and technical skills.

- The next paragraph begins with the sentence:

    *"Our principal concern is Arnold"* – therefore immediately addressing the requirement and highlighting Arnold as a key player going on to explain HOW and WHY he would be affected.

    So this is the first evidence of the implication of Arnold being a key stakeholder. At this point you could move on to another new point but it will be more useful to stop and think here of the implications and perhaps more importantly the justification of the points you have made. This will help you to delve deeper into the issue and add more value to your answer. It is often helpful to ask yourself the question at this juncture 'so what?'.

    We have made the point that Arnold is a key player but what does that mean for CAST? We can go on to say:

    *"A quotation is unlikely to have any benefit for Arnold, if only because his annual dividend is sufficient to make him a very wealthy person"*

    This explains the implication of our previous point and will earn an additional mark. This adds depth to our answer.

- Breadth of points is also important and so we can now move on to the next point which is the consideration of the next group of key stakeholders. It is important in your answer to prioritise as you are advising the CEO who will need to address the most serious elements first of any business concern:

    *"The other shareholders...none owns a sufficiently large block of shares to exert any significant power...their primary interest in a quotation is that their stake in CAST will be far more realisable...they may diversify their interests by selling shares in CAST and using the proceeds to invest in other companies"*

    This clearly satisfies the needs of the CEO and critically answers the requirement as set i.e. provide a list of stakeholders, along with an explanation of why each is affected and how their interests will be affected.

- This approach is then repeated for each stakeholder group identified making sure that the HOW and the WHY is both clearly addressed, plus any additional value added by adopting the principle of "stop and think". The main stakeholders affected would be:
    - Arnold
    - Other existing shareholders
    - Potential shareholders
    - Customers
    - Suppliers
    - Employees

    This list is not exhaustive and could be added to or split down further into subcategories e.g. employees could be managers, full time employees, part time employees etc all of which should earn credit. The key is to keep the list relevant to the proposal to seek a quotation.

    An example of this approach is demonstrated when considering the employees who have been classed as low power, high interest stakeholders, thus:

    *"Cast's employees will have little power over anything that the company does because they are unskilled and can easily be replaced (HOW). These changes are also very unlikely to interest the employees. The company does not treat its staff particularly well. The pressures arising from a quote to report strong earnings will not lead to the company reducing staff benefits because they could not be much poorer. Also, the company is unlikely to introduce a share-based incentive scheme, so the employees will not have any direct interest in the share price (WHY)"*

This approach is likely to earn one mark for identifying the stakeholder and then one mark for HOW and WHY they are affected by the business decision and one mark for suggesting how these stakeholders would be managed giving eighteen marks in total.

- At this point it is worth returning to the requirement to think about what to discuss next. We are looking at two tasks i.e. task (1a) and (1b)
    - Analysis of stakeholders affected by a business decision
    - Strategy for dealing with a major shareholder in the light of a business decision

Once we have covered the stakeholders identified in the initial Mendelow's matrix analysis we need to be sure that we address the other concern of the CEO, namely the development of a strategy for dealing with a major stakeholder and Key Player.

It is important therefore to draw the first part of the task (1a) to a close which is addressed by

*"To sum up, Arnold is the most important shareholder...the board will have to consider his interests very carefully to ensure the success of the quotation".*

This would earn a further mark and acts as an introduction to the next task.

We have now seen how the thirteen marks for the Business skills and five marks for Leadership have been allocated within this task. There are also integration marks available for this generic competency but we will consider integration later on in this chapter.

## Strategy for dealing with a major shareholder Arnold

This requirement is more focused on technical, people and leadership skills so it is going to be important to bring in your relevant technical knowledge but even more important that you apply it appropriately to the situation.

There are fewer marks available for this part of the first task (1b) – approximately 20 minutes so we are aiming for 6/7 well made points to be sure that we cover the requirement. It is worth checking the requirement again at this point..."I need you to think about a strategy for dealing with Arnold and to put your thoughts down on paper"

The requirement is very specific and your response should concentrate on Arnold entirely. We need to be sensitive in our response particularly as Arnold is the great grandson of the owner PLUS the shareholding that he has is significant and he has the potential to influence other shareholders and the opinion of the investment analysts if he reacts adversely to the potential for stock market flotation.

We will need to have clear structure to address the requirement – WHAT is the dilemma; WHY is it a dilemma and HOW would you recommend that CAST deal with the potential problem. Separate your answer plan into these three categories.

- The first point introduces the topic but makes a relevant link back to information from the pre-seen and will therefore earn a mark.

   *"I have been thinking ahead to the difficult problem of dealing with Arnold in the event that the proposal to pursue a stock market quotation goes ahead"*

- We can then go on to consider the dilemma in more detail beginning with an implication for CAST:

   *"Basic dilemma is that most shareholders are keen to seek a quotation which means that Arnold could be unable to prevent this even is he resists...resistance could prove both costly and disruptive. The market may be reluctant to pay a great deal for CAST's shares if Arnold threatens to sell a large block of shares..."*

   To earn marks here we need to think about the effect on CAST – it is important to avoid merely 'textbook' answers. So to crystallise the point we can introduce the key problem

   *"any attempt to defeat Arnold is likely to harm CAST...we need to work towards persuading him to work with us willingly"*

   thus earning a full mark.

- We can then go on to consider this point in more detail and address the practicalities to resolve the situation and earn further marks.

    It is important to recognise that the strategies need to be persuasive and sensitive both to the needs of the only surviving family member on the board and to CAST in seeking a stock market quotation. This is reflected in the use of appropriate language and choice of strategy. For example

    *"The first approach that we might pursue would be to persuade Arnold that pursuing a quotation is consistent with the company's underlying values. The business has grown successfully from humble origins as a small family business, but most large corporations started in the same way"*

    Again the example which links back to CAST is important to earning the mark here, avoiding another textbook answer.

- We can continue by providing an illustration how Arnold could retain his family connection but oversee the growth of the company which is consistent with the values of the founding fathers:

    *"Arnold's interests in the company's origins are due to his family connection to the founder. We could recognise that by offering him a non-executive directorship. Giving him a seat on the board would enable him to ensure that the company's values are maintained and pursued."*

    Then take a step back, return to the requirement and consider any other aspects which may help to persuade Arnold but maintain and retain his interest in the future development of the business.

- Finally we can present a few concluding points which together are worth 2 marks:

    *"It might be possible to persuade him to sell some of his shares as part of the placement on the stock exchange. Cast could persuade him to put the proceeds to some good use, such as the establishment of a charitable foundation, which Cast might also support as part of its ongoing development as a quoted company".*

We have now seen how the thirteen marks for technical, people and leadership skills are allocated within this section of the task – one mark for the introduction, one mark for identifying the dilemma, two marks for explaining why it is a dilemma, one mark each for identifying a relevant option to resolve the dilemma and a mark each for the pro's and con's of each option and two marks for concluding points...to a maximum of thirteen. As before there are integration marks within this generic competency which we will consider later.

Following this detailed analysis of the marking guide for the first section we will now show you a breakdown of the marks for the remaining tasks in the pilot exam.

## 3 Exam task 2

From the previous chapter we saw that this section required the following:

You are required to prepare a note for the CEO to brief the board covering:

- The suitability of each of four different valuation methods for the purposes of Cast flotation
- An explanation of the governance issues associated with flotation

| Requirement |  | Marks |
|---|---|---|
| Valuation models |  |  |
|  | **Asset based** – background and potential | 1 |
|  | Not resource intensive | 1 |
|  | Intellectual property (IP) | 1 |
|  | Share price would be undervalued if IP not included | 1 |
|  | **Earning based** – background and potential | 1 |
|  | Link to forecasts | 1 |
|  | Risk of unrealistic expectations to buyers | 1 |
|  | Need to offer a range for comparison purposes | 1 |
|  | **Dividends based** – background and potential | 1 |
|  | Suitability for family business | 1 |
|  | Lack of pressure from family members for regular dividends | 1 |
|  | Link to cash balance | 1 |

## Review of solution to pilot case and marking guide

|  | | |
|---|---|---|
| | **Cash based** – background and potential | 1 |
| | Problem with cash based and forecasts | 1 |
| | Ease of identifying free cash flows | 1 |
| | Realistic when compared to other valuation methods | 1 |
| *Total – technical skills* | | 16 |
| | Asset based – Effect of large underutilised cash balance | 1 |
| | Earnings based – Need to compare with suitable quoted company | 1 |
| | Dividends based – accuracy as a predictive tool for future dividend payments | 1 |
| | Cash based - Realistic when compared to other valuation methods | 1 |
| *Total – business skills* | | 4 |
| Governance issues | | |
| | Directors duties | 1 |
| | Directors responsibility to all shareholders | 1 |
| | Agency issue – adjusting share price? | 1 |
| | Stewardship and cash surplus issue | 1 |
| | Directors skills and knowledge | 1 |
| | Need for NED's | 1 |
| *Total technical skills* | | 6 |
| | Announcement form directors re cash surplus | 2 |
| | Directors competence – employ consultants or recruit | 1 |
| | Management of change | 1 |
| | Management of existing Chairman | 1 |
| *Total leadership skills* | | 5 |

# chapter 11

### Exercise 1

The following answer represents a possible student response to Section 2:

(a) **Valuation models**

The asset based valuation model values the company at the value of the net assets. Cast should not use asset-based valuation models because they ignore intangible assets. This might mean that CAST would be undervalued as a result.

Earnings-based valuations value a company based on the present value of the future post tax earnings of the business. Cast is profitable and should therefore generate returns for its shareholders. The company has not been operating in its present form for very long, so this could be a problem in determining future cash flows. This method also requires the identification of a suitable quoted company whose price/earnings ratio can be used as a base and applied to the valuation of CAST. There are lots of other online retail companies that CAST could research to see if there is any suitable comparison.

The dividend growth model essentially determines the net present value of future dividends on the basis of past observations of dividend payments and growth rates. Dividend-based valuations are probably unsuitable in this case because the company is a family business since its creation and only had to pay dividends to shareholders who had more long term interests in the company.

Cash-based models are much better. They are based on the calculation of the free cash flow and the establishment of the cost of capital. This will allow the value of the company to be determined by using the cost of capital multiplied by the free cash flow to establish the net present value of the company. There may be a problem in determining the cost of capital however which we need to look into.

## Review of solution to pilot case and marking guide

> **(b) Governance issues**
>
> The first complication is that CAST will become publicly owned and therefore be subject to changes in its governance arrangements.
>
> Agency issues would also arise as now there will be more shareholders involved. The newly formed CAST plc would also require more meeting to "comply or explain" any actions that the directors might take, e.g. what to do with the large cash surplus?
>
> The directors will have to ensure they are competent to manage this business because their recent experience is in the management of a private company (see pre-seen).
>
> It could be argued that Cast's board be required to increase the number of non-executive directors (see pre-seen) to maintain independence over decision making. Similarly CAST will need to decide what to do about the roles of CEO and Chairman. Arthur Brown may well continue as non-executive chairman, given his experience in banking. But the company would almost certainly have to appoint additional non-executives to support him.

**Required:**

Determine the likely marks awarded for this answer.

Remember that the marking guide is not rigid and any sensible and relevant point can score credit.

## 4 Exam task 3

This task required:

- Prepare a discussion document on the ethical implications of CAST's employment practices.
- Prepare a paper on how the share price maybe impacted by the allegations.
- Include in the paper an analysis of how the 30% shareholding of Arnold could affect the share issue price on stock exchange listing.

# chapter 11

| Requirement | | Marks |
|---|---|---|
| Ethical implications of CAST's employment practices | | |
| | Conflict of interest | 1 |
| | Directors duties – negative | 1 |
| | Directors duties – positive | 1 |
| | Ethical breach of duty | 1 |
| | Legal and economic responsibility? | 1 |
| Total – business skills | | 5 |
| | Refusal to recognise unions | 1 |
| | Safeguard against exploitation | 1 |
| | Uncaring employers? | 1 |
| | Willingness to negotiate? | 1 |
| | Shareholders' interest against employees | 1 |
| | Cost of labour increase | 1 |
| | Employee complaints realistic | 1 |
| | Company exploitation of circumstance | 1 |
| | Overtime not quaranteed | 1 |
| | Unfair dismissal? | 1 |
| | Intimidation of staff? | 1 |
| | Training to imporive – alternative? | 1 |
| | Dismissal affecting future careers | 1 |
| | Contrast allegations with CSR policy | 1 |
| | Maintain acceptable working conditions | 1 |

## Review of solution to pilot case and marking guide

| Requirement | | Marks |
|---|---|---|
| | Investment in CAST by ethical investors | 1 |
| | Poor record in employee relations | 1 |
| | Degree of abuse by CAST? | 1 |
| | Support of investors hard to redeem | 1 |
| *Total – people skills* | | *19* |
| Planning for strike | | |
| | History of strikes | 1 |
| | Perception of staff mood | 1 |
| | Potential volume of union members | 1 |
| | Job roles | 1 |
| | Opportunities for cover | 1 |
| | Safety issues | 1 |
| | Identify risk areas | 1 |
| | Contingency planning | 1 |
| | Temporary cover | 1 |
| | Implications | 2 |
| *Total – business skill* | | *11* |
| Arnold shareholding affecting the share issue price | | |
| | Active role in management of company? | 1 |
| | Perception of market on Arnold's actions? | 1 |
| | Potential poor publicity for Arnold | 1 |
| | Publicise treatment of workers | 1 |
| | Effect on profit of extra labour costs | 1 |
| *Total – leadership skills* | | *5* |

## 5 Integration

There are nine integration marks available in the pilot paper with marks spread across each of the generic competencies.

These marks will be awarded for the overall quality of your answer and use of available information. You should consider the style and language you use and ensure it is suitable for the intended recipient. It is also important that your responses are appropriately structured and logical.

You need to ensure that you integrate relevant parts of each of the three technical syllabi to score well.

## 6 Summary

You should now have an understanding of how the case studies are marked which is crucial if you are going to improve your performance. It is very important that you understand what will (and won't) earn credit in the exam.

You need to master the art of writing a clear and relevant response to tasks beforehand so that you can just get on with it once the real exam starts, without wasting time.

### Next steps:

(1) Revisit any chapters which you found tricky.
(2) Await the 'live' pre-seen for your exam.
(3) Re-perform the suggestions in this textbook using the real pre-seen to ensure you are prepared for the exam.
(4) Consider choosing a study option which gives you access to practice mocks – an important stage in your exam preparation.

# Review of solution to pilot case and marking guide

## Test your understanding answers

| Exercise 1 |||
|---|---|---|
| **Answer** | **Marker's comments** | **Marks** |
| Valuation Models | | |
| *The asset based valuation model values the company at the value of the net assets* | Knowledge based comment – does not address suitability of the model | 0 |
| *Cast should not use asset-based valuation models because they ignore intangible assets".* | Ignores the fact that CAST is not resource intensive rather driven by technology. No specific reference to Intellectual property (IP) but reference to intangible assets. | 1 |
| *This might mean that CAST would be undervalued as a result.* | Good conclusion following the earlier justification. | 1 |
| *Earnings-based valuations value a company based on the present value of the future post tax earnings of the business.* | Knowledge based comment – does not address suitability of the model | 0 |
| *The company has not been operating in its present form for very long, so this could be a problem in determining future cash flows* | There is an attempt to answer 'so what' in terms of suitability for CAST. (Vague and does not specifically refer to CAST) | 1 |

# chapter 11

| | | |
|---|---|---|
| *This method also requires the identification of a suitable quoted company whose price/earnings ratio can be used as a base and applied to the valuation of CAST.* | This explains the 'so what' of the above point | 1 |
| *There are lots of other online retail companies that CAST could research to see if there is any suitable comparison.* | This would have been better as part of the introduction. Indicative of a lack of planning perhaps? | 1 |
| *The dividend growth model essentially determines the net present value of future dividends on the basis of past observations of dividend payments and growth rates.* | Knowledge based comment – does not address suitability of the model for CAST | 0 |
| *Dividend-based valuations are probably unsuitable in this case because the company is a family business since its creation and only had to pay dividends to shareholders who had more long term interests in the company.* | There is an attempt to answer 'so what' in terms of suitability for CAST. A little vague and does not specifically refer to CAST | 1 |
| *......company is a family business since its creation and only had to pay dividends to shareholders who had more long term interests in the company.* | Lack of pressure from family members for regular dividends | 1 |

# Review of solution to pilot case and marking guide

| | | |
|---|---|---|
| *Cash-based models are much better. They are based on the calculation of the free cash flow and the establishment of the cost of capital. There may be a problem in determining the cost of capital however which we need to look into.* | Knowledge based comment – does not address suitability of the model for CAST | 0 |
| *This will allow the value of the company to be determined by using the cost of capital multiplied by the free cash flow to establish the net present value of the company.* | Knowledge based comment – does not address suitability of the model for CAST | 0 |
| **Marks awarded** | Fail | **7** |
| *Total available - technical skills* | | 16 |
| *This method also requires the identification of a suitable quoted company whose price/earnings ratio can be used as a base and applied to the valuation of CAST* | Earnings based – Need to compare with suitable quoted company | 1 |
| *company is a family business since its creation and only had to pay dividends to shareholders who had more long term interests in the company* | Dividends based – accuracy as a predictive tool for future dividend payments | 1 |
| *......Cash-based models are much better. They are based on the calculation of the free cash flow* | Cash based - Realistic when compared to other valuation methods | 1 |
| **Marks awarded** | Pass | **3** |
| *Total available – business skills* | | 3 |

## chapter 11

| Answer | Marker's comments | Marks |
|---|---|---|
| Governance | | |
| The first complication is that CAST will become publicly owned and therefore be subject to changes in its governance arrangements. | Knowledge based comment – does not address suitability of the model for CASTDirectors duties specifically | 0 |
| Agency issues would also arise as now there will be more shareholders involved. | Agency issue covered but vague and not specific to CAST – no mention of adjusting share price? | 1 |
| The newly formed CAST plc would also require more meeting to "comply or explain" any actions that the directors might take, e.g. what to do with the large cash surplus? | Knowledge based comment. Showing lack of application particularly to the stewardship perspective. No mention of action needed re cash surplus. | 0 |
| The directors will have to ensure they are competent to manage this business because their recent experience is in the management of a private company (see pre-seen). | There is an attempt to answer 'so what' in terms of relevance for CAST. | 1 |
| It could be argued that Cast's board be required to increase the number of non-executive directors (see pre-seen) to maintain independence over decision making. | There is an attempt to answer 'so what' in terms of need for additional governance measure for CAST | 1 |
| **Total marks awarded** | Fail | 3 |
| *Total available – technical marks* | | 6 |

259

# Review of solution to pilot case and marking guide

| The directors will have to ensure they are competent to manage this business because their recent experience is in the management of a private company | Directors competence – employ consultants or recruit | 1 |
|---|---|---|
| **Total marks awarded** | **Fail** | **1** |
| Total available – leadership skills | | 5 |

*Summary*

The answer has not achieved a pass because it has spent too long demonstrating pure knowledge of the different valuation methods and not enough time on the suitability for CAST.

Paying close attention to the task as described and then answering that task remains a key part of examination technique and success.

# chapter 12

## Pre-seen Material – Look

# 1 The benefits of practice case studies

We have already explained the benefit of practice case studies and guided you through the steps from start to finish using the Pilot exam, Cast. So that you have a chance to fully familiarise yourself with the process before embarking on your preparation of the real pre-seen we have also included a walkthrough of one of the variants sat in March 2015 using the Look case study.

The remainder of this chapter contains the Look pre-seen material. We would advise that you skim read this now before reminding yourself of the techniques from Chapter 5 where you were provided with guidance on how to familiarise yourself with the pre-seen material.

## Reference Material 1

### Background

You are a senior manager who works for the Look Group ("Look"). You report directly to the parent company's board and advise on special projects and strategic matters. You have compiled the following facts about the company.

### Look – company background

Look is a technology company that was founded by three software engineers in 1998. The company is still based in the European city where the founders were based when they met and agreed to go into business together. The company now has worldwide operations, with physical sites in five locations around the world and an electronic and commercial presence in virtually every country.

Look was created by Jay Bride, Martin Hong and Vijay Chatterjee (hereafter "Jay, Martin and Vijay"), who were studying computer science at a prestigious university. They were working on a project to improve internet search engines when Martin had an idea that led to a search algorithm that could find useful websites far more reliably than existing software. Jay and Vijay helped him to develop this idea into a viable product. They called the software "Look" and created a company of the same name to exploit the software's commercial potential.

Jay, Martin and Vijay each owned one third of Look's shares when the company was first created. The company generated very little revenue at first and many of the people who dealt with the company were offered shares instead of a cash payment. For example, a computer dealer received a 5% shareholding in return for six PCs and a programmer who assisted with the testing of the earliest version of the Look search engine received an 8% holding.

By the time that Look started to become commercially viable, the three founders held 75% of the shares and the remaining 25% were held by a number of suppliers and employees. Jay, Martin and Vijay attempted to buy these minority shareholdings back in 2002, but 10% of the company's equity shares were left in the hands of former employees at the time of the company's flotation.

Look was listed on the stock exchange in 2004. The equity shares in issue at that time were converted to a special class of equity share called founder shares. Each founder share receives the same dividend as the equity shares that were issued to the market during the flotation, but founder shares carry twenty votes per share. No further founder shares can be issued.

The flotation injected a significant cash inflow that has been used both to promote the Look search engine and also to finance an infrastructure:-

Look has two programming centres, one in India and the other in Eastern Europe. Each of those centres hires local programmers, who are generally extremely competent, to support the core businesses.

There are two major research and development centres, one in Europe and the other in the USA. These specialise in developing physical products.

Look also owns three major facilities that provide the company with the necessary data storage that it requires to provide its services and also to develop new features. Look records every search made using its search engine.

## Look's business strategy

Look's basic business model with respect to its search engine software has not changed since the company was founded. Users access the software using any internet browser. When they go to the Look site they can search on any term, such as "new car". Look's software presents users with a column of links to related commercial sites. For example, the user may be presented with links to sites for car makers and car dealerships. Look has taken great care to avoid this from becoming intrusive and many users find it useful to be offered these links. The links are sponsored by Look's advertisers, who pay Look a few Cents every time their link is activated by a user.

**Pre-seen Material – Look**

The secret to making this business model successful is to provide users with useful links to commercial sites. Look gathers information about users that enable the company to increase the likelihood of a link being followed. For example, Look can determine the location of the user's device and so any link to, say, a car dealership can be located within easy travelling distance. Look also stores details of past browsing history from that device and so a user who has looked at a particular model of car in the past may be provided with links to all of the dealers who sell that model within a reasonable distance, or to associated links such as sites of companies who provide car insurance or who provide finance on new cars. Look has been very successful in observing traits that can be used to predict users' interests.

The Look search engine is constantly being upgraded and refined. There are several competing search engines, although Look estimates that its engine is used for 60% of all internet searches. More than 120 billion searches are conducted using Look every month.

Look's principal competitors do not necessarily use search engines to generate advertising revenues. For example, there is a social media site called Friendtime, whose users post text and digital photographs to their Friendtime pages in order to exchange information with their friends. Friendtime users are presented with links every time they log onto the site and advertisers pay for clicks through to their websites. Friendtime does not compete with Look for users, but both companies are in competition for advertising revenue. A user who has accessed an advertiser's site via Friendtime will be less likely to access that same site via Look.

The Look search engine generates approximately 70% of the company's total revenue, but the company has diversified into other ventures:

Look Space is essentially a world map. Users can search for postal addresses and other locations anywhere in the world and the site can recommend a route for walking or driving between any two points. The basic business model is similar to that used by the search engine. Users who search for a particular address subsequently receive adverts relating to the surrounding area, such as hotels, restaurants and local attractions, and advertisers pay for clicks to their sites.

Look OS is a computer operating system that has been developed to power portable devices such as notebook computers, tablet computers and mobile phones. This operating system is "open source", which means that manufacturers can use the operating system in their own devices without paying for the privilege of doing so. There are more than 900 million Look OS devices in operation.

Look Apps is an online store that sells programs that operate under Look OS. Apps are typically simple games or software packages that have a very specific purpose. Each app is sold for very little, but it is a high volume market. Look will also sell third party apps in return for a commission from the seller.

Look Phone manufactures mobile phone handsets that use the Look OS operating system. The phones are highly featured and are intended to compete on the basis of innovation and build quality rather than price. Look Phone is the fourth largest manufacturer in terms of number of handsets sold. Look Phone does not have any manufacturing capacity. The phones are manufactured by subcontractors who specialise in making electronic devices.

Look Lens is a contact lens that can receive signals from the user's mobile phone and can create the impression of an image floating in space. That creates a number of possibilities, such as being able to view files stored on a mobile phone or being able to call up information such as arrows pointing to places of interest as defined by the phone's GPS receiver and local maps. Users will also be able to read emails and text messages without looking at their phones.

Look Media allows subscribers to rent or buy films, television programmes and music that can be played on subscribers' computers, tablets or mobile phones. Look Media pays a royalty to the copyright holder in return for the right to sell viewing or listening rights.

Look Cloud is an online storage system. Users of this service can obtain a free account that entitles them to store up to one gigabyte of data securely on Look's server, using their web browser to upload files and to access them. Many users pay a monthly subscription fee to rent additional storage capacity beyond this limit. This is not just an online storage service. Users can search their files to find, say, letters sent to a particular person.

Look regards each of these ventures as mutually supportive. Each new venture maintains a perception that Look is an inventive and exciting company and that any positive publicity that reinforces this perception benefits every line of business. There are also direct synergies, such as the future success of Look Apps depending on the strength of the user base for Look OS because selling more devices stimulates demand for apps and increasing the quantity and quality of apps makes owning a Look OS device more appealing.

## Organisation

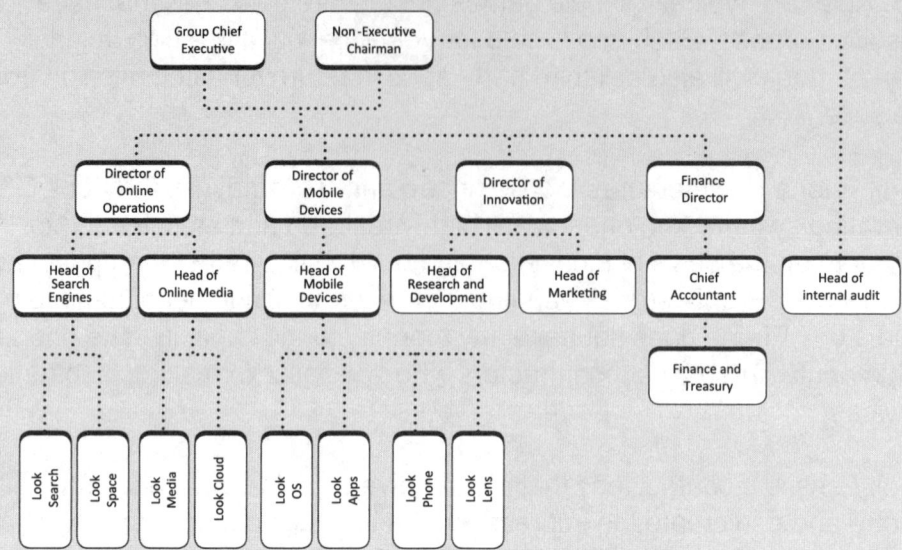

Jay is the Group Chief Executive, Martin is Director of Online Operations and Vijay is Director of Innovation. The board is supported by senior managers who take overall responsibility for the management of the eight revenue-generating divisions, such as Look Search, etc.

In practice, Jay, Martin and Vijay tend to work very closely together, focussing more on matters that interest them. They delegate much of the responsibility for the company's supervision to their fellow directors. The three founders argue that their vision created the company and continues to sustain it. For example, the Look Lens project is a speculative venture that would not have reached the stage of a product launch if Vijay had not convinced Jay and Martin of its potential before the three of them took the idea to the board with their firm commitment to proceed.

Finance and Treasury, Marketing and Research and Development are centralised service departments that support the whole group with respect to those functions. Other operational matters, such as human resources or health and safety, are left to the individual divisions to manage.

Mobile Devices is responsible for the manufacture of hardware, such as mobile phone handsets.

All matters relating to centralised information systems are the responsibility of Look Search. The two programming centres and the three data storage facilities are managed by Look Search and the other divisions are invoiced for any use that they make of their services. Look Space, Look Media and Look Cloud are heavy users of programming and data storage. The other divisions tend not to be heavy users because they have relatively modest data storage requirements and Look OS and Look Apps have their own specialised programmers, based at the programming centres, who are experts in the Look Operating System.

# chapter 12

The Board comprises two executive directors in addition to Jay, Martin and Vijay. There is also a non-executive chairman and three additional non-executive directors.

Looks employees are as follows

| | |
|---|---:|
| Look Search | 5,083 |
| Look Space | 803 |
| Look Media | 2,012 |
| Look Cloud | 651 |
| Look OS | 3,480 |
| Look Apps | 2,548 |
| Look Phone | 1,967 |
| Look Lens | 263 |
| Research and Development | 1,907 |
| Marketing | 598 |
| Finance and Treasury | 706 |
| Internal Audit | 234 |
| | 20,252 |

Look prides itself on being an excellent employer. Each of the company's sites offers an attractive working environment and includes facilities such as a good cafeteria and leisure facilities. Employees are well paid, although that is partly because Look needs to retain staff in the face of competition from other technology companies.

Look pays staff to develop themselves. The company will sponsor staff who wish to seek further qualifications and staff can apply for time to develop their own ideas, even if they do not have any immediate or obvious scope for commercial exploitation.

## Industry data

When Look was first established the internet was in a state of relative infancy. Usage has grown dramatically since, although the rate of growth has declined significantly as usage has gone towards saturation point.

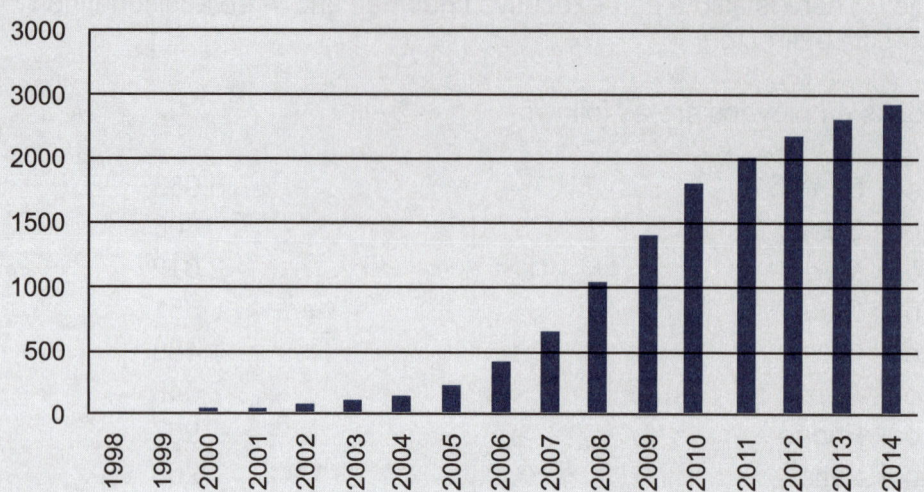

Look's analysts believe that internet users will tend to spend increasing amounts of time online, with the growth in the use of mobile devices, social media and online music and video for entertainment, but they will not necessarily conduct many more searches because of this.

Share prices over the past three years or so for Look and Friendtime are shown as follows:

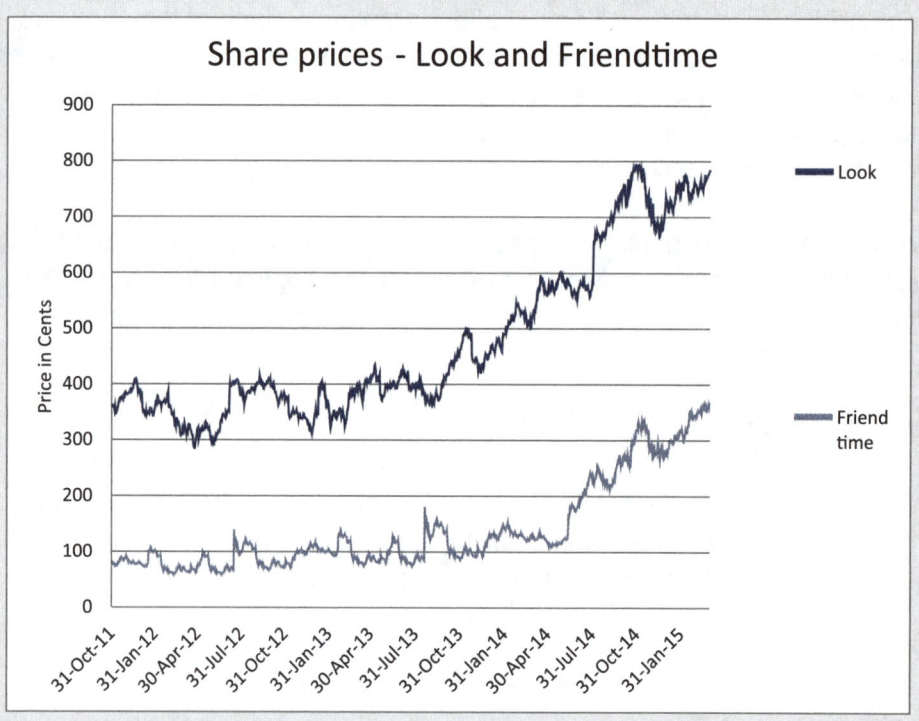

## Look's Mission Statement

Look is often credited with having two mission statements. The official mission statement is:

"Connecting people to the World."

Look's underlying intention is to make knowledge in almost any form instantly accessible to those using the company's services. The search engine is an obvious example of this, but the other divisions also contribute. Jay, Martin and Vijay believe that Look is a powerful force for enhancing the good of society.

Look also has an unofficial mission to "Do only good". This underpins an extensive ethical code:

Serve users

Respect others

Protect privacy

Respect external regulations

Work in Look's best interest (subject to the above)

## Look's strategy

Look's main strategic priority is to maintain market dominance. The company requires economies of scale and scope to attract users and so attract advertisers in order to generate revenues from its services. The loss of significant market share to a competitor could lead to disproportionate losses.

Look's directors have prepared the following outline SWOT analysis:

| Strengths | Weaknesses |
|---|---|
| • Significant user base<br>• Highly recognisable brand | • Dependence on programmers and other specialists whose skills are in demand<br>• Dependence on availability of internet for delivery of service |
| **Opportunities** | **Threats** |
| • Innovative new products can capitalise on existing brand image<br>• Growing presence of the Look OS platform in the home and workplace | • Growing concerns about online privacy<br>• Increasing concerns about regulation<br>• Relatively low barriers to entry for potential competitors |

**Look's board of directors**

**Jay Bride, Co-founder and Group Chief Executive**

Jay Bride co-founded Look in 1998. Today he serves as Group Chief Executive.

Jay has a Bachelor of Science degree in Computer Science and a PhD in Software Engineering. He holds honorary doctorates from three leading universities.

Jay has been credited with developing the business model upon which Look's success has been built.

## Martin Hong, Co-founder and Director of Online Operations

Martin Hong co-founded Look in 1998. Today he serves as Director of Online Operations.

Martin has a Bachelor of Engineering degree in Electronic Engineering and a PhD in Software Engineering. He serves as a visiting Professor of Systems Architecture at a prestigious university and he has published many academic papers on the mathematics of search algorithms.

Martin wrote the algorithm that is the basis for Look's search engine.

Martin's role as Director of Online Operations requires him to maintain his strategic vision for Look's systems architecture.

## Vijay Chatterjee, Co-founder and Director of Innovation

Vijay Chatterjee co-founded Look in 1998. Today he serves as Director of Innovation.

Vijay has a Bachelor of Science degree in Mathematics and Statistics, a Master of Science degree in Statistical Analysis and a PhD in Software Engineering.

Vijay has successfully patented many ideas that have been brought to the market by Look, including three patents that protect the intellectual property embedded in the Look Lens device.

## Amanda Wilson, Director of Finance

Amanda Wilson has been Look's Director of Finance since 2007. She is an accountancy graduate and is a professionally qualified accountant. She has held senior position in accounting and finance at two manufacturing companies and was the Finance Director of a small commercial bank before she joined Look as Finance Director.

## Victor Lee, Director of Mobile Devices

Victor Lee has been Look's Director of Mobile Devices since the division was first created in 2011. Victor has a Master of Engineering degree in Design Engineering. He worked in product design and in marketing at a major global mobile telephone company before he joined Look.

Victor joined Look in 2008 to take charge of the development of mobile devices. He was promoted to Director in 2011 when the Mobile Devices Division was created in response to the growth in this line of business.

### Charles Anstruther – Non-executive Chairman

Charles Anstruther has been Look's Non-executive Chairman since 2012. He was previously Chief Executive of a major multinational retailer. He has served as Finance Director of two other quoted companies during his long and successful career.

Charles is a qualified accountant and he holds a Master of Arts degree in Politics, Philosophy and Economics.

Charles chairs the Audit and Remuneration Committees.

### Alison Gordon – Non-executive Director

Alison Gordon has been a non-executive director since 2011. She has a background in software engineering and has held senior managerial positions with a number of companies in the telecommunications industry.

Alison has a PhD in Systems Architecture.

Alison is a member of both the Audit and Remuneration Committees.

### Michael Yip – Non-executive Director

Michael Yip has been a Non-executive Director since 2012. He has had a long career in the telecommunications industry. He served as Director of Technical Operations in an unquoted company before joining Look.

Michael has a Master of Science degree in Software Design and a Master of Business Administration degree.

Michael is also a Non-executive Director of an unquoted bank.

Michael is a member of both the Audit and Remuneration Committees.

### Mara Reynolds – Non-executive Director

Mara Reynolds has been a Non-executive Director since 2010. She was previously one of Look's longest-serving employees, having joined the company as a secretary in 2000. She was Martin Hong's Personal Assistant from 2005 until her retirement in 2010. She was offered a non-executive seat on the Board in recognition of her long service and loyalty to the company.

Mara does not sit on any Board committees.

## Internal Audit Department

Look's Internal Audit Department has offices at every site from which the group operates. The department comprises a mixture of qualified staff and trainees. Given the nature of Look's business activities, internal auditors are recruited from a mixture of backgrounds, mainly accounting or computer science. The Head of Internal Audit believes that there are benefits in having a range of skills in the department and that those without an accounting background can learn to apply their skills in an audit context and those who started as auditors can learn about the IT issues required for their role.

The Internal Audit Department focuses on compliance audits, as is traditional, but there is a heavy emphasis on compliance with IT operations to ensure that the security and privacy of data is safeguarded in accordance with Look's standard operating procedures.

The Internal Audit Department uses the risk-based approach to planning and conducting its investigations.

## 2 Reference Material 2

The following information has been extracted from Look's financial statements for the year ended 30 September 2014

### Look Group Consolidated statement of profit or loss

|  | Notes | Year ended 30 September 2014 $ million | Year ended 30 September 2013 $ million |
|---|---|---|---|
| Revenues | [1] | 62,488 | 50,615 |
| **Costs and expenses:** | | | |
| Cost of revenues | [1] | (22,496) | (16,197) |
| Research and development | | (8,654) | (6,795) |
| Sales and marketing | | (6,528) | (5,222) |
| General and administrative | | (3,524) | (3,216) |
| Total costs and expenses | | (41,202) | (31,430) |
| | | | |
| Operating profit | | 21,286 | 19,185 |
| Interest and other income, net | | 256 | 452 |
| Profit before tax | | 21,542 | 19,637 |
| | | | |
| Tax expense | [2] | (3,468) | (3,875) |
| | | | |
| Profit for year | | 18,074 | 15,762 |

## Pre-seen Material – Look

### Look Group Consolidated statement of financial position

| | Notes | As at 30 September 2014 $ million | As at 30 September 2013 $ million |
|---|---|---|---|
| **Assets** | | | |
| **Non-current assets** | | | |
| Property, plant and equipment | [3] | 14,500 | 19,987 |
| Intangible assets | [4] | 8,756 | 4,871 |
| Goodwill | [5] | 12,874 | 9,478 |
| | | 36,130 | 34,336 |
| **Current assets** | | | |
| Inventories | | 485 | 412 |
| Trade receivables | | 8,874 | 9,852 |
| Deferred tax | | 1,144 | 1,526 |
| Marketable securities | | 38,971 | 32,746 |
| Cash and cash equivalents | | 8,973 | 7,625 |
| | | 58,447 | 52,161 |
| **Total assets** | | 94,577 | 86,497 |
| **Equity** | | | |
| Share capital | [6] | 20,000 | 20,000 |
| Retained earnings | | 54,967 | 45,839 |
| Total equity | | 74,967 | 65,839 |
| **Non-current liabilities** | | | |
| Long-term debt | | 4,800 | 4,800 |
| Net pension scheme liability | | 1,624 | 1,328 |
| Total non-current liabilities | | 6,424 | 6,128 |
| **Current liabilities** | | | |
| Trade payables | | 2,258 | 2,364 |
| Short-term debt | | 2,897 | 3,874 |
| Accrued expenses and other current liabilities | | 3,586 | 3,412 |
| Deferred revenue | [7] | 1,200 | 1,005 |
| Income taxes payable | | 3,245 | 3,875 |
| Total current liabilities | | 13,186 | 14,530 |
| **Total equity and liabilities** | | 94,577 | 86,497 |

## 3 Reference Material 3

### Basis of consolidation

The consolidated financial statements include the accounts of all subsidiaries controlled by the parent company. All intragroup balances and transactions have been eliminated.

### Cost of revenues

Cost of revenues includes the expenses associated with the operation of data centres, including depreciation of hardware, staff costs, energy, and bandwidth costs, credit card and other transaction fees related to processing customer transactions, as well as content acquisition costs.

### Property, Plant and Equipment

We account for property, plant and equipment at cost or valuation less accumulated depreciation. We compute depreciation using the straight-line method over the estimated useful lives of the assets, generally two to ten years. We depreciate buildings over periods up to 25 years.

Depreciation for equipment commences once it is placed in service and depreciation for buildings commences once they are ready for occupation. Land is not depreciated.

### Software Development Costs

The costs of developing software, including costs to develop software products or the software component of products to be marketed to external users, are written off before the technological feasibility of such products is determined.

Software development costs also include costs associated with programs for our own internal use and with cloud-based applications used in the delivery of our services.

### Note 1 – Segmental analysis

| | Look Search $ million | Look Space $ million | Look Media $ million | Look Cloud $ million | Look OS $ million | Look Apps $ million | Look Phone $ million | Look Lens $ million | Total $ million |
|---|---|---|---|---|---|---|---|---|---|
| Revenues | 42,492 | 9,373 | 4,374 | 1,875 | 0 | 1,250 | 3,124 | 0 | 62,488 |
| Cost of revenues | (6,297) | (5,624) | (2,025) | (2,475) | (1,575) | (1,125) | (2,025) | (1,350) | (22,496) |
| Revenues less cost of revenues | 36,195 | 3,749 | 2,349 | (600) | (1,575) | 125 | 1,099 | (1,350) | 39,992 |

|  | USA $ million | Europe $ million | Africa and Middle East $ million | Asia and Australia $ million | Total $ million |
|---|---|---|---|---|---|
| Revenues | 26,245 | 17,496 | 11,248 | 7,499 | 62,488 |

## Note 2 – Tax expense

|  | $ million |
|---|---|
| Current tax | 3,086 |
| Net movement in deferred tax | 382 |
|  | 3,468 |

## Note 3 – Property, plant and equipment

|  | Property $ million | Plant and equipment $ million | Total $ million |
|---|---|---|---|
| Cost or valuation |  |  |  |
| As at 30 September 2013 | 9,484 | 36,011 | 45,495 |
| Additions | 1,296 | 2,989 | 4,285 |
| Disposals | 0 | (2,374) | (2,374) |
| Impairment adjustment | (1,536) | (2,996) | (4,532) |
| As at 30 September 2014 | 9,244 | 33,630 | 42,874 |
| Depreciation |  |  |  |
| As at 30 September 2013 | 876 | 24,632 | 25,508 |
| Charge for year | 83 | 5,793 | 5,876 |
| Disposals | 0 | (874) | (874) |
| Impairment adjustment | (128) | (2,008) | (2,136) |
| As at 30 September 2014 | 831 | 27,543 | 28,374 |
| Net book value |  |  |  |
| As at 30 September 2014 | 8,413 | 6,087 | 14,500 |
| As at 30 September 2013 | 8,608 | 11,379 | 19,987 |

## Note 4 – Intangible assets

|  | $ million |
|---|---:|
| Cost or valuation |  |
| As at 30 September 2013 | 27,564 |
| Additions | 9,751 |
| As at 30 September 2014 | 37,315 |
| Amortisation |  |
| As at 30 September 2013 | 22,693 |
| Charge for year | 5,866 |
| As at 30 September 2014 | 28,559 |
| Net book value |  |
| As at 30 September 2014 | 8,756 |
| As at 30 September 2013 | 4,871 |

## Note 5 – Good will

Goodwill increased as a result of the acquisition of Memory Games.

## Note 6 – Share capital

|  | $ million |
|---|---:|
| Founder shares | 1,980 |
| Equity shares | 18,020 |
|  | 20,000 |

## Note 7 – Deferred revenue

Deferred revenue arises because many Look's advertisers pre-pay for advertising.

## 4 Reference Material 4

**Risk factors**

| | |
|---|---|
| Competition | We have several lines of business, each of which faces significant competition for market share. Our businesses operate in markets that are constantly evolving and our competitors are often capable of finding new and unforeseen ways to strip us of market share. We must respond by developing our own strategies in order to maintain revenues. |
| Investment on new business | The Look Group is always keen to develop new lines of business and develop existing lines through investment. This process often yields significant benefits, but it can also prove disruptive to ongoing business activities. |
| New technologies | The Look Group's core business activities centre on the internet. This is an area of rapid development and the technologies that affect our business are constantly changing. New devices and platforms, such as smart televisions, are being introduced to access the web. Such new platforms have the capacity to impact on our business model. |
| Advertising revenues | Much of our revenue comes from advertising consumer products. Economic factors can affect the demand for the products that we advertise and that can have an impact on our advertisers' willingness to pay for our services. |
| Regulations and scrutiny | Legitimate concerns about the security and privacy of our users often lead to changes in the law and in other forms of regulation. Such changes can prove to be disproportionate and disruptive to our operations. |
| Political motives | Governments have acted to curtail or disrupt free access to the internet by their citizens. That can have a detrimental effect on our ability to provide a high standard of service. It can also leave us open to accusations of political bias when we act alongside governments in order to minimise the disruption that such restrictions may create. |
| Legal liabilities | We are open to an increasing volume of claims associated with the services that we provide. Users can have claimed that links suggested by our search engines are either misleading or defamatory. There are concerns about privacy issues. Our liability is also increasing through the growing importance of cloud-based storage and the consequential liability associated with the loss or corruption of data |

# chapter 12

| Joint liability | In many cases, our products and services are used in conjunction with devices or software provided by third parties. We can be left facing accusations of negligence by a user who claims to have suffered a loss because of a malfunction in a device or program that may have been supplied by a third party. |
|---|---|
| Manufacturing and supply chain | We are heavily dependent upon third parties for the supply of bought in goods and services, both to service our web-based products and also the physical devices sold by us. Many of our products are manufactured in developing countries where there are concerns about poor working conditions |
| Security and quality of service | Third parties may attempt to disrupt and interfere with our online services. Malicious access can be motivated by criminal intent or simply a desire for notoriety. |
| Interruption of communications | Our services are vulnerable to disruption of the links that form the basis of internet activities. While inherently robust, those systems do have a finite capacity to cope with disruption. Our reputation will be severely undermined if our services are disrupted, particularly if such disruption occurs at a time when a natural disaster stimulates demand for access to relevant information. |
| Key personnel | The Look Group was founded by three individuals who continue to provide a significant input into developing and expanding the business' vision. We also depend heavily upon the skills of engineers and programmers to maintain and enhance the high quality service with which we are associated. |
| Ad blocking | Many users would prefer to access our services without the associated download of advertising links. There are various techniques that can be used to block ads, which would severely curtail our revenues from advertising. |

## 5 Reference Material 5

**Look's Corporate Social Responsibility Report for the year ended 30 September 2014**

Look's motto "do only good" runs through every aspect of the company's operations, including minimising the company's environmental impact.

Look's carbon footprint

Since the company's foundation, we have acknowledged responsibility for our impact on the environment.

The fact that a typical internet search generates a little less than half the $CO_2$ emissions of boiling a kettle is frequently repeated. Look accepts that operating any data-based activity consumes electricity and so generates externalities. We have responded in several ways:

- Look's data centres are managed with care to reduce energy consumption. Our servers are the most energy-efficient that we can source. We work with suppliers to ensure that hardware excels in energy performance. Efficient servers generate less waste heat and so require less energy to be consumed directly in operations and indirectly through cooling and air conditioning.

- We conduct regular energy audits and our data centres use approximately 50% less energy than comparable centres.

- Look has been carbon neutral since 2005. We invest heavily in carbon offsets that exceed our estimated $CO_2$ emissions.

- Look funds research into the development of renewable energy sources. In 2014 we funded projects to the value of $1.1 billion. We work directly with leading universities to identify research projects that might not otherwise attract funding but that do stand a realistic prospect of success in the long term.

**Case study: Western Data Centre**

The Western Data Centre has recently completed a rolling programme to upgrade the power management of the Centre's servers. This was actually more expensive than the installation of new machines, but Look has a policy of upgrading and repairing equipment whenever possible to avoid the consumption of energy and scarce materials required for the manufacture of electronic equipment.

The Western Data Centre draws water from a nearby river to augment temperature control. The water is filtered, run through clean pipes that absorb waste heat from operations and discharged back into the river. An independent environmental audit established that this arrangement increased ambient river temperature by a negligible amount and had no net effect on plant or animal life. The water running through this system is actually cleaner when discharged back to the river than when it is drawn into the Centre.

The Western Data Centre offers a free bus service to local railway stations and other public transport links so that staff can use public transport whenever possible.

The food served in the Western Data Centre's cafeteria is sourced locally and the menu changes to make the best use of local produce when it is in season.

**Look's products**

Many of Look's products reduce users' environmental impact significantly.

Our mission of "Connecting people to the World" means that information that would previously have been accessible only through a journey to a library or a book shop can now be accessed from a computer or mobile phone.

The efficiency of Look's search algorithms make fewer demands of the infrastructure and so reduce energy consumption (in addition to providing users with a fast and efficient service).

Look Space enables users to plan journeys that follow the shortest route and so reduce fuel consumption (or encourage them to walk or cycle rather than drive for shorter journeys). We are working on an upgrade to Look Space that will integrate journey searches with bus and rail timetables so that users are automatically offered a viable public transport alternative whenever one exists.

Look Media offers users the ability to access content without the need to manufacture a physical disk and associated packaging and burden the environment with the carbon footprint of buying and delivering that disk.

Look Cloud ensures that data is secured securely and efficiently, again without the need for users to buy hardware that would require a footprint in its manufacture, distribution and operation.

**Look's people**

Look's reputation as an employer is emphasised both by the very low rate of staff turnover and the very large number of applications that are received for every job that is advertised.

Look has a clear policy of treating staff with respect and of providing them with opportunities to grow and develop. Look has a formal training scheme for all staff that is designed to ensure that professional skills are maintained and extended. New staff are encouraged to participate in external training that is relevant to their roles and all staff can reclaim the cost of any external classes or training, regardless of its relevance to their roles, once they have been in post for more than two years.

Look provides excellent benefits, including competitive salaries and other rewards. All sites have free pre-school childcare facilities. Cafeterias are heavily subsidised. Every site has a well-equipped gym and some sites have swimming pools and other leisure facilities.

### Look in the community

Look sponsors a number of activities that are intended to show support for local communities.

Every member of staff is free to participate in a scheme where Look provides training in programming and information systems to local schools. Interested staff are granted one or two working days per month to assist in this programme and full travel expenses are paid.

Look supports a number of charities by providing data management services and other services free of charge.

Look provided logistical support to the charities which assisted in the recent tragedy in Central Africa.

Look's assistance meant that food, medicine and building materials offered by aid agencies were quickly directed to the areas of greater need. Look established a temporary data centre at the nearest major airport within 72 hours of the news of the tragedy and provided skilled programming and operations staff to maintain the centre. The head of a charity that was also involved commented that Look's assistance had been invaluable and she hoped that Look could be called upon to provide similar support in the event of a future disaster of this scale.

## 6 Reference Material 6

### Look in the news

The following article was published recently by a leading business newspaper.

> **Whither Vijay?**
>
> Vijay Chatterjee, Look's charismatic design guru, seemed somewhat subdued at the launch of the latest iteration of the Look Lens product. The product may have been his brainchild, but he did little more than introduce the head of the design team to the assembled hordes of press and took little further interest in proceedings.
>
> It has long been suspected that Vijay is becoming a little disenchanted with life at the very top of the internet giant. He was clearly at his happiest when the internet was a wild and exciting place and Look was regarded as innovative and iconoclastic. Now it is just another large corporation that is answerable to the capital markets. Even Look's no-suit, cheerful cafeteria with free coffee culture is not that different from that of many other businesses.
>
> Vijay has been rumoured to be interested in stepping down from Look's board. He is a keen sailor and he would clearly love to spend more time competing for trophies in the competitive world of yachting.

## 7 Reference Material 7

**Competitor analysis**

Look's primary business is in the area of online search, both through the Look Search product and the Look Space (which is essentially a search engine that adds the dimension of mapping to the basic idea). Both of those products generate revenue indirectly through the sale of advertising on a "pay per click" basis.

Look faces a diverse range of competitors in this field:

Firstly, there are the traditional search engines, such as Wellfind and Webrun. While Look is far more popular than any of the direct alternatives, it costs users nothing to experiment with other engines and some comments in the computer press have identified benefits to be had from switching.

Secondly, there are more specialised search engines that focus on specific areas. For example, Planeweb is designed to search for flights and Webmedic can be queried for health advice. These sites are usually linked to sales portals offered by advertisers. For example, Planeweb's users can find the cheapest flight on the day they wish to travel and they can book and pay for tickets without leaving the site.

Thirdly, many e-commerce sites fulfil a similar purpose to Look Search. For example, users can search the Buyfind site for products that interest them. They can read the specifications of the products in that category and also reviews posted by users who have already purchased those products. Purchases can be made directly through the Buyfind site and paid for using a credit card.

Finally, other content providers can attract users and offer them adverts that interest them. For example, social media sites such as Friendtime or Picpost are frequently used to promote products. Users on these sites have accounts that they can use to communicate with their friends by posting information that can be accessed by other account holders who have been granted access. Users generally upload personal news and photographs. Advertisers sometimes pay to create commercial accounts that users can link to in order to download product information and advertising links are shown on users' browsers when they are reading their friends' posts. These sites do not compete with Look for users, but advertisers have limited advertising budgets and so they do compete for advertising revenues.

Look's other business activities are far smaller, but are important because they are growing and have the potential to expand dramatically.

Look Media is a logical progression for Look. It enables the company to generate income by making sales directly to its users. Look Media competes in a relatively crowded market, but the company's strong brand recognition means that they may choose to download their favourite film or music from Look Media rather than a competitor. Volume is the key to this market because Look Media has to pay a royalty to the companies which own the copyright in these media files. Higher volumes make it easier to negotiate keener royalty payments, which can be passed on to users in the form of lower download prices.

Look Cloud is also a business that generates regular fees from users and is also a business that is crowded with competition. Look has the advantage of being a known and trusted name and that is important when the company is asking users to entrust their personal data to a remote server.

Look Phone, Look OS and Look Apps are effectively one business that has three symbiotic elements. When Look decided to enter into the crowded marketplace for mobile phone handsets it was faced with the reality of a single, dominant supplier that had captured consumers' imagination. That competitor remains the dominant force in the market, but Look has made significant inroads by developing a viable alternative operating system that is popular with users. Look's operating system would never have captured market share unless Look had stimulated demand by offering a range of phones on which to run it. Making the operating system open source and giving it to other manufacturers was an inspired move because it has underpinned the credibility of the Look Phone as a viable alternative. Much of Look's success in this market has been due to the fact that other manufacturers have adopted Look OS. The growing base of Look OS users has created a ready market for Look Apps.

Look Lens is a rather confusing business proposition because sales will depend on whether users are prepared to use contact lenses. The company will produce prescription lenses for those who need them anyway, but many of the young people at whom this device is targeted will not require contact lenses and may be unwilling to wear plain lenses just for the sake of accessing the output from their phones. The Look Lens has been criticised by many commentators as providing a solution to a problem that does not really exist, but it does have the advantage of appealing to early adopters and it may train wearers to believe that they need to be connected to the internet, their texts and emails on a more or less continuous basis.

## 8 Reference Material 9

### Extracts from Friendtime's financial statements

Friendtime Group Consolidated statement of profit or loss

|  | Year ended 30 September 2014 $ million | Year ended 30 September 2013 $ million |
|---|---|---|
| Revenues | 49,990 | 35,431 |
| Costs and expenses: |  |  |
| Cost of revenues | (13,498) | (8,908) |
| Research and development | (1,358) | (1,749) |
| Sales and marketing | (9,248) | (8,237) |
| General and administrative | (2,491) | (2,214) |
| Total costs and expenses | (26,595) | (21,108) |
|  |  |  |
| Operating profit | 23,395 | 14,323 |
| Interest and other income, net | (587) | (479) |
| Profit before tax | 22,808 | 13,844 |
|  |  |  |
| Tax expense | (2,444) | (2,357) |
|  |  |  |
| Profit for the year | 20,364 | 11,487 |

## Friendtime Group Consolidated statement of financial position

|  | As at 30 September 2014 $ million | As at 30 September 2013 $ million |
|---|---:|---:|
| **Assets** | | |
| **Non-current** | | |
| Property, plant and equipment | 9,852 | 9,674 |
| Intangible assets | 4,200 | 4,200 |
| Goodwill | 896 | 896 |
|  | 14,948 | 14,770 |
| **Current assets** | | |
| Trade receivables | 4,478 | 4,685 |
| Deferred tax | 986 | 921 |
| Cash and cash equivalents | 874 | 1,129 |
|  | 6,338 | 6,735 |
| Total assets | 21,286 | 21,505 |
| **Equity** | | |
| Share capital | 1,000 | 1,000 |
| Retained earnings | 9,652 | 10,997 |
| Total equity | 10,652 | 11,997 |
| **Non-current liabilities** | | |
| Long-term debt | 4,400 | 3,800 |
| Net pension scheme liability | 486 | 412 |
| Total non-current liabilities | 4,886 | 4,212 |
| **Current liabilities** | | |
| Trade payables | 1,078 | 984 |
| Short-term debt | 1,000 | 1,000 |
| Accrued expenses and other current liabilities | 845 | 654 |
| Deferred revenue | 682 | 584 |
| Income taxes payable | 2,143 | 2,074 |
| Total current liabilities | 5,748 | 5,296 |
| Total equity and liabilities | 21,286 | 21,505 |

# chapter 13

# Summary of the Pre-seen – Look

**Chapter learning objectives**

# 1 Introduction

In Chapter Five we showed you some techniques to help you in your analysis of the pre-seen. Once you have completed your analysis of the pre-seen for the March 2015 sitting, Look, you can review this chapter to ensure you have identified the key points. We will take you through each exhibit highlighting the key conclusions before bringing this together into a summary using the SWOT framework.

# 2 Exhibit by exhibit conclusions

### Reference material 1 – Introduction and overview of Look

### Look – Company Background

Look is a diversified technology company based in a European City with worldwide operations and five physical locations.

Look started as a web search software company and this still represents a large proportion of revenue.

The company is listed and on flotation 10% of the shares were held by former employees – these 'founder share' arrangements, whereby the original shareholders maintain more votes, are generally unpopular with investors.

Look employs 'extremely competent' programmers in its centres in India and Eastern Europe.

Along with two R&D centres the company also has three data storage facilities. Data storage requirements are likely to grow as Look records EVERY search made using its engine – this creates opportunities, for harnessing this 'Big Data' and also exposes Look to additional risks.

### Look's business strategy

The Look search engine makes money through sponsored links so it is crucial that they are useful and relevant in order to earn 'click through' revenue. To make the links relevant Look gathers information about the users e.g. location from the device and past browsing history.

It is estimated that 60% of searches taking place use Look which give the company a powerful market share against competitors. However it is important to think carefully about who the competition is as they are not necessarily all other search engines. For example, Friendtime, a social network, will also compete with Look for advertising revenue. Look must protect this advertising revenue as 70% of Look revenue is from the search engine.

The rest of the product portfolio comprises:

**Look Space** (basically Google Earth) – again earning revenue through adverts

**Look OS** is an open source operating system used on 900 million devices worldwide. This provides Look with a ready-made testing environment and allows them to make improvements to any final software product before full launch.

**Look Apps** is an online store selling apps. Third party apps are sold for commission revenue whilst native Look apps are sold for small amounts of revenue in (hopefully) huge volumes.

**Look Phone** manufactures handsets using the Look OS. The phones are high quality and with a range of features and are manufactured by subcontractors.

**Look Lens** is the contact lens version of Google glasses enabling users to access the internet based on what they see and where they are.

**Look Media** is a live media streaming service which earns revenue through a pay per view system and incurs cost in the form of royalties.

**Look Cloud** is a web based storage system which offers a certain amount of free storage before a fee is charged.

It is evident that many synergies exist between the various revenue streams and so any decisions Look makes must take into account all aspects of the business.

**Organisation**

With a range of different integrated divisions, Look will experience transfer pricing issues with respect to recharges of shared services.

The company employs a workforce of 20,000 staff and is keen to be considered an excellent employer. Look provides good working conditions and is very strong on staff development offering financial support for staff wishing to develop their skills and knowledge. This may lead to innovation and new ideas identified by employees. Google employees used to have one day a week given to side projects and it was claimed that this was 'responsible for the company's most significant advances'.

### Industry data

Look's share price is rising (as is that of Friendtime). In fact Look has seen share price growth of over 100% in the last four years. It is important that they are able to maintain the positive investor relationship. Friendtime's growth has been more recent showing a threefold rise in the last nine months.

### Look's Mission Statement

Look has an official mission statement, 'Connecting People to the World' and unofficially 'Do only good' highlighting their desire to be a socially responsible organisation.

### Look's Strategy

Look aims to maintain market dominance. Economies of scale and therefore market share are crucial to success – otherwise advertisers will not be encouraged to spend money with Look.

### Look's Board of directors

The Board comprises highly technical, well-educated founders as well as other well qualified executive directors. The only real weak area in terms of board composition is the appointment of Mara Reynolds as a non-executive as she seems to lack relevant skills and experience – this calls into question Looks' director recruitment policy.

### Internal Audit department

The internal audit department has offices at every physical location with a team made up of qualified staff and trainees from a range of backgrounds. The department adopts a risk based approach and seems to carry out a lot of information security work which should be reassuring as this is likely to be a key area of risk given the amount of data which Look gathers and stores.

**Reference material 2 – Financial Statements for the year ended 30 September 2014**

| Ratio | 2014 | 2103 |
|---|---|---|
| Revenue growth | 23.5% | – |
| Gross profit margin | 64% | 68% |
| Operating profit margin | 34.1% | 37.9% |
| Return on capital employed | 25.8% | 25.7% |
| Asset turnover | 0.76 | 0.68 |
| Effective tax rate | 16% | 20% |
| Gearing | 9.3% | 11.6% |

Revenue increased to $62,488m ($50,615m) an increase of 23.5%. This was lower than Friendtime's rate of revenue growth of 41%. This may indicate that Look could be losing market share and not keeping up with competition.

Revenue generation has improved with asset turnover rising to 0.76 from 0.68 highlighting that Look is generating greater revenue per $ invested.

Cost of revenues has worsened to 36% of revenue (32%). The 4% increase in revenue costs has cost Look $2,500m in gross profit and the reasons for the increase need investigating as Look's business should be about economies of scale and it would arguably be expected for the % cost to revenue to reduce following growth in sales.

In addition, given the nature of Look's business, a very high proportion of its costs would be assumed to be fixed and consequently the high operational gearing should have resulted in a higher rate of profit growth than sales growth, not the decrease observed. There could however be increases in fixed costs which have contributed to the reduced growth in profit but detailed cost breakdowns are not available.

At operating profit level we can see the effect of the increase in costs with only an 11% increase in operating profit compared with the 23.5% increase in revenue. Similarly, the operating profit margin has slipped from 37.9% to 34.1%. Further detail on the cost lines would be required to analyse this.

The decrease in operating margin and increase in asset turnover have negated one another to produce a static return on capital employed of 25.8% (25.7%).

## Summary of the Pre-seen – Look

The effective rate of tax decreased by 4% in 2014 to 16% of profit before tax (20%). This could be due to efficient tax planning or R&D tax incentives which may have been introduced but without further information this cannot be determined. Given Look's unofficial mission to "do only good" and to respect external regulation, hopefully the reduction in tax is not due to tax-avoidance schemes that may have been entered into which could harm Look's image and reputation.

The gearing figure highlights the very low level of debt that Look is utilising in financing its activities. This brings both advantages and disadvantages.

The first advantage of Look's low gearing will be a lower annual interest obligation, which will keep the financial risk to Look's shareholders low. Secondly, there will be a lower required rate of return by Look's shareholders compared with Friendtime's shareholders, as Look's shareholders are exposed to less risk to their earnings. Finally, the low level of debt is likely to mean that there will be relatively few covenants imposed on Look by its debt-holders. This will result in greater freedom for Look in its financial decision making.

Although Look's gearing appears low, their ability to raise further debt would depend upon their debt capacity, particularly its asset strength for providing security/collateral for the debts. Without any security the cost of unsecured debt borrowing is likely to be high.

According to the Statement of Financial Position, while Look has just over $36 billion of non-current assets, only $14.5 billion of this is tangible, the remainder consisting of intangibles such as patents and consolidated goodwill. Whether the patents have any open market value and could be realised would be a key determinant in whether these could be used as security for new debt. The goodwill is unlikely to be suitable unless its value could be easily realised by lenders.

The tangible non-current assets consist of property as well as plant and equipment. The plant and equipment is likely to be mainly the IT infrastructure at its data centres which are unlikely to be suitable for security purposes due to their rapid loss in value.

Raising an additional $15,518 million of debt could therefore be a problem for Look as it is likely to exceed their current debt capacity according to the financial statements.

### Reference material 3 – Accounting policies extract

The company currently expenses all software development costs. More information is required to determine if this is in line with accounting and industry standards.

### Segmental Analysis

| Business Unit | % of total revenue |
| --- | --- |
| Search | 68 |
| Space | 15 |
| Media | 7 |
| Cloud | 3 |
| OS, App and Phone | 7 |
| Lens | 0 |

### Reference material 4 – Risk factors

#### Competition

By diversifying the products, Look is already reducing its risk by not focusing in one area where market share may be eroded. One of the founding board members, Vijay Chatterjee, is Director of Innovation and has a track record of creating new products. Look also has a specific policy encouraging staff to research and develop their own ideas which may result in commercial opportunities.

#### Investment in new businesses

A balance may need to be struck between ensuring ongoing business activities are not ignored over developing new ideas. Financial and non-financial targets via a balanced scorecard may help communicate and focus activity. For instance, ensuring income is maintained from old products may be in the financial quadrant, while no. of new products in development may come under innovation and learning.

Updating and developing existing products may be essential but disruptive. However, as staff are encouraged through HR policies to develop themselves and keep up-to-date with IT changes, the need to embrace change becomes part of the culture rather than demotivating.

### New Technologies

New technologies/devices/platforms may result in current Look products being incompatible or undesirable. This risk cannot be transferred, avoided or simply accepted. Look must try to reduce this risk by monitoring the innovations in the way the internet is used. This is already being done via some of the measures mentioned above.

### Advertising revenue

The impact of negative economic conditions can be reduced through making Look's products more inelastic: advertisers may then use Look no matter what the price. This can be achieved through having a strong brand and through the effectiveness of its search engine. For instance, through the use of controls, Looks search engine can provide the most relevant and tailored results. Look will have the ability to see which "clicks" end up with a purchase. The more accurate the search result, the more likely the customer is to purchase. During hard economic times, advertising is most likely to continue where it is most effective.

### Regulations and scrutiny/Political motives/Legal liability

The political, regulatory and legal risks cannot be avoided or transferred to another party. Neither would it be possible to simply accept these risks and do nothing, due to the reputational and financial damage it may cause. However, managing these risks is not straightforward.

Look can work with political governments and their regulatory bodies to ensure existing laws are not broken and new laws are not onerous. Look may also consider working with its peers e.g. Friendtime when lobbying governments to increase its power and influence.

Staff with relevant expertise may be hired to advise and work in different countries and legal systems. Each country and situation may require a different approach in order to mitigate the risk accordingly.

Specifically regarding the legal claims, Look's legal team can develop terms and conditions for users to agree to, which may reduce the risk of legal claims. There ought to be a clear complaints procedure for users. Look has an unofficial mission of "Do only good" which should help guide staff on how to resolve issues in an efficient and ethical manner, therefore potentially reducing the number of legal claims.

### Joint liability/Manufacturing and supply chain/Security & quality of service

Having (partially in some cases) transferred the risk associated with manufacturing and service provision, Look need to reduce the risk of third party failure through contracts, service level agreements and inspections. It may also consider buying the manufacturer to maintain more control over production.

### Interruption of communications

Look ought to have plans in place for resilience in its services such as backup, business continuity procedures and incident management capability. These ought to be reviewed and tested frequently.

### Key personnel

Look may monitor non-financial information that may help reduce this risk of losing key staff, such as staff turnover. In addition, through staff surveys and exit interviews, Look may find out what motivates staff to stay so that Look can take required action.

The three founder directors remain a "Key man" risk. A succession plan ought to be developed for a smooth exit and transition.

### Ad blocking

As the bulk of income come from advertising on the search engine, Look need to monitor this risk closely. Continued system controls and improvements may lead to search engine service provision that is so accurate, customers see less unnecessary or inapplicable advertising, reducing the need for ad blocking.

### Reference material 5 – Look's Corporate Social Responsibility Report for the year ended 30 September 2014

As we have already noted, Look have an internal 'do only good' motto which highlights their social responsibility stance. Amongst other things their data centres have managed to reduce energy consumption and have been carbon neutral since 2005. Look also funds renewable energy R&D – the amount invested in 2014 was $1.1bn.

### Reference material 6 – Case Study: Western Data Centre

This exhibit shows an example of some of the initiatives which Look have implemented. They include upgrades to the power management of servers, water cooled via a nearby river, a free bus which allows staff to use public transport to commute and locally sourced cafeteria food.

### Reference material 7 – News article

This brief article shows that there are rumours that Vijay may be thinking of stepping down from the board as he is bored with corporate life. This highlights the risk of losing key personnel which has been discussed already.

### Reference material 8 – Competitor Analysis

Look has a range of different types of competition to deal with including:

- other traditional search engines
- specialised search engines e.g. flight searches
- e-commerce sites such as Amazon
- sites like Facebook which also aim for advertising revenue

It is crucial that all types of competitor reaction are considered when making strategic decisions.

### Reference material 9 – Extract's from Friendtime's financial statements

Friendtime has grown much quicker than Look in recent times with a 41% year on year revenue growth to 2014. This has not been at the expense of profitability as operating margin has also increased from 40% to 46% and so the company has been able to pay out big dividends. A large pension deficit could cause concern for any potential purchaser of Friendtime.

### 3 SWOT analysis

A SWOT analysis is a useful tool to summarise the current position of the company. It is simply a listing of the following:

- The STRENGTHS of the organisation. These are internal factors that give the organisation a distinct advantage.
- The WEAKNESSES of the organisation. These are internal factors that affect performance adversely, and so might put the organisation at a disadvantage.

# chapter 13

- The OPPORTUNITIES available. These are circumstances or developments in the environment that the organisation might be in a position to exploit to its advantage.
- The THREATS or potential threats. These are factors in the environment that present risks or potential risks to the organisation and its competitive position.

Strengths and weaknesses are internal to the organisation, whereas opportunities and threats are external factors.

A SWOT analysis can be presented simply as a list of strengths, followed by weaknesses, then opportunities and finally threats. It would be useful to indicate within each category which factors seem more significant than others, perhaps by listing them in descending order of priority. Alternatively a SWOT analysis, if it is not too long and excludes minor factors, can be presented in the form of a 2 × 2 table, as follows:

| Strengths | Weaknesses |
|---|---|
|  |  |
| Opportunities | Threats |
|  |  |

With this method of presentation, the positive factors (strengths and opportunities) are listed on the left and the negative factors (weaknesses and threats) are on the right.

### Exercise 1 – SWOT analysis

Prepare a SWOT analysis of Look based on the summary of each exhibit and the guidance above.

# Summary of the Pre-seen – Look

## Test your understanding answers

### Exercise 1 – SWOT analysis

| Strengths | Weaknesses |
|---|---|
| • Brand name<br>• Range of products<br>• Market share<br>• Revenue growth<br>• Strong CSR policies | • Shares owned by former employees<br>• Lots of power in the hands of founding directors<br>• Restless director<br>• Reliance on key skilled staff<br>• Reliance on reliability of browsers etc.<br>• NED recruited based on loyalty and long service |
| **Opportunities** | **Threats** |
| • Acquisition of similar companies and small app developers<br>• New product innovation<br>• Expansion in Chinese market<br>• Use of the Big Data gathered through searches | • Smaller niche products with greater levels of innovation attacking individual products<br>• Regulation (e.g. Spain's ruling over online news channels)<br>• Backlash by users re use of data |

# chapter 14

# Unseen Material – Look

# Unseen Material – Look

This chapter reproduces the unseen information for Variant 2 of the March 2015 exam sitting. It is recommended that you skim read the materials and then work through Chapter Fifteen to prepare your answers before reviewing the solutions and analysis in the final chapter of this textbook.

Strategic case study exam

Maximum Time Allowed: 3 Hours

This examination is structured as follows:

| Section number | Number of tasks | Time for section (minutes) |
| --- | --- | --- |
| 1 | 1 | 60 |
| 2 | 1 | 60 |
| 3 | 1 | 60 |

The time available for each section is for reading, writing and planning your answer(s).

Note that in the exam these are not labelled as 'tasks' or 'triggers' but are presented simply as exhibits, emails, articles and so on. Similarly exhibits are not numbered.

chapter 14

**Combined Trigger and Task 1**

The following email was flagged as being urgent when you arrived at work this morning:

**From:** Amanda Wilson, Director of Finance

**To:** Finance Manager

**Subject:** Press interview

Hi,

I need you to help me with something before you do anything else this morning. I have attached an article that appeared on an online business news site late last night.

Jay probably won't be in for another hour, but the first thing he does every morning is run a search for news stories about Look and he will be furious about this. We need to be ready with a draft press release to respond to this article, otherwise we will have to deal with a very grumpy Chief Executive for the rest of the week.

Please draft a paper that I can use to hold an informed discussion with Jay concerning the following matters:

- Is there a strategic logic to Look's extensive portfolio of business interests?
- Assuming that we were prepared to divest any of these lines of business, what should our approach be to deciding which ones to discontinue?

I need you to be positive because we need to be ready to impress Jay on this one.

# Unseen Material – Look

### Reference Materials 1

**Look through the Lens**   by Pete Lawrence

Most of us have been using Look as our preferred search engine for many years. The software has becomes such a major part of our lives that we often use the company's name as a verb, so that 'Looking' for something can be very different from 'looking'.

I find myself increasingly bemused by Look. Ironically, for a company devoted to finding things, Look seems to have lost its way. The company developed its own operating system, which it then decided to give away free to anybody who was prepared to use it. It manufactures mobile phones that are as good as those produced by the market leader, but it makes very little profit from their sale. Now the company is trying to interest us in its new Look Lens, a product that has been developed to deal with a problem that does not yet exist.

Look's raft of new ventures extend to web-based businesses as well and include cloud based storage and other content.

My big concern is that Look will lose sight of the one thing that it makes money from (and so can claim to be successful at it). My motives for saying so are selfish. I remain the biggest fan of Look's search engine and I would hate to have to get used to using one of the many alternatives that are keen to take even a small percentage of Look's share of this lucrative market.

# chapter 14

**Combined Trigger and Task 2**

The following message was on your voicemail:

"Hi, it's Amanda here. I need your help quite urgently. Jay, Martin and Vijay don't feel that we are getting the best possible value out of our relationships with the other companies who manufacture devices for Look OS. While I agree with them, I think that the best way to handle things is to manage the relationship so that it is win-win for us and the manufacturers.

We need to do this quickly because Martin has suggested that we could simply stop updating and upgrading Look OS for a while and then release a significantly improved version that has a different name ("Look Mobile"), which would render Look OS obsolete. We are working on a major upgrade anyway and Martin is arguing that so much has changed we could say that it is a different product.

Draft a paper for me that deals with the following:

- I want to be very clear about the risks to Look arising from this arrangement.
- I am keen to have your thoughts on how best to manage our relationship with the manufacturers AND the ethical implications of implementing Martin's suggestion concerning the release of a new operating system".

# Unseen Material – Look

### Reference Materials 2

**LOOK OS**

(1) Anyone who wishes to use Look OS is free to do so, for either personal use or commercial gain.

(2) Commercial users can supply the LOOK OS as part of a physical device or platform that is sold for profit and they can provide purchasers of such products with updates and upgrades.

(3) Users can modify the source code provided that any improved or enhanced version of the software is made available to download and use on the same basis as the original Look OS.

(4) Notwithstanding 3 above, users can modify the user interface in order to enhance the usability of any device that runs the Look OS. Such modifications can be treated as proprietary and protected by copyright.

(5) Look retains the right to apply its own user interface on any device that uses the Look OS and that interface will remain Look's intellectual property.

(6) These rights to copy and use the Look OS will not lapse and will apply to any future versions that are published.

# chapter 14

## Combined Trigger and Task 3

You have received the following email:

**From:** Amanda Wilson, Director of Finance

**To:** Finance Manager

**Subject: Analyst briefing**

Hi,

I had a meeting with an investment analyst who specialises in the technology sector on behalf of one of the big investment institutions. These meetings are really important because analysts' opinions can have a significant impact on the share price. I am really annoyed with myself because I was unprepared for his very first question and it made me sound incompetent.

Look OS is freely available to anyone who wishes to download it and use it, even if they plan to sell it as part of a commercial product. Look OS is becoming increasingly popular with consumers and so more device manufacturers are adopting it and adapting it to their own requirements.

We have made the Look OS computer code and all of the documentation freely available, but manufacturers need programmers who are experts in Look OS to make use of that. There is a danger that third parties will recruit skilled staff from Look OS.

The analyst was concerned that we could lose key staff from Look OS and asked what plan we had in place to prevent that from happening. I gave a very weak and unconvincing answer, but it was obvious that we had not really thought about the question. I am afraid that I sounded like an amateur, which is hardly going to reassure the capital markets!

I need you to reply with your thoughts on the following:

- How might we ensure that we have a coherent and contented team of programmers in Look OS?

- Related to the previous issue, but continuing from it, how might we ensure that the individual programmers are inspired and motivated to stay with us?

- How likely is it that the share price will slip because of concerns about us losing our programmers? How concerned is the analyst likely to be that I couldn't answer this important question?

305

Unseen Material – Look

# chapter 15

# Walk through of the unseen – Look

# Walk through of the unseen – Look

## 1 The Aim of a Walkthrough

The aim of this chapter is to give you a chance to practise many of the techniques you have been shown in previous chapters of this study text. This should help you to understand the various thought processes needed to complete the full three hour examination. It is important that you work through this chapter at a steady pace.

Don't rush on to the next stage until you have properly digested the information, followed the guidance labelled 'Stop and Think!' and made your own notes. This will give you more confidence than simply reading the model solutions. You should refer to the unseen produced in the previous chapter as you proceed through these exercises.

The following chapter will then guide you through the suggested solutions and marking key.

## 2 Summary of trigger 1

A newspaper article has been published suggesting that Look has 'lost its way' and should focus on the core products which make money i.e. Look Search. The article also criticises the decisions to offer Look OS as an open source product, therefore not charging a fee for use.

### Stop and think!

(1) What do we know about the Look portfolio and the importance of each product?
(2) What tools do we have available to analyse the product portfolio?
(3) What arguments have been made to support Look OS as open source?

## 3 Overview of task 1

You are required to prepare a paper covering:

- Strategic logic of the product portfolio
- Approach to making divestment decisions

### Let's plan

We need to create a planning page that ensures you identify and respond to all parts of the requirement. You can use the techniques discussed in Chapter eight or develop your own method. In this chapter we will use the ordered list approach.

Split your planning sheet (use your wipe clean whiteboard) in two – one half for each part of the task as follows:

## chapter 15

**Strategic logic of product portfolio**

**Approach to making divestment decisions**

Note that the first section is roughly the same size as the second as each sub part of a task will be equally weighted in terms of mark allocation.

You now need to brainstorm all the relevant points you can think of under the above headings, making sure you are bringing together your knowledge from the relevant syllabus as well as your analysis of the pre-seen information.

Let's break down the requirements and consider all the key phrases to try and understand what the examiner is looking for. Remember that a failure to answer the question set is a key reason for failing the case study exam so be careful!

So the question is asking if there is a 'strategic logic' to the company's 'extensive portfolio'. It would be handy at this point in the exam to have the relevant reference material explaining each product in Look's portfolio. There is a temptation to home in on the word 'portfolio' and write a very knowledge based answer about the BCG matrix or the Product Lifecycle. This is not what the examiner is looking for in the case study exam as this kind of knowledge has already been tested in the Objective Tests. What you do need to be comfortable doing is applying these models if (and only if) they support and enhance your answer. Do not take a prepared list of models into the exam with intention of 'shoehorning' them into your answer!

# Walk through of the unseen – Look

You could apply either of the models mentioned above. Think about what we can learn from each. The BCG matrix helps us to understand the balance of cash generation and future potential in the portfolio. The Product Lifecycle makes us think about whether we have suitable products at all stages of growth, development and maturity. For a company like Look in the technology space, the lifecycle model is particularly useful and may be most appropriate to consider when planning your answer. Remember not to get so stuck on this model that you can't think about anything else. There are lots of other reasons for Look having the range of products they do - make sure you try and think of as many as possible.

We also need to think about the phrase 'strategic logic'. In simple terms we could rephrase this as 'does the portfolio make sense'. Think about trying to justify the reasons for each product being necessary to Look. This should help you to address the logic.

As a rough rule of thumb you should spend about 15-20% of the time available for reading and planning. So for this section of the exam, where you are given 60 minutes, you should be spending approximately 10 minutes planning your answer before you complete the exercise below. This would leave you about 45 minutes to write your answer and a few minutes spare to check through what you have written.

Overall it is worth noting that that if you give a good answer to each part that links together and answers the questions you will also earn integration marks. If you do it well you will get three marks per task.

### Exercise 1

**Prepare a response to the first task in this variant of Look.**

## 4 Summary of trigger 2

In this section you are presented with a single document containing both the trigger and task (as well as some additional reference materials). We have considered the trigger and task elements separately for consistency.

The board have suggested an approach to maximising the value from Look OS. The suggestion is to gradually retire the current product and then launch a 'new' product called Look Mobile. The terms of the original open source operating system are included as reference materials and include the item 'these rights to copy and use the Look OS will not lapse and they will apply to any future versions that are published'. One of the directors, Martin, is suggesting that Look Mobile will be a completely new product rather than simply a new version of Look OS.

**Stop and think!**

- You can start to think of the advantages and disadvantages of such a strategy
- Think about what Look is trying to achieve
- Consider why you have been given the terms and conditions of Look OS

## 5 Summary of task 2

You are asked to prepare a paper covering the following:

- Risks involved in relaunching Look OS as Look Mobile
- How to manage the relationship with manufacturers
- Ethical implications of the relaunch

**Let's plan**

Set up your whiteboard with two sections to begin with as the examiner presented the requirements for this task as two bullet points. We have split the second requirement into two parts to ensure we remember to cover the ethical part as well. So you can split the second half of your whiteboard into two sections.

# Walk through of the unseen – Look

| Risks of strategy to relaunch Look OS |
|---|
|  |

| Managing manufacturer relationship |
|---|
|  |

| Ethical implications |
|---|
|  |

Be careful not to paraphrase too much as you could end not properly planning your answer or addressing the requirement when you write it up. For example if you just wrote 'strategy to relaunch Look OS' it is very likely you would go off on a tangent thinking about evaluating the strategy and not fully focusing on answering the question.

When you are trying to think of risks the best approach is to take a step back and think 'what could go wrong'. This should give you plenty of ideas here!

Managing the manufacturer relationship simply requires some common sense and a focus on answering the question rather than desperately trying to repeat some vaguely connected theory.

When you get on to the ethical section it may be helpful to think about CIMA's Fundamental Ethical principles. They are unlikely to all apply but it may help to generate some ideas and provide a framework for your answer.

Now spend 10 minutes completing your plan before attempting Exercise 2. You would then have 45 minutes to write your answer and a few minutes to check through what you have written before reviewing the solution.

### Exercise 2

Prepare a response to the second task in this variant of Look

## 6 Summary of trigger 3

Amanda Wilson (Finance Director) has just returned from a meeting with an investment analyst where she discussed the issue of losing staff skilled in Look OS programming. The analyst asked about plans in place to prevent this from happening but Amanda wasn't confident that her response was very convincing.

**Stop and think!**

(1) How can Look ensure they retain these key staff?

(2) Consider market reaction to this situation

## 7 Summary of task 3

This task requires a discussion of:

- How to ensure a coherent and contented team of programmers
- How to ensure programmers are inspired and motivated to stay with Look
- How likely is it that the share price will slip as a result of concerns about losing programmers
- How concerned is the analyst likely to be

**Let's plan**

Remember that you are aiming to get your main thoughts down with some kind of structure, ensuring you address all parts of the requirement. Note that for the first two requirements you are asked for an evaluation of 'how'. So your answer must consider the issues involved and focus on actions the company can take.

Give yourself about 10 minutes to plan and then you can attempt exercise 3. You will then have approximately 45 minutes to write your answer, leaving a short amount of time to check through what you have written. Remember to allocate the time equally across the requirements.

| Exercise 3 |
|---|
| Prepare a response to the third task in this variant of Look |

Overall it is worth noting that that if you give a good answer to each requirement that links together and answers the questions set you will also earn integration marks. If you do it well you will get three marks per task.

These answers have been provided by CIMA for information purposes only. The answers created are indicative of a response that could be given by a good candidate. They are not to be considered exhaustive, and other appropriate relevant responses would receive credit. CIMA will not accept challenges to these answers on the basis of academic judgement.

chapter 15

# Test your understanding answers

### Exercise 1

**Strategic logic**

There is no single approach to the justification of Look's product portfolio. The following discussion relies on the product lifecycle and also the availability of synergy.

The first factor that we might usefully explore is the product lifecycle. Internet search is now a mature market, as evidenced by the reduction in the growth of searches. It is reasonable to expect revenues from this source to stagnate and decline because there are relatively low barriers to entry.

Look Space is a clear and synergistic extension to our search engine business. The technical issues are very similar because they are both essentially search engines and so we can apply the skills and much of the coding that we already possess. Look Space opens this line up to a whole new revenue stream because we can sell location-related services, which may make our service attractive to smaller advertisers than might be interested in Look Search. For example, customers searching Look Space for directions to a particular town could be offered links to hotels, restaurants, petrol stations and other businesses in that town.

The Look OS is a natural extension to Look's core business. Firstly, it is essentially a software product that enables us to apply skills developed in the course of creating and developing our search engine. Secondly, this is a product that could open up new markets for internet search, thereby creating direct synergy. Hardware is becoming increasingly portable, with devices such as tablets and even phones being used as the consumer's device of choice for internet access. This also creates a very direct link to our Look Space product, with consumers using their phones or tablets as navigation aids. Advertisers can exploit this phenomenon by advertising directly on the map interface.

Our strategy of giving free access to Look OS is commercially sound because it means that Look OS is more likely to become a de facto standard in the market for portable devices. We will be at the forefront of new developments in the creation and exploitation of new versions and upgrades to existing versions of Look OS.

The Look Phone and Look Apps products are both closely tied to the success of Look OS. If we had not launched a phone then it would have been more difficult to showcase the merits of the operating system. Our launch of the operating system would have been delayed by the need to find at least one launch partner to supply the necessary hardware.

# Walk through of the unseen – Look

Look Phone has the potential to become a major source of revenue in its own right, although we could decide to either sell the subsidiary or merge it with another manufacturer once we are certain that the Look OS has reached a critical level of adoption.

Look Apps is a further method of adding value to Look OS, in addition to generating revenues. Consumers expect to be able to personalise their devices with apps and so the OS would have limited value unless we could be certain that there was a good range of apps available. Publishing our own apps gives us control over quality and pricing.

Finally, Look Lens fits into the overall strategy through it being at an early stage in the product lifecycle and so it is evidence that Look is developing new and innovative products to supplement those that are moving into maturity. The vision for Look OS, Look Phone and Look Apps is that hardware will be increasingly portable and accessible and so the development of a wearable computer interface that is always available is totally consistent with our existing market strategy. It remains to be seen whether Look Lens will prove popular, but it has the capacity to prove the concept of wearable technology and it will provide Look with an appreciation of features that the market values.

Look Media and Look Cloud are both businesses that have well-developed competitors. Look could claim that these services are both capable of offering synergies, each in its own way. Look Media can exploit Look's knowledge of the searches undertaken by its users, so a search on a particular musical artist could lead to a link to that artist's albums on Look Media. Conversely, Look Cloud could apply Look's search technology to personal files. Users could be offered the option of using Look search to search their own files for, say, correspondence with a specific person.

### Divestment decisions

There is no single decision criterion that would enable us to reach a final decision about which divisions to divest. The most immediate factor would be the potential selling price. For example, it is likely that the search engine could be sold for far more than any of the other lines of business. Selling a more valuable subsidiary would generate more cash that could be applied to future expansion on areas that are potentially more lucrative.

The shareholders' perceptions of any disposal will have to be managed, otherwise Look's Board will lose credibility. Ideally, any disposal would have to yield more than the subsidiary's value to Look, although that might be difficult to demonstrate because of the synergies between various aspects of the business. It could be argued that some buyers can afford to pay a premium because of synergies with their existing businesses, for example it may be possible to sell Look Phone at a good price to a phone manufacturer who is seeking economies of scale or a quick route into the market in Look OS phones. In the absence of such a justification, the shareholders may be concerned that Look's Board is effectively admitting that it cannot maximise the commercial potential of the various lines of business.

It could be argued that Look should dispose of businesses to which it can add little value. For example, the search engine is a mature business and it is unlikely to deliver any further growth. Divesting the company of its biggest business would be a risky move, but it could be argued that Look should focus on innovation and the development of new products and that mature lines of business could be sold in order to finance the potentially more lucrative areas where growth is a possibility. It may be possible for such arrangements to be structured as joint ventures, whereby Look would retain an ownership interest and a degree of control while the venture partner provided most of the expertise. Such partial disposals could have the effect of revitalising Look's smaller subsidiaries at minimal risk to Look and without diverting senior management attention from more important matters.

In the same vein, Look may struggle to generate significant profit from either Look Media or Look Cloud because both businesses face significant competition in fairly crowded markets. It could be that either business could be sold to a direct competitor who could then combine Look's customer base with their own and who might be willing to pay a fair price. Look could justify such a disposal on the basis that it would remove a potential distraction from the company's portfolio of business interests.

Look should consider the intangible losses associated with disposals, such as the loss of programming teams which could otherwise have been available for other projects within the company. The converse of this could be that selling the subsidiary may also equip a potential competitor with expertise that could be of value in any future competition with Look.

Finally, Look should consider the implications for other stakeholders. For example, it may be unsettling to Look's other employees if the company is disposing of subsidiaries. That will be particularly true if the buyer is keen to acquire intellectual property and is unlikely to retain the employees whose contracts have been acquired. Staff morale may decline if there is a threat of redundancy.

# Walk through of the unseen – Look

### Exercise 2

## Risks

The most immediate risk is that there will be very little interest in the operating system, in which case Look's credibility will be undermined. Look has underpinned a number of other ventures with Look OS, particularly Look Phone. Look's reputation as an innovator and developer will be undermined if the other manufacturers choose to stick with their own operating systems or to adopt those offered by Look's competitors.

Look OS is competing with established operating systems that have already been shown to be commercially successful. If Look fails to gain adequate market share then the investment in this project may be lost.

Look risks further reputational damage arising from the applications developed by the companies that adopt the operating system. The manufacturers who adapt Look OS to meet their needs could introduce bugs or security risks that could harm users. This could result in adverse publicity for Look, even if the problems were due to the modifications.

Look could be opened up to claims if the operating system is blamed for losses borne by users. The responsibility for such losses may be difficult to allocate because users may be running apps for sensitive functions that had not been envisaged by Look's programmers.

The users who adopt Look OS may take the idea of modification to an extreme level, to the extent that look may struggle to retain control of ongoing development. Some manufacturers may choose to update and upgrade their own versions of Look OS and so there could be one or more parallel versions of the Look OS that could prove more popular than Look's own.

Other software companies could decide to compete directly with Look by offering their own operating systems on the same basis, which could force Look to invest significant amounts of time and money in upgrading Look OS to ensure that it remains competitive.

There is an upside risk that this arrangement will lead to the widespread adoption of the Look OS as a leading platform. This could be in Look's long-term interests even if the OS itself generates no income. It could, for example, boost sales of the Look Phone or any other devices that Look develops to promote the operating system.

### Managing relationships

Firstly, the key is to ensure that the relationship generates value to both parties. If Look's partners profit from this arrangement then they will be more likely to remain loyal to the OS and to cooperate and assist Look in future developments.

Look should discuss manufacturers' needs and expectations of the operating system. Ideally, Look should build any functionality into the operating system so that the most the manufacturers need to do is add their own interface. If Look can maintain a single line of upgrades then it may be less expensive in the longer run because there will be only one basic variant to be maintained and updated.

Look should aim for a consensus over the optimal rate at which new versions of the operating system should be developed and released. Constant change may require manufacturers to develop new hardware and could disrupt retail sales with consumers being unwilling to buy devices based on operating systems that will soon be replaced with updated versions. Manufacturers will, however, also wish to see new versions developed from time to time so that users will have an incentive to replace their phones and tablets with updated versions.

Look should aim to facilitate a discussion between all manufacturers so that they agree on the manner in which the operating system should be promoted. Ideally, they will compete on the basis of the features offered by their devices, or on price. They should be discouraged from competing on the basis of their implementation of Look OS, otherwise there is a risk that the market will start to feel disenchanted with some versions of the operating system and its overall popularity will decline.

### Ethical issues

There isn't necessarily a single framework that can be used to evaluate ethical dilemmas. The Code of Ethics for Professional Accountants sets out some general principles that could inform this discussion.

It would be difficult to justify Martin's proposal from an ethical point of view. We may use the fundamental ethical principles of integrity and professional behaviour as our benchmarks.

## Walk through of the unseen – Look

Integrity requires that business relationships be conducted in a manner that is straightforward and honest. Look has encouraged manufacturers to invest time and effort in the adoption of an operating system, which is a fundamental component of their products. A straightforward' interpretation of those facts would be that Look has made a commitment to the manufacturers that all reasonable steps will be undertaken to maintain that operating system. An 'honest' application of the open-source conditions would be to respect the spirit as well as the letter of the agreement.

It would be dishonest to claim that a revised version of Look OS was a different product altogether even if the law would permit such an argument. Even if Look is having reservations about the benefits of this agreement, it would suggest a degree of unacceptable recklessness in granting the open-source rights in the first place. Look should have carefully considered its interests before signing off on the agreement and should have made any possibility of its support being withdrawn explicit in the document.

Professional behaviour suggests that Look's management should avoid discrediting the company's reputation. Most observers would regard the exploitation of a loophole in a legal contract as morally unacceptable, even if it could be viewed as legal. There could be an argument that the publication of open-source code implies a gift that could not be withdrawn without damaging Look's reputation. Apart from manufacturers, many consumers will have purchased expensive devices on the understanding that they will be able to download updates and upgrades to the operating system and so Martin's suggestion could be viewed as being against the public interest.

### Exercise 3

**From:** Finance Manager

**To:** Amanda Wilson, Director of Finance

**Subject:** Analyst briefing

**Coherent and contented team of programmers**

Ensuring that the team is coherent is a matter of leadership and structure. It may not be appropriate to have a rigid hierarchy in a programming department because staff may find that stifles their creativity, but there should be clarity over lines of communication and reporting. Given the interactive and collaborative nature of programming, it may be worth creating ad hoc project teams to tackle specific tasks and each team should be led by a designated person so that there is both leadership and accountability. Locating all Look OS programmers at one location might help because it would enable them to interact informally, although it is perfectly feasible to collaborate on code using electronic communication provided the tasks are clearly specified. Relocating all Look OS programmers to one site would almost certainly mean making the programmers at one site redundant and hiring and training replacements at the other site, which could prove disruptive.

Programming staff will be contented if they are properly resourced and rewarded. If the programming department is understaffed then assignments will be pressured and staff will be demotivated. Resourcing should also extend to providing the necessary facilities in terms of hardware and software, suitable workstations, etc., otherwise staff will feel undervalued. Salaries should reflect local market conditions, so that staff do not feel underpaid. Programming staff should also receive acknowledgement for their contribution because the operating system will quickly become out of date and insecure without their input. Look OS management should make it clear to their programming staff that they appreciate the fact that they remain loyal to the company despite the opportunities that are available elsewhere.

**Inspiring and motivating staff**

The key to inspiring and motivating staff is to provide them with stimulating and interesting challenges in their work on the system. That could be difficult because of the fact that the operating system has been developed and launched and much of the work will now be routine maintenance.

It might help to ask the programmers to take a more proactive role, such as attempting to pre-empt security weaknesses in the operating system and closing them before they can be exploited. Staff could be rewarded in some way for identifying weaknesses and developing fixes.

It would be encouraging to involve the programmers in the development process, beyond the actual coding. If the programmers could be involved in developing new features and capabilities then they would realise that there was still scope to make a significant input into the system.

It could help to exchange programmers between Look OS and Look Apps. That would enable all programmers to have the opportunity to develop small programs on their own, while remaining involved with the development of the operating system. Apart from the change of emphasis, this would give all programmers the opportunity to see whether their apps were well received by consumers and so commercial successes.

The Look OS programmers should be trained in the latest programming techniques and have the opportunity to apply those to future updates to the system. The very fact that the training is happening confirms that the programming staff need to have their skills maintained if they are to keep the software up to date. The training also confirms that Look values the skills and experience of the programming team, because the alternative could be to make older staff redundant and then hire younger replacements who have been trained in the most recent techniques.

**Verbal slip**

The impact on the share price and the possibility that the analyst would be concerned are actually two very different issues and should be addressed separately.

The capital markets value shares on the basis that they will be held in a diversified portfolio. The possibility that the programmers will leave Look OS is a non-systematic risk. The point of diversification is that non-systematic risks can be diversified away and so the share price should not be affected.

If concerns emerged then there could be some shareholders who might sell their shares and that might depress the share price slightly in the short term. Generally, the markets will interpret the purchase or sale of shares as suggesting the possibility that somebody could be acting upon price-sensitive information.

Analysts are in a slightly different position from the shareholders because they are required to express an opinion on the company in isolation. The analysts have to consider the total risk facing the company, both systematic and unsystematic and so the fact that the programmers could depart would be an issue. Having said that, Look OS is only a small part of Look as a whole and the programmers could be replaced, albeit at some inconvenience. Thus, the impact of their departure should not be very pronounced.

The analyst might be more concerned that the finance director had not been adequately briefed on an important risk that could affect a potentially important subsidiary. Board members should not necessarily know the terms and conditions of every member of staff, but they should be conscious of the need to retain key employees. The fact that the programmers in question are based overseas makes it even more important that the risks are understood and are under review. The analyst may feel that the weak answer implied a more serious question about governance.

# Walk through of the unseen – Look

# chapter 16

# Analysis of marking key – Look

**Chapter learning objectives**

# Analysis of marking key – Look

## 1 Introduction

As we have already explained in previous chapters the case study examinations are marked against a series of competencies. It is important that you understand this process to ensure you maximise your marks in the exam.

Once you have reviewed Chapter Fifteen, attempted the exercises and reviewed the suggested solutions, this chapter takes you through the detail of how these exercises would be marked.

## 2 Section 1

As we saw in the previous chapter, in the first section you were required to prepare a paper covering:

- Strategic logic of the product portfolio
- Approach to making divestment decisions

Let's examine each of these areas in turn.

### Strategic logic of the product portfolio

It is important to recognise that such a strategic analysis is largely testing your Business skills. You therefore need to consider your understanding of this organisation, the external environment in which it operates and any industry analysis which you may have performed when working through the pre-seen information.

This part of the requirement is asking you to consider the reasons behind including each of Look's divisions in the portfolio. This whole section is allocated 60 minutes so for this part of the exercise you have approximately 30 minutes. Working on a rough ratio of 2 marks for every point you make, this implies you need to make about 15 points. However this is not necessarily 15 separate discrete ideas. At this level a large part of the value of your answer is in explaining the implications of what you are saying.

The first few sentences of the suggested solution introduce the context and topic of the paper and the concept of the product life cycle. We then have a section explaining:

*Internet search is now a mature market, as evidenced by the reduction in the growth of searches. It is reasonable to expect revenues from this source to stagnate and decline because there are relatively low barriers to entry.*

Identification and explanation of the maturity of this product will earn a mark but this paragraph also goes on to give the **implication** of this which will earn a further mark. Thinking 'so what' for each point you make can help to identify the implications and therefore earn more marks.

The answer then moves on to the next product:

*Look Space is a clear and synergistic extension to our search engine business. The technical issues are very similar because they are both essentially search engines and so we can apply the skills and much of the coding that we already possess.*

This addresses a key part of the requirement – the logic of the portfolio. Again you should be thinking of the **implication** of this and the following point earns a further mark:

*Look Space opens this line up to a whole new revenue stream because we can sell location-related services, which may make our service attractive to smaller advertisers than might be interested in Look Search.*

A further mark can be gained by giving a well thought out example – some real world common sense can often help with this:

*For example, customers searching Look Space for directions to a particular town could be offered links to hotels, restaurants, petrol stations and other businesses in that town.*

Moving on to the next product in the portfolio:

*The Look OS ... is essentially a software product that enables us to apply skills developed in the course of creating and developing our search engine. Secondly, this is a product that could open up new markets for internet search, thereby creating direct synergy.*

Explaining the logic of this product earns a mark. Again we can follow the pattern of making and explaining the point and then considering the implication:

*Hardware is becoming increasingly portable, with devices such as tablets and even phones being used as the consumer's device of choice for internet access.*

This product is then linked back to other aspects of the portfolio for a further mark:

*This also creates a very direct link to our Look Space product, with consumers using their phones or tablets as navigation aids. Advertisers can exploit this phenomenon by advertising directly on the map interface.*

## Analysis of marking key – Look

The next paragraph considers the appropriateness of the Look OS strategy. You may not have thought of making this point but it does highlight the importance of thinking widely, without straying away from the requirement. One of the most common reasons for failing this exam is not answering the question set so it is important to be very clear about what the examiner is asking you to do.

*Our strategy of giving free access to Look OS is commercially sound because it means that Look OS is more likely to become a de facto standard in the market for portable devices. We will be at the forefront of new developments in the creation and exploitation of new versions and upgrades to existing versions of Look OS.*

We then consider the Phone and Apps parts of the business and make the point and explain it:

*The Look Phone and Look Apps products are both closely tied to the success of Look OS. If we had not launched a phone then it would have been more difficult to showcase the merits of the operating system. Our launch of the operating system would have been delayed by the need to find at least one launch partner to supply the necessary hardware.*

before considering the implication:

*Look Phone has the potential to become a major source of revenue in its own right, although we could decide to either sell the subsidiary or merge it with another manufacturer once we are certain that the Look OS has reached a critical level of adoption.*

A further two marks is awarded for linking back to other parts of the portfolio again:

*Look Apps is a further method of adding value to Look OS, in addition to generating revenues. Consumers expect to be able to personalise their devices with apps and so the OS would have limited value unless we could be certain that there was a good range of apps available. Publishing our own apps gives us control over quality and pricing.*

The answer then turns to the final product and its stage in the lifecycle:

*Finally, Look Lens fits into the overall strategy through it being at an early stage in the product lifecycle and so it is evidence that Look is developing new and innovative products to supplement those that are moving into maturity.*

It is important that a discussion like this is properly concluded. Here the answer considers two sides to the portfolio with each fully explained conclusion earning a mark:

*The vision for Look OS, Look Phone and Look Apps is that hardware will be increasingly portable and accessible and so the development of a wearable computer interface that is always available is totally consistent with our existing market strategy. It remains to be seen whether Look Lens will prove popular, but it has the capacity to prove the concept of wearable technology and it will provide Look with an appreciation of features that the market values.*

*Look Media and Look Cloud are both businesses that have well-developed competitors. Look could claim that these services are both capable of offering synergies, each in its own way. Look Media can exploit Look's knowledge of the searches undertaken by its users, so a search on a particular musical artist could lead to a link to that artist's albums on Look Media.*

*Conversely, Look Cloud could apply Look's search technology to personal files. Users could be offered the option of using Look search to search their own files for, say, correspondence with a specific person.*

We have now seen how the fifteen marks for Business skills have been marked within this task. There are also integration marks available but we will consider integration later on in this chapter.

### Approach to making divestment decisions

This requirement is more focused on People skills so it is going to be important to think about appropriate decision making but also how these decisions might affect the staff and other stakeholders.

As we are assuming that there are a similar amount of marks available for this part of the section we are aiming for approximately fifteen points again.

Again the answer starts with an introductory sentence before going on to explain the first consideration when determining which division to divest:

*The most immediate factor would be the potential selling price. For example, it is likely that the search engine could be sold for far more than any of the other lines of business.*

At the risk of being repetitive we can then consider the **implication** of earning the highest price:

*Selling a more valuable subsidiary would generate more cash that could be applied to future expansion on areas that are potentially more lucrative.*

## Analysis of marking key – Look

Remember to think about stakeholders when evaluating decisions. Consideration of the shareholders is often appropriate:

*The shareholders' perceptions of any disposal will have to be managed, otherwise Look's Board will lose credibility. Ideally, any disposal would have to yield more than the subsidiary's value to Look, although that might be difficult to demonstrate because of the synergies between various aspects of the business.*

We can then consider the sale from another key stakeholder, the prospective purchaser:

*It could be argued that some buyers can afford to pay a premium because of synergies with their existing businesses, for example it may be possible to sell Look Phone at a good price to a phone manufacturer who is seeking economies of scale or a quick route into the market in Look OS phones.*

Linking this back to the implications for the shareholders earns a further mark:

*In the absence of such a justification, the shareholders may be concerned that Look's Board is effectively admitting that it cannot maximise the commercial potential of the various lines of business.*

Moving on to the next consideration:

*It could be argued that Look should dispose of businesses to which it can add little value. For example, the search engine is a mature business and it is unlikely to deliver any further growth.*

And the implication of this:

*Divesting the company of its biggest business would be a risky move, but it could be argued that Look should focus on innovation and the development of new products and that mature lines of business could be sold in order to finance the potentially more lucrative areas where growth is a possibility.*

It is worth thinking practically and considering how any suggested divestment could be achieved:

*It may be possible for such arrangements to be structured as joint ventures, whereby Look would retain an ownership interest and a degree of control while the venture partner provided most of the expertise.*

And considering the wider implications of such a structure:

*Such partial disposals could have the effect of revitalising Look's smaller subsidiaries at minimal risk to Look and without diverting senior management attention from more important matters.*

A further point is explained:

*In the same vein, Look may struggle to generate significant profit from either Look Media or Look Cloud because both businesses face significant competition in fairly crowded markets.*

Along with the implication:

*It could be that either business could be sold to a direct competitor who could then combine Look's customer base with their own and who might be willing to pay a fair price. Look could justify such a disposal on the basis that it would remove a potential distraction from the company's portfolio of business interests.*

Consider the key strengths of Look and how they may be lost through divestment:

*Look should consider the intangible losses associated with disposals, such as the loss of programming teams which could otherwise have been available for other projects within the company.*

Sometimes you may be able to consider two sides to an argument. A point like this shows your ability to reason and present a balanced argument:

*The converse of this could be that selling the subsidiary may also equip a potential competitor with expertise that could be of value in any future competition with Look.*

We can then return to the consideration of stakeholders to earn a mark for a well explained point:

*Finally, Look should consider the implications for other stakeholders. For example, it may be unsettling to Look's other employees if the company is disposing of subsidiaries. That will be particularly true if the buyer is keen to acquire intellectual property and is unlikely to retain the employees whose contracts have been acquired.*

## Analysis of marking key – Look

And a further mark for the final implication:

*Staff morale may decline if there is a threat of redundancy.*

We have now seen how the fifteen marks for people skills are allocated within this section of the task. As before there are integration marks included here too.

These marks can be summarised in a marking grid as shown here:

|  |  | Marks |
|---|---|---|
| **Strategic logic** |  |  |
|  | Search – mature | 2 |
|  | Space extends PLC | 2 |
|  | Look OS use of skill | 2 |
|  | Link OS to Space | 3 |
|  | Look OS as open source linked to Phone and apps | 2 |
|  | Look Lens – introductory stage | 2 |
|  | Conclusions | 2 |
| Total – business skill |  | **15** |
| **Divestment decisions** |  |  |
|  | Relative values | 2 |
|  | Synergies | 3 |
|  | Divestment of mature business | 2 |
|  | Joint venture arrangements | 2 |
|  | Competition | 2 |
|  | Intangible losses | 2 |
|  | Employees | 2 |
| Total – people skill |  | **15** |
| Integration |  | 3 |
| Max awarded |  | **33** |

Following this detailed analysis of the marking guide for the first section we will now show you a breakdown of the marks for the remaining tasks in the pilot exam.

## 3 Section 2

From the previous chapter we saw that this section required a paper covering the following:

- Risks involved in relaunching Look OS as Look Mobile
- How to manage the relationship with manufacturers
- Ethical implications of the relaunch

| Requirement | | Marks |
|---|---|---|
| **Risks** | | |
| | Product risk | 3 |
| | Reputational | 3 |
| | Litigation risk | 2 |
| | Lack of control | 2 |
| | Competition | 3 |
| | Upside risk | 2 |
| Total – technical skills | | **15** |
| **Relationship with manufacturers** | | |
| | Joint value | 2 |
| | Simplicity | 2 |
| | Release rate | 2 |
| | Promotion | 2 |
| Total – business skills | | **8** |
| **Ethical implications** | | |
| | Integrity | 4 |
| | Professional behaviours | 3 |
| Total – people skills | | **7** |
| Intergration | | 3 |
| Total marks | | **33** |

# Analysis of marking key – Look

## 4 Section 3

This task required an evaluation of:

- How to ensure a coherent and contented team of programmers
- How to ensure programmers are inspired and motivated to stay with Look
- How likely is it that the share price will slip as a result of concerns about losing programmers
- How concerned is the analyst likely to be.

| Requirement | | Marks |
|---|---|---|
| **Coherent and contented programmers** | | |
| | Structure | 2 |
| | Project teams | 2 |
| | Location | 2 |
| | Resources | 2 |
| | Rewards | 3 |
| Total – Leadership skills | | **11** |
| **Inspiring and motivating staff** | | |
| | Nature of the work | 2 |
| | Proactive role | 2 |
| | Development | 2 |
| | Job exchanges | 2 |
| | Training | 3 |
| Total – Leadership skills | | **11** |
| **Share price/analyst concerns** | | |
| | Non-systematic risk | 2 |
| | Market reaction | 2 |
| | Reaction of analysts to staff leaving | 2 |
| | Reaction of analysts to lack of information | 3 |
| Total technical skills | | **9** |
| **Integration** | | 3 |
| **Total marks** | | **34** |

## 5 Integration marks

There are 9 integration marks available in this variant paper with marks spread across each of the tasks. These marks will be awarded for the overall quality of your answer and use of available information. You should consider the style and language you use and ensure it is suitable for the intended recipient. It is also important that your responses are appropriately structured and logical. The integration marks are also for how well your answer joins together the different subjects and competencies. This will show understanding of all the subject areas. It is important that you are not just competent in E3 or F3 or P3. You must show understanding and application of all subjects. By doing this you will also cover all the competencies and link them together in a meaningful way.

# Analysis of marking key – Look